IMPERIAL

BENEVOLENCE

Jane Samson

IMPERIAL

BENEVOLENCE

Making British Authority

in the Pacific Islands

University of Hawai'i Press

Honolulu

03 02 01 00 99 98   5 4 3 2 1

Library of Congress Cataloging-in-Publication Data

Samson, Jane, 1962–
    Imperial benevolence : making British authority in the Pacific islands / Jane Samson.
        p.   cm.
    Includes bibliographical references (p.   ) and index.
    ISBN 0–8248–1927–6 (alk. paper)
    1. Islands of the Pacific—History—19th century. 2. Islands of the Pacific—Relations
—Great Britain. 3. Great Britain—Relations—Islands of the Pacific. 4. Great Britain—
Colonies—Oceania. I. Title.
    DU40.S26   1998
    990—dc21   97–48936
                                                          CIP

Design by Diane Gleba Hall

For Simon

Contents

Maps

Abbreviations

ADM	British Admiralty, and ADM Records, PRO
APS	Aborigines' Protection Society
APL	Auckland Public Library
AONSW	Archives Office of New South Wales
ATL	Alexander Turnbull Library, Wellington
BCRO	Buckinghamshire County Record Office
BEL	Bellasis and Oliver Papers, NMM
BLK	Blake Papers, NMM
BLO	Bodleian Library, Oxford
BM	British Museum
BUL	Birmingham University Library
CAF	Central Archives of Fiji and the Western Pacific High Commission
CMS	Church Missionary Society
CO	British Colonial Office; and CO Records, PRO
CUL	Cambridge University Library

CWM	Council for World Mission Records, School of Oriental and African Studies, London
CY	ML microfilm copy reel
FBN	Microfiche box number
FM	ML microfilm
FO	British Foreign Office; and FO Records, PRO
FR	Fremantle Papers, BCRO
HBM	His/Her Britannic Majesty
JMMS	Journal Manuscripts, RGS
LMS	London Missionary Society
ML	Mitchell Library, Sydney
MRK	Markham Papers, NMM
NANZ	National Archives of New Zealand
NLA	National Library of Australia
NMM	National Maritime Museum, Greenwich
NSW	New South Wales
P.P.	*Great Britain Parliamentary Papers*
PMB	Pacific Manuscripts Bureau
PRO	Public Record Office, Kew
QMS	ATL manuscript sequence
RGS	Royal Geographical Society, London
RNAS	Royal Navy Australia Station
SCL	Selwyn College Library, Cambridge, U.K.
SOAS	School of Oriental and African Studies, London
STK	Stokes Papers, NMM
WMMS	Wesleyan Methodist Missionary Society; and Society Records, SOAS

Orthography and Nomenclature

MANY place names changed during and after the nineteenth century, and could be spelled in a variety of ways. For clarity and consistency, this study uses the following designations: Australia (formerly New Holland); New Guinea (now Papua New Guinea and/or Irian Jaya); New Hebrides (now Vanuatu); Samoa (formerly Navigators Islands, now Western Samoa and/or American Samoa); Sandwich Islands (now Hawai'i), Tonga (formerly Friendly Islands). Place names within quotations have not been altered. The spelling of proper names for Pacific islanders follows the islander's own wishes (if known), as when someone took a new name after baptism. Readers should note that in Pacific Studies convention, the word "European" refers to Americans as well as Europeans.

In Fijian orthography the following letters are pronounced as shown below:

"b" as "mb" ("number")	"c" as "th" ("that")
"d" as "nd" ("end")	"g" as "ng" ("singer")
"q" as "ng" ("finger")	

Samoan orthography pronounces "g" as "ng" ("bang"). Tongan orthography used "b" and "p" interchangeably, as well as "g" and "ng" until these were recently standardized as "p" and "ng" respectively.

Finally, readers should note that all spelling, punctuation, and emphasis in quotations is original.

Acknowledgments

M ANY people have helped me write this book. Sara Joynes, of the now-defunct Australian Joint Copying Project, led me to many archives in Britain that I would otherwise have missed. Other archivists and librarians, especially at the Alexander Turnbull Library, Auckland Public Library, National Library of Australia, and Mitchell Library, have helped me beyond the call of duty. Also in Australia and New Zealand, Alan Frost, Niel Gunson, David Mackay, David Routledge, Deryck Scarr, Dorothy Shineberg, and Nicholas Thomas have all given me invaluable advice and feedback. At the University of British Columbia in Canada, a Killam Postdoctoral Fellowship made writing up possible and enabled me to research comparative issues in the Pacific region. In Britain, I have long enjoyed the support of the National Maritime Museum, most recently as Caird Junior Research Fellow, and for advice and encouragement I am particularly endebted to Glyn Williams, Peter Marshall, Chris Bayly, and all members of the Imperial History and Maritime History seminars in London. The Menzies Centre for Australian Studies, also in London, has given me vital professional and administrative support.

I must also thank my parents for their editorial and moral support during the final stages of writing up. My editor at the University of Hawai'i Press, Pamela Kelley, has encouraged this project from its early stages, as have the editorial staff of Melbourne University Press. Finally, the book is dedicated to my husband Simon, not because he typed the manuscript or prepared the index, but because he never doubted that it would be written.

JANE SAMSON has traveled widely in the Pacific, crossing disciplinary boundaries and national preoccupations to pursue the challenges of Pacific history. Her current research interests focus on British seaborne exploration, culture contact, and empire from the perspectives and methodologies of anthropology and maritime and imperial history. She has held research fellowships at both Canadian and British universities and is currently in the history department at the University of Alberta. She is coeditor, with Alan Frost, of *Pacific Empires: Discovery and Colonisation in the Eighteenth Century*.

Introduction

PERSPECTIVE is everything. Pacific Studies, imperial history, maritime history, and anthropology tend to form worlds of their own; sailing among them over the past few years, I have often felt a sense of dislocation. Theoretical and methodological approaches can differ radically between disciplines, and sometimes different academic cultures are in open opposition to one another. Pacific Studies, for example, was spawned amid a general rejection of imperial historiography in the 1960s. Recent British imperial history has tended to neglect the Pacific in its preoccupation with Africa and Asia, and with studies of economic imperialism, racist and gendered discourses of hegemony, and the role of law, police, and military force in those parts of the world. Social scientists' traditional denunciations of the excessive subjectivity of history have given way (in some quarters) to denunciations of history's excessive empiricism. Everywhere are calls for greater interdisciplinary cooperation, but too often this cooperation is discouraged by specialist jargons obviously meant to distinguish "us" from "them." Essentialism can act as another centrifugal force, declaring that an academic's profession, gender, or race should enhance or exclude particular fields of study. At this point, L. P. Hartley would remind us that "the past is a foreign country" in which we are all strangers.[1] I am an English speaker, with white skin, but mid-Victorian Britain and the floating cultures of its warships are alien to me. My history must acknowledge their otherness as well as that of the Pacific islanders they encountered. It must also find its own path through today's academic debates about culture and representation. Some voices call for the scrutiny of all texts with an oppositional eye and a rejection of both the privileging and the judging of particular histories. Others call for an academic politics that unequivocally condemns imperialism and all its works. Behind all of this is a familiar tension between metropolitan and peripheral approaches to imperial history, refocused by postmodernist and postcolonial critical theory. My own history suggests that some metropolitan documents have been neglected for too long and that (like most texts) they are full of surprises and unexpected riches; to that extent it is unapologetically empirical. My study will also find constructions of imperial authority that invite debate. It is an oppositional analysis, resisting monolithic categories like "the islanders' side of the story" or "British interests." It notes Pacific islanders' responses to British expansion, where we can glimpse them through (mainly) European documentation, but it emphasizes the diversity of those responses. It identifies British rationalizations of empire, and it confronts the ambivalence and contradictions of rationalization: it is an approach that yields more hard questions than easy judgments.

Any study of European exploration and culture contact in the Pacific invites the crossing of boundaries, as does the maritime environment of the Pacific itself. In maritime histories, the ocean and its communities take center stage, with ships and beaches as the setting for Greg Dening's "ethnographic moment" when worlds and histories collide.[2] A burgeoning literature is currently examining Europe's maritime exploration of the Pacific, but a curtain comes down after Cook, Vancouver, and Bligh leave the stage. Later ship's captains explored, meddled, dreamed, and lost their lives in the Pacific, but we know almost nothing about them. Nineteenth-century missionaries, traders, and beachcombers have all found their historians, but Captain Cook's Victorian successors remain almost inscrutable.

There was no general history of nineteenth-century British naval operations in the Pacific islands until John Bach's 1963 thesis was published as *The Australia Station* in 1986. Bach's book is exactly what it claims to be: a general overview "perhaps written with too much admiration for its subject" that invokes naval assertiveness as a foil for "our current society, with its confusion between racism and culturalism and its pathological lack of confidence in its own values."[3] It is salutary to compare the findings of the Earl of Pembroke, whose tour of the Pacific islands in 1870 inclined him to champion British traders and labor recruiters against their naval detractors. Pembroke denounced "the astounding liberties taken by sentimentio-religious captains of men-of-war" whose evangelical liberalism made them the willing tools of missionaries and islanders.[4] The earl longed instead for "the good old times of Conquest and Colonization," when "the civilized nations of the day . . . maintained that it was the savage's business to understand and conform to their notions, and not their business to regard the savage's."⁵ Just as Pembroke invoked a golden age of martial conquest to reproach the liberalism of his own times, so the Victorian navy can symbolize a cultural confidence perceived to be absent today. These projected anxieties underline the importance of navies as symbols of national virility; where the maritime environment prevails, as in the Pacific, relationships between naval activity and imperialism must be closely scrutinized. In two provocative pages about Europe's navies in *Paradise Found and Lost*, O. H. K. Spate notes that "many officers shared the humanitarian sentiments proper to gentlemen in the Age of Feeling."⁶ We must explore what this meant to them, conscious of the temptation to moralize about what it means to us.

What was "British authority" in the Pacific, and how did the Royal Navy attempt to create it? John Ward wrote in 1948 that "matters of island government [were] . . . effectively coerced, where necessary, by British men-of-war,"⁷ and nearly fifty years later historians have barely begun to question the presumed role of "gunboat diplomacy" in the Pacific. A handful of case studies have made it clear that there was a vast gulf between British and islander interpretations of naval activities, but this has produced no general revision of concepts like "commodore justice" and "naval policing." Also to be considered are the navy's divided opinion on the use of force and the way its hesitations in the Pacific reflected domestic anxieties about how imperial power should be displayed.

My own approach to these questions reflects imperial history's current interest in the ambiguities and contradictions of British expansion. Many passionate critiques of empire have been written in a variety of disciplines to show how the British deployed class, gender, and race as strategies of power. On the other side of the frontier, area studies specialists have emphasized indigenous agency, especially through collaboration and resistance. These complex findings are, in turn, raising questions about the supposedly unified, relentless nature of imperialism. Current work on British domestic history has begun to scrutinize humanitarianism and liberalism; military history has exposed a shifting series of masculinities and images of national vigor; legal history has deconstructed concepts like "law and order" and "the rule of law." These issues have had a profound effect on the study of empire, which now must include both indigenous agency and British mutability in its analysis.⁸

Some scholars have suggested that it is time for a more extensive examination of these issues in the Pacific island context,⁹ and the activities of the Royal Navy provide an ideal focus. The development and dilemmas of British involvement in the islands can be traced clearly through the naval record, which contains everything from islanders' letters and depositions to correspondence from British traders and missionaries. By considering these various voices, together with the officers' reports that enclosed them, we can observe a process of transmission, interpretation, and feedback. I want to show how the British government was drawn into greater involvement in the Pacific through the crafting of a humanitarian mission to protect islanders. Between the eras of culture contact and colonial rule lies the hazy territory of "informal empire," where the definition of British influence lay in the hands (and pens) of Britain's most conspicuous representatives: naval officers. We will see that their self-assigned mission drew upon evangelicalism, antislavery sentiment, and contemporary debate about the nature of race; in other words, it was a contradictory mixture of fears and ideals.

This is not meant to be a comprehensive study of British imperialism in the Pacific, nor is it a technical study of naval operations there. Rather, it is an examination of the navy's sense of mission in the Pacific islands: a phenomenon directed at different island groups at different times. Tahiti and New Zealand were important at the beginning of the nineteenth century, but changing circumstances made naval involvement there more formal; less self-defining. French influence was paramount in Tahiti after 1842. New Zealand became a British colony in 1840, with a government that had its own priorities. In other areas, British naval involvement can be traced over decades without the distraction of international rivalry or the complications of formal colonization. Accounts of Tonga, Samoa, Fiji, and the New Hebrides will predominate. The story will end with the British annexation of Fiji in 1874 because this (or the creation of the Western Pacific High Commission the following year) is where imperial historians have tended to *begin*. The last quarter of the nineteenth century is widely recognized as a time of extensive British expansion, while the imperial activities' preceding seventy-five years are often described as reluctant and limited. I want to turn this story on its head. There was nothing reluctant about the moral empire British representatives sought to make in the Pacific islands, and I want to show the degree of continuity that links the early years of the nineteenth century with the formal territorial expansion of later decades.

Humanitarian representations of island conditions depended both on a misunderstanding of the vigor and adaptability of island cultures and on an exaggerated view of the influence of white men. But more practical difficulties also stood in the way of attempts to protect islanders from physical and moral contamination. These included the absence of legal jurisdiction and the home government's reluctance to transform informal influence into territorial empire.

An exception was made for New Zealand at a time when humanitarian influence in the British government was strong, but the results of the Treaty of Waitangi discouraged those who had hoped that idealistic intentions would produce racial harmony. Elsewhere in the islands, British missionaries and their naval supporters attempted to uphold the concept of indigenous sovereignty by encouraging the ambitions of leaders who might bring centralized government to their societies. However, the official response to their efforts was ambivalent and the recognition of island governments problematic. There was little room in the British imagination for islanders that no longer seemed like children. There was also little support for nonmissionary white men; even British consuls found themselves under attack by naval officers for sympathizing with British subjects rather than islanders. When a former plantation owner in Fiji, John Bates Thurston, became an influential minister in the Cakobau government of the 1870s, traditional humanitarian suspicions did much to influence Commodore James Goodenough's confrontation with him. By the time Goodenough forced the cession of Fiji in 1874, imperial benevolence had been shaping Britain's role in the Pacific islands for decades.

1

Measures of Benevolence

EIGHTEENTH-CENTURY Europe's "Pacific craze" populated the Pacific Ocean with beings from the anthropophagi of *Gulliver's Travels* to Rousseau's noble savages. Dutch and French voyage narratives gave the appearance of realism to various theories about islanders, but erratic publication lessened their impact. Each time Captain Cook returned from the Pacific, however, a veritable publishing industry sprang up to ignite the imaginations of British artists, philosophers, missionaries, and writers of pantomime. Cook's observations drew new lines across the Pacific: a grid of latitude and longitude that fixed the positions of islands now no longer free to roam with Europe's imagination. Observations of islanders, more regular and comprehensive than ever before, invited natural philosophers to assign them a place on the Enlightenment's map of human civilization.[1]

Cook's mission was to replace speculation with certainty; but to members of the new London Missionary Society (LMS), he was more of a prophet than a scientist. His narratives spoke of a paradise lost and a call to redemption. Traders, too, found prophecies in the prices fetched at China for sea otter fur from the northwest coast of North America and in Cook's accounts of the abundant whale and seal populations of the south Pacific Ocean. When missionaries themselves began to publish accounts of the islands, traders arrived to seek sandalwood in Hawai'i and Fiji, while ships' deserters and convicts sought a life of ease and freedom as beachcombers. There were more than two worlds—island and British—meeting in the Pacific. Just as Pacific islanders manifested a wide range of responses to European contact, so Britons spoke of the Pacific with many different voices. British missionaries and their supporters told stories very much like the old satirical parables about savagery and civility. The forces of darkness were no longer monsters, but cannibal feasts and human sacrifice. After islanders began converting to Christianity, the stories changed again to tell of innocence victimized by European lusts.

"Noble savages" got fairly short shrift in Britain, where evangelicalism tended to emphasize the fallen nature of indigenous societies.[2] By Cook's time natural philosophers in Scotland had developed a rudimentary system of classification that ranked societies according to their mode of subsistence—the ethnological equivalent of Cook's navigational grid. Known as the "four-stage" system, it assumed that technologically advanced societies based on private property were superior to nonindustrial or communal ones. The four stages of civilization began with subsistence hunting and gathering, followed by pastoralism, agriculture, and commerce. This approach, as it developed in the writings of Adam Ferguson, Lord Kames, and John Millar, stood Rousseau's idealized savagery on its head, placing "the rude forests of nature" below "agreeable and fertile plains" in the scale of civilization.[3] Rousseau's theories were routinely disparaged in ninteenth-century travel accounts, naval reports, and missionary correspondence, giving the impression that they had once been

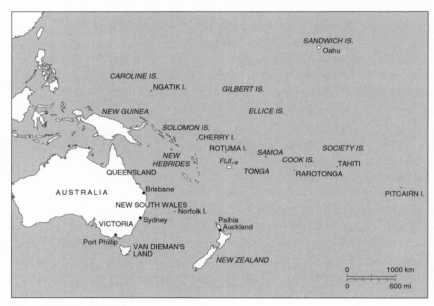

Map 1. The South Pacific

widely accepted. But even in France Rousseau's ideas had been challenged: Napoleon returned from Egypt declaring, "L'homme sauvage est un chien."[4] The noble savage was more useful as a foil than a working theory in British writings. It was a way of emphasizing Britain's accomplishment in bringing Christianity to Pacific islanders while other nations theorized at home.

The first LMS missionaries arrived at Tahiti in 1797; after that, they and other organizations spread steadily throughout the Polynesian islands. The missionaries represented different ecclesiastical points of view: the establishment Anglican Church Missionary Society (CMS), the congregationalist LMS, and the Wesleyan Methodist Missionary Society (WMMS). Each had its own jealously guarded territory. The LMS expanded from Tahiti throughout the Society Islands and on to Samoa, the Marquesas, and the Cook Islands; while the Methodists established bases in Tonga and Fiji in the 1830s. In 1820, the American Board of Commissioners for Foreign Missions, known as the "Boston Mission," arrived in the Sandwich Islands. From Australia the Anglicans moved into New Zealand in 1814 and Melanesia in the 1840s, avoiding the territory of the Presbyterian New Hebrides Mission founded in 1850. There were open clashes about territory and much privately voiced criticism of theology and method. Nevertheless, there was a remarkable degree of consistency in mission attitudes toward islanders—and toward the great enemies, beachcombers and Catholicism.

Britain's four-stage cultural theories easily accommodated missionary interpretations of island societies; the Evangelical revival simply added a moral dimension to the existing material classification system by using biblical allegory to describe Pacific backwardness and British superiority. Missionaries to the Pacific often saw islanders as living examples of antique humanity, a view that emphasized that it was the circumstances of time and space—not differences of race—that had allowed Western Europeans to advance. LMS missionary William Ellis' influential book *Polynesian Researches* (1829) attempted to link Polynesian origins with ancient Semitic or Hindu migration, working from the premise that, after the biblical Flood, all peoples shared a single language and culture.[5] This was little different from John Locke's famous statement that "in the beginning all the World was America" or Adam Ferguson's belief that by observing non-Europeans "we are to behold, as in a mirror, the features of our own progenitors."[6]

Victorian ethnologists simply incorporated new peoples into this framework. The work of James Prichard, a founding member of the Aborigines' Protection Society (APS), had a particular significance for the humanitarian movement.[7] Prichard's emphasis on "one blood" for all peoples complemented the Anti-Slavery Society's slogan "Am I Not a Man and a Brother?" and the APS's own motto "Ab Une Sanguine." Prichard's approach was not new—it recalled the biblical anthropology of early modern natural philosophy—but it appeared in the new context of the antislavery movement, the developing science of comparative anatomy, and growing British patriotism.[8] After Prichard's death in 1849, Robert Latham carried on his work by adding a fifth stage to the scale of civilization in which the "influences of religion, literature, science, and political and social morality" produced the highest stage of development—as in Britain.[9]

Since slavery itself could claim biblical sanction through the curse of Ham (supposed ancestor of black Africans), much ink was spilled countering this with references to Genesis, Christ's universal sacrifice, and the shared humanity theories of ethnologists and missionaries. The result for Pacific islanders was a flurry of articles in humanitarian journals like the *Journal of Civilization,* which declared in 1841 that "there is no peculiarity in any of these islanders, which shuts them out from the pale of Christianity and civilization."[10] For missionaries on the spot in the south Pacific, it was not always easy to believe in equality of potential. After seeing his first cooked human body in Fiji, William Moore wondered whether Fijians had souls at all, let alone the capacity for redemption, and sternly reminded himself: "O yes! This is man without the Gospel, 'A beast in body, A demon in mind,' but there is still hope. . . . My commission extends even to these, for they are still out of Hell, although at its very jaws."[11] The theories of Darwin, which seem to tower over the Victorian period in retrospect, did not make a significant impact on British thinking about Pacific islanders until much later in the nineteenth century.[12] Questions of culture and environment, rather than "race" in a purely biological sense, dominated British accounts of Pacific islanders in the early and mid-nineteenth century. Besides, British humanitarians sought both connections and distinctions between themselves and islanders. That was the general nature of the British paternalism often dubbed "Exeter Hall," after the London venue for missionary and benevolent societies. It emphasized brotherhood and sisterhood, but its whole purpose was to assist those categorized as disadvantaged.[13] We must examine British humanitarianism in the Pacific islands in all of its contradictory zeal.

War with Napoleonic France concluded the "Age of Discovery" as exemplified by Cook, but already Britain had established a Pacific presence stretching from its Chinese trading base at Canton to the colonies of New South Wales and Van Dieman's Land and across the Pacific to the northwest coast of America.[14] These developments had been a piecemeal response to circumstances rather than a formal policy of colonial expansion. The establishment of New

South Wales in 1788 had taken place only after extensive debate, and Britain had asserted its influence on the northwest coast only after the Nootka Sound controversy nearly provoked war with Spain in 1790. It was often subordinate officials or colonial governments themselves who pushed for imperial expansion. East India Company hydrographer Alexander Dalrymple advocated collaboration with the Hudson's Bay Company to keep the growing north Pacific fur trade in British hands and revived the question of a northwest passage between the Atlantic and Pacific oceans. At the turn of the nineteenth century, naval surveyors like Matthew Flinders and Philip Parker King helped the New South Wales government to consolidate Britain's claim to the whole Australian continent through the patronage of Joseph Banks at home.

New South Wales had begun trading with Pacific islanders almost at once, and a number of problems arose that would become all too familiar in later decades. In the Australian colonies themselves, the position of Aboriginal peoples was unclear. New South Wales had been colonized on the principle of *terra nullius,* literally "no one's land," but the land was already inhabited, and legal confusion about the status of the indigenous population would often overwhelm attempts to treat them as British subjects.[15] Confusion increased as British traders, missionaries, and beachcombers began moving into the Pacific islands in greater numbers after the 1790s. I will return to this subject again, but for now it is important to note that virtually all of the problems of culture contact in the islands, as interpreted by the British, were first played out in the Society Islands and New Zealand. Escaped convicts required capture, the need for provisions and goods like timber or flax required collaborative relationships with island leaders, and British missionaries required protection. Before the European peace of 1815 brought the Royal Navy back into the Pacific, beach communities and mission stations had already sprung up with their attendant questions of jurisdiction and sovereignty.

When naval exploration recommenced after 1815, the evangelical revival and paternalistic ideas about race and empire had begun to infiltrate naval wardrooms. Already associated with Britain's moral victory against slavery, the Royal Navy now took the humanitarian crusade of "Christianization and Civilization" to the Pacific. Britain's maritime supremacy seemed to be an endorsement of that mission, as the Society for the Diffusion of Useful Knowledge proclaimed: "The extention of civilization throughout every region of the earth where the people are ignorant and wretched, appears to be the peculiar duty which Providence has imposed upon a maritime and commercial nation."[16] From 1829 onward there were regular patrols of the larger island groups once a year; either from the Pacific Station, based in South America, or the East Indian Station, based at first on Ceylon and later at Hong Kong.[17] The duplication of effort combined with concerns about French expansion produced a semi-independent Australian Division in 1848 with its headquarters at Sydney. As the navy's role in the islands grew, the Division became the Australia Station in 1859.

An increasingly sophisticated organization did not provide naval captains with detailed direction about their island duties, however. Their standing orders, which changed little during our period, urged them to demonstrate respect for indigenous societies by conforming "strictly to the established Regulations & Customs of the Place."[18] Emphasis on island sovereignty was consistent with current humanitarian thinking and with the Royal Navy's role in negotiating antislavery treaties in other parts of the world, but it placed captains in an awkward position with regard to the protection of British interests in the Pacific islands. The Admiralty directed the commander in chief of the Pacific Station to protect British subjects, but his captains were "limited to affording an Asylum on board Ship in cases of extreme necessity."[19] Captains were to defer to the local British consul, who would attempt to negotiate a settlement of grievances. The Admiralty especially discouraged the use of firepower to resolve disputes, since this would "defeat the maintenance of those amicable terms of commercial intercourse, which the presence of a Naval Force is intended to cherish and protect."[20] Captains puzzled about how to apply these instructions in areas without British consuls or even identifiable governments. Although Richard Charlton had been appointed British Consul for the Sandwich and Society Islands in 1824, he never left his base at Honolulu. Consul George Pritchard did not arrive at Samoa until 1845—and not until 1858 did the Foreign Office approve a third consulate at Fiji. There were no jurisdictional treaties, as there were in West Africa, and few competent interpreters. Thus captains relied on their own initiative to guide them through their encounters with islanders—a situation that makes a study of their own perceptions imperative.

Like other Britons, naval officers were influenced by pre-Darwinian ethnological theories, especially Prichard's. In the first edition of the *Admiralty Manual of Scientific Enquiry*, published in 1849 as mandatory reading for Royal Navy officers, Darwin appears as a geologist; it was Prichard who contributed the ethnological essay just before his death. The *Manual*, which went through many editions in the nineteenth century, was meant to be a guide to naval observations about every aspect of scientific investigation—and officers prepared themselves to observe indigenous peoples through the lens of Prichard's humanitarianism. Their own religious beliefs already predisposed them toward that point of view in any case. Although Cook and many of his immediate successors had not been noticeably pious men, the situation was altogether different by 1840.

Instructed to protect all British subjects in the islands, naval officers took a particular interest in missionaries, at first because they and their superiors were suspicious about mission activities. The early years were difficult for the LMS and CMS pioneers; experiments with different forms of proselytism had provoked controversy, especially when the numbers of converts seemed to be unusually large or mission trading operations uncomfortably profitable.[21] In a disastrous operation that almost led to the collapse of the CMS mission to New Zealand, Samuel Marsden tried to introduce Western economic and cultural practices before teaching Christianity. The LMS, too, had chosen its first missionaries from farming and artisan backgrounds, hoping to civilize before it Christianized, but they soon began to seek better theological and pastoral qualifications of its applicants. Both of these societies eventually settled on a blend of religious and cultural instruction, believing that waged labor, Western marriage, and literacy were important factors in facilitating conversion to Christianity. John Williams, the best known of these early missionaries, purchased a schooner to carry LMS teachers and supplies to the islands, and to sell the coconut oil being produced by island labor on LMS mission stations.

It was the apparently excessive form of the "civilizing" process that some naval officers, and the British public, found reprehensible. In 1830, the East Indies Station despatched Commander Sandilands of HMS *Comet* to "report especially on the present state of those places and the Progress of the Inhabitants in Civilization and Christianity, their intercourse with other places and the effect apparently produced on them by the visits of the Traders or Missionaries."[22] Other captains conducted their own investigations. Captain Frederick Beechey of HMS *Blossom*, who published the journal of his surveying voyage in 1831, claimed that missionaries exaggerated their successes and were autocratic toward island converts, forbidding amusements such as dancing that he believed were harmless.[23] HMS *Alligator*'s officers, at New Zealand in 1834, had read Augustus Earle's denunciation of the CMS.[24] The ship's devout assistant surgeon, William Marshall, warned missionary Henry Williams that "Earl's narrative had been the general topic of conversation for many weeks and that they would scrutinize us with much severity."[25] Williams was summoned to the wardroom and interrogated about Earle's allegations.[26] Sir Edward Belcher of HMS *Sulphur*, surveying the Pacific in 1837, was particularly critical of the LMS in Tahiti and the Sandwich Islands, where the missions monopolized trade and fostered "the tyranny of fanatics."[27]

In response to these criticisms, mission societies began keeping a tighter rein on their far-flung brethren,[28] and the opinions of naval officers themselves began to change as a larger number of captains began supporting missions out of a personal commitment to Christianity. For some, south Pacific duty proved to be a spiritual turning point. Ellis and his colleagues recalled that Captain Gambier of HMS *Dauntless* was "not prepossessed in favour of them" and "in a measure suspicious of their reports."[29] After only a few days and the inspection of what appeared to be a model English village amid the palm trees, it seemed to Gambier that paradise had indeed been regained and that the beautiful island scenery reflected the way "the blessings of Christianity were diffused amongst the fine people who inhabited it."[30] Captain William Waldegrave of HMS *Seringapatam* was also skeptical about the LMS when he arrived at Tahiti in 1830. He disapproved of mission involvement in trade and suspected the mission's honesty in reporting such large numbers of converts. The missionaries were insulted when the captain, catechism in hand, began questioning their flock.[31] By the time he reached Tonga, Waldegrave had become more supportive, striking Methodist missionary George Turner as "the decided friend of Missionaries," who "seems resolved to remove every impediment out of our way that lays in his power."[32] The captain's enthusiasm grew at Rarotonga, where he met John Williams, and he returned to England a changed man. He attended the next annual meeting of the LMS to tell the story of his voyage and became a lifelong subscriber to the society. An Anglican, he also became an active member of the CMS and served on several of its committees.[33]

Junior officers, too, found themselves profoundly affected by the piety of newly converted islanders. Lieutenant Frederick Walpole of HMS *Collingwood*, seeing a rainbow over Apia during his visit to Samoa in 1848, described it as "an earnest of [God's] promise to the savage and the sage, the east and the west,— to all nations and all tongues, for they are alike to be partakers in the great inheritance; and the naked heathens, now my companions, are fellow-heirs with the polished European, and equally with him, sons of God."[34] Ashamed that his own religious observances compared so unfavorably with the dedication of Samoan Christians, Walpole found it ironic that he, an Englishman, was finding islanders' Christianity more vital than religious practice his own country. It was men like Walpole who inspired the *Journal of Civilization* to declare that naval officers "did not forget that they were also enlisted under the more glorious banner of the Lord of Hosts."[35]

One officer's excessive zeal recalled the *Gentleman's Magazine* warning about naval officers "better fitted for the organ loft than the quarter deck."[36] Walter Croker, commander of HMS *Favorite,* was so inspired by the activities of the Methodists in Tonga that he promised to address their annual meeting at Exeter Hall after returning to Britain.[37] In the meantime, discovering that the Christian communities on the island of Tongatapu were under attack from pagan rivals, Croker decided to lend military assistance to the cause of Christ. Like a crusader, he drew up a combined British and Tongan force near the pagan headquarters at Pea and charged the fortifications with a sword.[38] He was killed at once and his ordnance captured. Croker seems to have realized that his decision would be controversial, for he had told the missionaries that "the Providence of Almighty God had directed him in coming to the place" and "with what pleasure he should lose his commission in HM Service if in doing this work his conduct should be disapproved."[39]

If less enthusiastic than Croker, most captains and Senior Officers of the Australian Division after the 1840s seem to have been pious men who went out of their way to assist the various missionary societies. They helped transport new missionaries to their stations, made handsome donations to mission funds, and made a splendid show of gold braid and epaulettes at island church services. Although they were more restrained in expressing it, they also shared a suspicion of the French Roman Catholic mission activities that had begun in 1827. Captain Home of HMS *North Star* noted with approval that the Methodist missionaries at Tonga had "very comfortable houses with good gardens," built and tended for them by Tongan servants. At the French Roman Catholic mission station on Wallis Island, however, even the resident bishop "lived entirely in the Native fashion." From this, Home concluded that "they are behind our Missionaries in all respects, and the Natives gain but little advance in Civilization through their means."[40] These responses to French activities in general must be distinguished from the treatment of French missionaries as individuals. The French navy made relatively few patrols of the islands, forcing French missionaries to turn to the Royal Navy with their grievances: lack of transportation, supply shortages, and undelivered letters.[41] In 1849, Captain Erskine of HMS *Havannah* met Bishop Pompellier at the Isle of Pines just before the reestablishment of the French mission at Yengin in New Caledonia. The bishop was waiting for transportation and seemed embarrassed as he admitted that "he was to have left

Tahiti in a ship of war, if one could have been spared."[42] The captain was glad to hear that "he and his companions had often received valuable attention and assistance from Captains of English merchant vessels both here and at Aneityum," as this seemed to be the only way the bishop was able to continue his activities.[43] At Tonga, Erskine found the Catholic mission at Moa badly in need of medicines and did his best to provide supplies from his ship's stores.[44] Less virulently anti-Catholic than their missionary compatriots, naval officers usually preferred some sort of Christianization over none at all.

While contemplating the outspoken faith of officers like these, we must refrain from judging by twentieth-century standards of service "professionalism." A present-day officer would be censured for acting officially out of personal religious conviction, but the nineteenth-century concept of "duty" was much more flexible. At issue was what Captain Stephen Fremantle called the "high and chivalrous feeling"[45] that should guide naval officers in their dealings with Pacific islanders. As sentimental and unprofessional as this romanticism seems in late twentieth-century eyes, it must be taken seriously as an important component of naval humanitarianism in the nineteenth-century Pacific. One of the most Victorian of words, "duty," governed a man's conduct as an officer, a gentleman, a Christian, and a Briton; during most of this period, Christian duty was considered as important as any other aspect of character.[46] Influenced by romanticism and neo-chivalry, and by the growing legend of Lord Nelson, most naval officers believed that they had moral responsibilities far exceeding their instructions. Captain Francis Crozier visited the south Pacific before his tragic death in the Arctic during Franklin's last search for the Northwest Passage. Reporting to the Admiralty in 1836, Crozier declared, "Above all things, I hope I have exalted the character of the British Nation among uninstructed savages, by examples of Morality, firmness, and Moderation."[47] Captain Patrick Blake of HMS *Juno* rebuked Consul George Pritchard for his unenlightened view of Samoans, believing that "there was something due from us to a half-savage uninstructed people, such as justice, charity and moderation, especially on the part of ourselves . . . belonging to a country whose fame and whose power is spread throughout the world, and whose justice, if I am conscious of it, in the station I hold, I will not be a willing instrument to sully."[48] Blake's contemporary, Captain Edward Fanshawe of HMS *Daphne*, left for his Pacific cruise vowing to be "a sort of knight errant,"[49] and he was not alone in viewing his role as a heroic one. The first Bishop of New Zealand, Augustus Selwyn, looked favorably on the fervor of his naval friends, hoping they "would be like Shakespeare's sun, to make glorious summer out of the winter of discontent." Better still, he added, "the days of Captain Cook would return again. . . . England enjoys at present the best reputation of all the naval powers; and it is for her to take the lead in making this Ocean as Pacific in its moral character as it is already in its climate and in its name."[50] It was no coincidence that Captain John Erskine, the first Senior Officer of the Australian Division, sailed for Sydney with only two portraits in his cabin: those of Cook and Nelson.[51] To Cook's navigational skill and humane leadership was joined Nelson's heroic, Christian patriotism.

The Great Navigator had almost divine status among his naval successors.[52] They sought echoes of his presence through elderly islanders who remembered him or the descendants of individuals about whom he had written. At Tahiti in 1829, Commander William Laws met Mahine, heir of Omai, "the Native who visited England and returned to his country with and under the protection of Captain Cook." Laws was delighted when Mahine showed him items Omai had brought back from England, including two muskets and a fowling piece given to him by Lord Sandwich.[53] Captain Robert Fitzroy was so attached to Cook's reports that he clung to the anachronistic name "Otaheite," because "our immortal countryman, Cook, wrote Otaheite, and it is difficult to hear or see the word without thinking of him."[54] Relying on Cook's pioneering surveys well into the nineteenth century, captains like Fitzroy also followed the track of his first encounters with islanders and his death at their hands. Like pilgrims, they called at Tahiti and the Sandwich Islands to stand where he landed, to weep where he fell, and to seek relics of his passing. In 1839, Captain John Shepherd and the crew of HMS *Sparrowhawk* labored to preserve the remains of a coconut tree growing near the spot where Cook died. After tarring the stump and installing a commemorative plaque, they broke pieces of rock as mementos while "endeavouring to call to mind the scenes of which this most interesting spot had once been the theatre."[55] The British were not the only ones who found sacredness in this place: after his crew had trimmed the stump of "Cook's Tree," Captain Shepherd observed an elderly islander reverently carrying the discarded wood away to a nearby burial site.

There were other naval pilgrimages: to Dillon's Bay, Eromanga, where missionary John Williams was murdered; and to Pitcairn Island, where chaplain George Nobbs recorded the visits and correspondence of the dozens of officers to whom the Pitcairn community represented a miracle of survival and redemption. Nobbs received their gifts and donations, welcoming their assistance during the islanders' temporary move to Norfolk Island. "Your beloved flock have won my heart" said Admiral Fairfax Moresby in 1853, and he wrote to Nobbs and to the children of Pitcairn until his death.[56] Like the wake of Cook, the track from Pitcairn to the British mission stations and the sites of British martyrdom became part of a Pacific Christian geography.[57]

This study focuses on the captains who directed their ships' dealings with islanders, but we should note that not all junior officers or sailors were as devout or humanitarian as their commanders. At Fiji in 1850 Lieutenant Henry Swainson of HMS *Bramble* ridiculed the "cant & d———d sanctified bosh" of missionaries like "that crying Bitch" James Calvert.[58] By 1875 the noble purpose of the navy's antislavery activities had paled for Lieutenant Frank Henderson; on his first cruise of the south Pacific in HMS *Sappho,* he was pleasantly surprised to find that islanders were better looking than he expected and wondered whether "after the Coast of Africa I am more easily pleased as regards coloured races than most people." He contemplated "the Exeter Hall Mob," wishing they could be transported from their comfortable British homes to where "this tropical heat & hard faces would do their godly stomachs good."[59] Below decks, missionary passengers occasionally noticed examples of piety and praised captains' successes in restricting the use of foul language.[60] But it is difficult to document the beliefs of sailors or soldiers directly. Bishop Selwyn's view was that, although the men were "clean, orderly and attentive," there was a long way to go "before we shall have such a navy as would be a true protection to our empire, composed of men who themselves seek and rely upon the protection of the Most High."[61] Perhaps the best summary of the situation was Fremantle's, when, after unsuccessful attempts to get his cook to attend church in Sydney, he remarked that "amongst the men generally, as compared with other ships, there is some good disposition to pay attention to religion, always improving when at sea, and always falling off when in Port."[62]

Yet it was sometimes a junior officer who pressed for a more Christian agenda. Returning to England in 1835 from service in *Alligator,* William Marshall published his criticisms of the ship's recent mission to New Zealand.[63] The governor of New South Wales had instructed Captain George Lambert to rescue an Englishwoman and two children being held captive by Maori near Cape Egmont, New Zealand. The mission was successful but at the cost of Maori lives and property, consequences Marshall believed could have been avoided had the expedition used missionary interpreters and taken a more conciliatory approach. His views attracted the attention of the House of Commons' Select Committee on Aborigines, chaired by the humanitarian Fowell Buxton. Both Marshall and Captain Lambert were called to give testimony in 1836, but it was Marshall's humanitarian view that the committee's final report reflected.[64] Condemning Lambert's handling of the expedition, it declared that he had obstructed "those measures of benevolence which the Legislature designs to native and barbarous tribes" by failing to act according to humanitarian principles with missionary support and advice.[65] The committee recommended official changes to the navy's involvement with Pacific islanders; as Britain's representatives in the islands, naval officers should act with tolerance toward islanders, while promoting the spread of Christianity.

The investigation of *Alligator's* New Zealand operations revealed shared humanitarian concerns, but it also underlined divisions of opinion. Lambert told the Select Committee that missionaries like Henry Williams in New Zealand had supported his use of force. CMS superiors in Sydney had deplored it. This ambivalence would become typical of the naval-mission relationship in future decades. Missionaries often praised naval captains for their support, while expressing doubts among themselves about accepting assistance based on the influence of guns and powder. Sometimes a mission would plead for naval intervention when its stations were threatened by islanders, discounting the navy's role once danger had passed or the intervention had proved unprofitable. Having invited Captain Croker's ill-fated support, then appalled by his death, Tonga's missionaries began disowning him at once. Lamenting his "rashness and imprudence," they suggested that he had gone mad.[66] In other cases, individuals contradicted themselves. The Methodist mission superintendent Walter Lawry declared, "We know that the Gospel needs not the aid of great guns," but wrote bitterly about the lack of naval support for his missionaries during the mid-1840s.[67] Even in dangerous Fiji, missionaries were unsure about the navy. Richard Lyth, amid renewed civil war in 1838, hoped for the early arrival of the *Herald* and recalled the successful peacemaking activities of previous captains. However, he continued, "in general, ships of war have not materially served our cause. An arm of flesh is not to be trusted to for the great work of subjugating human minds to the obedience of faith."[68] Although missionaries and their naval patrons were both committed to "Christianization and Civilization," the partnership was sometimes an uneasy one.

One goal humanitarians all shared was the challenge "to improve the character of the barbarous but energetic races of men" in the Pacific islands, something possible only if islanders were capable of "improvement."[69] We have already seen how they were described as "uninstructed savages" whose failings stemmed from heathenism rather than inherent inferiority. However, as European contact with the islands increased, attacks on white men threatened to cause a backlash against these images of childlike dependency. Samoa, for example, had already acquired an ominous reputation after the murder of members of the

French explorer La Pérouse's crew on the island of Tutuila in 1787. Although the captain left without taking revenge (he tacked for two days attempting to get within cannon range), he later published an embittered report describing Samoans as treacherous savages.[70] His account was so convincing that in 1829 Laws of the *Satellite* refused to pursue some escaped convicts to Samoa, declaring that the savage cannibals of that place would already have killed them.[71] In 1838, Bethune reported a different interpretation of the La Pérouse incident. Published in the *Nautical Magazine,* Bethune's explanation (obtained from missionaries) insisted that Samoans had retaliated against the French after one of them had been murdered by a sailor.[72] The American explorer Charles Wilkes repeated this interpretation, quoted in turn by John Erskine.[73] This reconstruction of the La Pérouse episode was self-conscious; Erskine, at least, had read the original French account. Apparently mindless savagery had been transformed into vulnerability, creating a Samoa in need of protection from European aggression— a complete reversal of La Pérouse's perspective.

Even "The Cannibal Islands" of Fiji were redeemable, despite their reputation for ferocity. Captain Crozier mentioned the murder of French and American traders by Fijians in his 1836 report but added that "the visit of a Man of War occasionally among them will tend much to their improvement."[74] Captain Henry Worth of HMS *Calypso,* visiting in 1848, reported: "It might be judged that but little can be said respecting the character of a people so degraded as the Feejeeans evidently are: what character can cannibals have, it might be asked, but that of the wild beast? That they are deeply degraded admits of no denial; yet they are not without characteristics of an intellectual, and even moral kind."[75] Despite their cannibal propensities, Erskine thought Fijians were "the finest & most improvable people we have seen,"[76] while Home reported Fijian "abominations" in 1852 "to shew that every exertion of Christian and humane nations is required to turn these people (who are as capable of humanity as any other amongst the islands) from the habits which they now follow."[77]

Parts of Melanesia were virtually unexplored by Europeans until the middle of the nineteenth century, and although the sandalwood trade brought some European traders to the New Hebrides, the suspicious and often hostile behavior of the islanders prompted descriptions of them as "deceitful and treacherous . . . savage and frightful."[78] Humanitarians strove to dispel these negative images. Eromanga, infamous for its murder of LMS missionaries John Williams and John Harris in 1839, was given special consideration. Philip Vigors, an army officer aboard *Havannah,* observed that it was only a matter of time before "proper means" enabled Eromanga to be settled by Europeans "living in friendly intercourse with the natives, who are now accounted very savage and have at several times murdered boats crews."[79] Erskine noted that several Eromangans, including "a friendly chief," had been shot by unscrupulous sandalwood traders and invited greater attention to white "atrocities."[80]

This view of islanders was protective: islanders were potentially improvable but in need of sympathetic guidance. Naval reports sometimes emphasized islanders' capacity for improvement by comparing them to ancient Britons. Mediterranean missionaries had Christianized and improved Britain's Celtic and Saxon inhabitants, beginning the process that many believed accounted for Britain's present position of international influence.[81] The Fijian chiefs Cakobau and Gavidi reminded Captain Erskine of Scottish highlanders, a comparison often made by readers of Sir Walter Scott's *History of Scotland* and its descriptions of the "Christianization and Civilization" of one of Britain's first imperial frontiers.[82] Captain Home took a different approach when congratulating Tāufaʻāhau of Tonga on the defeat of his enemies, calling him the "Alfred the Great of the Friendly islands."[83] Through metaphors like these Pacific islanders were defined as kin to their British observers, but in the manner of children whose elders were guiding their education and development.[84] Images of islander dependency were reinforced by ethnographic theories about the vulnerability of less advanced societies. Prichard's ethnology, which did so much to shape the objectives of the APS, was meant to obtain more information about "the feeble uncivilized races of mankind," and the society itself declared that its object was "to assist in protecting the defenceless."[85] Mission and naval reports frequently cited declining population figures as "evidence" of approaching extinction, blaming European traders for the introduction of venereal disease and firearms into the islands. Only humanitarian efforts stood between the "feeble races" and extermination, not by the process of natural selection—that theory came later—but through the moral negligence of civilized Europe.[86]

It was to avoid such negligence that Britain agreed to colonize New Zealand through the Treaty of Waitangi in 1840. British missionaries and traders had been colliding with the Maori and with each other throughout the 1820s, prompting the New South Wales government to request regular naval patrols there.[87] Although governors King and Macquarie attempted to ensure Maori consent for the building of trading establishments in New Zealand by Australian traders, stories of atrocity continued to pour in from the CMS missionaries. The most shocking was that of the *Elizabeth*, a New South Wales trading vessel whose master had encouraged his Maori friends to go to war in order to provide him with a supply of preserved heads destined for the lucrative curiosities market. The

Select Committee on Aborigines heard testimony about the *Elizabeth* affair and probed the ineffectual role subsequently played by British Resident James Busby. Busby was appointed by New South Wales governor Darling in 1831 after the *Elizabeth* scandal, but his lack of legal authority made his position untenable. During the *Harriet* investigation in 1834, Captain Lambert of the *Alligator* virtually ignored him. To some Maori leaders, however, Busby represented their best hope of direct communication with the British government. Busby had arrived with a letter from the Secretary of State for the Colonies, Lord Goderich, which promised the Maori "friendship and alliance with Great Britain" in return for their support of the new Residency. For a while some of the North Island chiefs collaborated with Busby to foster Maori political unity: in March 1834 a group of twenty-five chiefs chose a flag from a selection brought by HMS *Alligator* on the ship's first visit to New Zealand. Their choice was the English flag (white with red Cross of St. George) with a blue upper-left quadrant showing a red Christian cross and four white stars. The warship hoisted it along with the Union Jack and gave it the twenty-one-gun salute of a sovereign state.[88] Later, when the French adventurer Baron de Thierry announced his plans for large-scale land acquisition in New Zealand, the chiefs signed a declaration of independence whose language was designed to appeal to its paternalistic British readers. The chiefs invited King William IV to be "the parent of their infant state," which they had named "The United Tribes of New Zealand."[89] The Maori alliance soon disintegrated, however, along with Busby's influence.

Meanwhile, the New Zealand Company was attempting to organize an emigration scheme conceived by Edward Gibbon Wakefield. After the Select Committee's minutes and report were published, humanitarians reacted angrily to the idea that any private organization, "however benevolent," had the ability to accomplish "the arduous task of raising the New Zealanders to the enjoyment of the blessings of a Christian and civilized State."[90] Instead, the position of British Resident should be strengthened in order to control misbehaving British subjects.

Although they joined the chorus of Busby's critics, New Zealand's missionaries were adamantly opposed to the colonization, believing it would victimize the Maori and jeopardize Christianization. The House of Lords agreed, advising against British rule in its 1838 report on New Zealand.[91] However, British-based Anglicans like Bishop Samuel Hinds were in favor of British rule, because it would control the behavior of white men and because "civilized man is the guardian of the savage—God and nature appoint that it should be so."[92] Only a preemptive strike by Edward Gibbon Wakefield's New Zealand Company broke the deadlock.[93] When the company's first emigrant ship left England in 1840, the British government decided that colonialism was preferable to "the accumulating evils of a permanent anarchy" that Busby and members of the Committee on Aborigines were predicting.[94] Direct rule would permit Britain to control emigration and land sales, and, it was hoped, the Treaty of Waitangi would give the Maori all the rights of British subjects. Some British officials, like James Stephen at the Colonial Office, had always hoped for colonization and set about attempting to make it as benign as possible.[95] The path to colonization displays the complicated relationship between humanitarianism and imperialism, and the ambiguous definition of "British interests" in the south Pacific. On one point, however, all humanitarians were agreed: white villains were reponsible for the most troubling aspects of culture contact in the Pacific islands.

2

White Savages

CAPTAIN Cook first arrived at Tahiti in 1769, after the visits of Wallis and Bougainville, and was interested in the effects of European contact on Tahitians. In 1773, on his second voyage, he was also able to observe the consequences of his own activities. The prognosis was not good: Cook noted evidence of recent warfare and new faces in the highest social ranks. In New Zealand, where Maori men offered their female relatives to the visitors, James King wrote a passionate condemnation of the European visitors who debauched "morals already too prone to vice."[1] Cook himself admired many aspects of the societies he encountered, not least their freedom from materialism, and was saddened by what he perceived to be the contaminating effect of European contact. By his third voyage, the venereal diseases were spreading "which will for ever embitter their quiet & happy lives, & make them curse the hour they ever saw us."[2]

If islanders were victims, then who victimized them? Cook seldom shrank from the ironies or the tragedies of his quest for knowledge, but later British travelers were more inclined to point the finger. Victorian naval and mission reports were full of claims about the perfidious influence of French sailors, who were held responsible for everything in the islands from alcoholism to sodomy. However satisfying for nationalist sentiment these claims might have been—and the French gave as good as they got—the French presence in the south Pacific was simply too small to be held responsible for the wide-ranging consequences of culture contact. New and better villains were found in the beachcombers, escaped convicts, and traders who competed with British missionaries for the attention and labor of islanders. Traders, after all, brought a different set of referents to the islands: the best price for seal fur, the Chinese demand for sandalwood, the British market for whale oil. Islanders were a source of labor and supplies, and their aptitude for trade was more important than their religious beliefs. A willingness to exchange sandalwood for muskets represented a commercial opportunity rather than a moral dilemma for most traders; and some features of indigenous society, notably the sexual availability of women, were positively welcomed. For missionaries no compromise was possible, either with islanders' indigenous practices or with the white men who helped perpetuate them.

The humanitarian interpretation of island conditions contained two interdependent themes: a benevolent, protective view of islanders and the condemnation of white men defined as threats to "Christianization and Civilization." This viewpoint had its own internal logic, whereby islander behavior at odds with their presumed backwardness and passivity could be explained with reference to outside agency. The energy with which islanders sought European trade goods like firearms, for example, or the efficiency with which they made war was generally credited to the corrupting influence of the European men who lived among them in increasing numbers during the nineteenth century. Although these beachcombers were sometimes escaped convicts, most were seamen who had deserted or been abandoned by their own shipmasters. Shipowners in Britain were well aware of how often their captains put men ashore to avoid reponsibility for medical treatment or pay, and by 1836 shipowners in the British whaling industry were asking the Admiralty for help in controlling the excesses of some of their ships' masters.[3] The total number of European beachcombers numbered about two thousand by mid-century, and they congregated near the most popular ports of call in the Sandwich Islands, Tahiti, and New Zealand.[4]

Since Tahiti featured the islands' first British missions, it also produced the earliest humanitarian accounts of the beachcomber threat. New South Wales' pork trade with Tahiti, which lasted until about 1820, brought escaped convicts to the Society Island group and gave the LMS missionaries ready-made symbols of moral depravity.[5] A similar story unfolded at other islands, and naval officers, often asked to search for escaped convicts by the New South Wales authorities, sometimes became preoccupied by this aspect of their duties and exaggerated the scale of the problem. Captain Waldegrave's 1830 report led Rear Admiral Baker of the Pacific Station to report that "the Friendly and Society Islands are at present infested by great numbers of worthless characters calling themselves Englishmen, from New South Wales and elsewhere, who keep the natives in constant dread of their depredations."[6] It is difficult to tell which upset the Admiral more, the fact that islanders were living "in constant dread" or that convicts were "calling themselves Englishmen." They were Englishmen, for the most part, but the Admiral was making a distinction between those he believed were a credit to their country—like missionaries—and those who were not. Rear Admiral Owen of the East Indies Station took a similar view, remarking to one of his officers that the "misconduct" of white men outside mission stations in the south Pacific was "digraceful to the British name and character as well as to the Christian religion and to Humanity."[7] Such individuals were not worthy of the name Englishmen. Time and again we observe this pattern of exclusion: humanitarians defining themselves as the true defenders of Christianity and civilization against the treacherous white men who betrayed their own culture.

Owen's captains would be the first of many to criticize British whaling crews and other traders, and details of the controversial *Alligator* expedition seemed to confirm the impression that white misbehavior lay behind outbreaks of violence with islanders. In his account of the episode, Marshall suggested that the *Harriet*'s crew had provoked the Maori to violence; he noted that *Harriet*'s captain was a former convict who proclaimed that "a musket ball for every New Zealander is the only way of civilizing their country!"[8] The report of the Select Committee on Aborigines, which drew attention to Marshall's interpretation, obscured distinctions between traders, escaped convicts, and other undesirables in the islands: "Our runaway convicts are the pests of savage as well as of civilized society; so are our runaway sailors; and the crews of our whaling vessels, and of the traders from New South Wales. . . . In proof of this we need only refer to the evidence of the missionaries."[9]

The missionaries' evidence frequently pointed to the exchange of liquor for food and other supplies as prime evidence of "the demoralization and impediments to the civilisation and prosperity of the people."[10] In Samoa, where La Pérouse's savages were becoming model converts, the islanders had also been curious about European trade goods. After whalers, deserters, and escaped convicts began doing business and taking up residence in the beach community of Apia in the 1830s, missionary John Thomas testified to the Committee on Aborigines that "our hearts almost bleed for the poor Samoa people; they are a very mild, inoffensive race . . . but the conduct of our English savages has a tone of barbarity and cruelty in it which was never heard of or practised by them."[11] The committee did not invite testimony from traders, who were simply lumped together with the rest to form a featureless group of lawless reprobates. The evidence of the missionaries was accepted without question.

The fact that most of the beachcombers "infesting" the islands were merchant sailors of low social status helps explain the virulence of complaints against them by missionaries and naval officers. Many of the earliest LMS missionaries to Tahiti had been from artisan backgrounds, but even these sought to distance themselves from the beachcombers in social rank. Some complained that the clothing the society gave them was so inferior in quality and cut that they were "no better dressed than common Seamen."[12] From the 1830s onward, after the mission societies decided to distance their members from trade and give them additional educational qualifications, missionaries became even more upwardly mobile. Social distinctions grew between the "old guard," with their artisan or trading backgrounds, and a new breed of missionary with middle-class aspirations began to emerge from the mission societies' theological colleges.[13] The differences between missionaries and beachcombers, proclaimed in purely moral terms in the mission journals, had roots in class prejudice as well.

The social background of Royal Navy officers was also changing. When regular naval cruises of the Pacific islands began in 1829, wardrooms no longer featured men like James Cook, who had risen from a humble background and service below decks to reach the rank of captain. Only the sons of naval officers or those with influential aristocratic connections were able to find midshipmen's berths and promotion in the crowded naval service after 1815.[14] Such officers were both morally and socially inclined to view missionaries as the only "respectable" white men in the islands. Although Erskine once referred to the sandalwooder James Paddon as "a gentleman," few others received such marks of respect. The captain pointed out the debauchery and arms trading of Charles Pickering, a notorious character who had been exiled by the white community at Levuka in Fiji, by drawing attention to the fact that Pickering was "a native of New South Wales" and concluding that "the aggravation of the previously barbarous state of the Feejees dates with the arrival of the first white settlers, who, although of the lowest and most abandoned class of men, maintained . . . the character of chiefs, whose example was worthy of all imitation." The captain blamed the introduction of firearms and the practice of cannibalism on these men, preferring to emphasize the depredations of "this vagabond class" rather than acknowledge Fijian warriors' desire for European weaponry.[15] Sometimes traders from New South Wales or New Zealand did much more than trade liquor for food or women. Captain Home observed a European-supervised trade in "Feejee wigs, and Human teeth" taken from Fijian battlefields, which he concluded would "tend to promote [Fijian] wars and consequently retard civilization."[16] Worse, such items were finding a market in the Australian colonies, recalling the trade in human heads between New Zealand and Sydney that had so exercised the New South Wales and British governments. The comparison was not lost on observers like Erskine, who warned that "should, therefore, no precaution be taken by the Government, a few years will probably produce . . . questions as troublesome to settle as occurred in New Zealand."[17]

In Melanesia, missionary complaints about other Europeans arose in part from the insecurity of their own position. Relying on advance preparation by pairs of Samoan or Rarotongan teachers, many of whom lost their lives during this period, the LMS tried to move into the New Hebrides by sending George Turner and Henry Nisbet to Tanna in 1842. The multiplicity of languages, suspicion of strangers, absence of paramount chiefs, and resentment at the introduction of disease all operated against the mission's success, and a Tannese attack on their station forced the missionaries with their Samoan teachers off the island after only one year.[18] This contrasted strongly with the mission experience in the eastern and central Pacific, where island societies were much more stratified, and the apparent disorganization of western islanders prompted humanitarians to view them as cruel but vulnerable children needing careful supervision. That protectiveness, in turn, invited the agents of benevolence to look askance at the sandalwood trade as it developed in the western Pacific in the 1840s. Sandalwooders now joined escaped convicts, deserters, and whalers in the humanitarian hall of infamy, and familiar descriptions of white depravity and islander victimization followed.

In the eastern Pacific, missionaries usually preceded trade, but in Melanesia they followed in its wake and found it easy to blame trade violence for their hostile reception. Mutually supportive mission and naval reports were all the more effective, because members of the trading community usually did not— or could not—publish their side of the story.

One of the most important individuals to shape British perceptions of Melanesia during this period was Captain John Erskine, whose published account of his 1849 voyage provided British readers with their first detailed view of the sandalwood trade. It also invited humanitarians to defend Melanesian islanders against the white villains who defrauded and murdered them. Explaining that, with every new island touched by the sandalwood trade, "the usual results of vessels being cut off and crews massacred have followed," Erskine concluded that these "outrages" were "to be traced in many cases to revenge for injuries inflicted by the undisciplined crews, whose superiority to the blacks is often limited to the knowledge of gunpowder."[19] Often quoting Erskine, missionaries reinforced these images of systematic, violent exploitation. Aneityum missionary John Geddie noted with approval that Erskine seemed "determined to check the cruel outrages of the white traders on the natives," convinced that Paddon's nearby sandalwood establishment had a destructive effect.[20] One of Paddon's employees, a Malay named Kange, tried to rape the widow of a missionary teacher in 1851, confirming Geddie's suspicion that, although it was "strange that civilized men could harbour among them such a savage," it seemed that "such characters seem to suit them best here. The awful depravity of the traders among these islands must be witnessed to be known. Their wickedness is one of the greatest barriers to the extension of the gospel on this island."[21]

Humanitarians were determined to put white agency at the center of the story, confining islanders' motives to an easily understood "retaliation theory." Missionaries and their supporters had already developed the retaliation explanation elsewhere in the Pacific; Ellis' defense of British missions in 1831 had noted that there were many explanations for clashes between Europeans and islanders, inlcuding "the oppression of preceding visitors."[22] Daniel Wheeler, a Quaker who visited several Polynesian mission stations in the 1820s, believed that the recent murder of crew members from the shipwrecked vessel *Active* at Fiji had been precipitated by the "harsh and imprudent conduct" of the sailors.[23] The Rarotongan LMS teacher Ta'unga, who visited various Melanesian islands in the 1840s, believed that victimized islanders were determined to avenge themselves on white men, and "it is due to this spirit of vengeance that the Europeans are killed in these islands."[24] As a Christianized Polynesian, Ta'unga found the western islanders as primitive and baffling as his British patrons did. I will examine the retaliation theory in greater detail later, but from what we can gather of the islanders' own perspective, Melanesian behavior had its own motives that were related indirectly, at best, to European actions. We also need to turn the construction of trade villainy back upon itself to discover the contradictions inherent in this apparently straightforward concept. Wasn't "Commerce" one of the partners of "Christianization and Civilization"?

Missionaries regularly preached the virtues of "industry," knowing that trade could create a market for European goods in the islands and encourage the development of British social and labor practices. Connections between Christianization, civilization, and commerce were often defended by John Williams, who purchased and supervised the building of several trade schooners for mission use. He hoped that they would help him teach islanders about laboring and trading for profit by bringing cargoes of European clothing and tea-drinking equipment for island converts who paid for them in coconut oil. Williams' ships reflected his belief that "wherever the Missionary goes, new channels are cut for the streams of commerce";[25] and in an age dominated by the idea of the dignity of labor, the Protestant work ethic formed a large part of the civilizing mission. Bishop Selwyn worried: "There seems to be one prevailing complaint throughout the South Seas that the Polynesian race cannot be induced to work, and without that how can they become a civilized people?"[26] After the New Hebrides Mission obtained its first foothold in Melanesia, enjoying remarkable success at Aneityum in the 1850s, John Inglis proudly declared that this Christianized island was "the only island on this group on which life & property are everywhere secure."[27]

Traders found it safer and easier to deal with islanders used to European notions of purchase and sale, and often praised this aspect of missionary work. In New Zealand in the 1820s, Benjamin Morrell recalled the unpredictable and sometimes violent Maori response to trade activity, remarking: "Since that period, the nature and disposition of these people have undergone a most wonderful change for the better, through the unwaried labours of benevolent and pious missionaries. They are now a civilized, rational business people, having a very brisk intercourse with the British settlements at New South Wales, and Van Dieman's Land."[28]

British naval officers were also enthusiastic about the effect of Christianization on British trade. Erskine believed that trade could "improve," in principle, observing of Mare islanders that "under other circumstances, their eagerness for barter, which seemed to us greater than among any other islanders, would probably have been the means of hastening their civilization."[29] A humane trader like James Paddon, whose fair dealing at sandalwood stations on Aneityum and the Isle of Pines was endorsed by Erskine and his friend Selwyn, were examples of commerce at its best; Paddon's employer Robert Towns wrote to tell him that the Royal Navy was happy "to protect you on your legitimate trade."[30] However, it was the "constant disputes, attended with bloodshed on both sides,"[31] that dominated Erskine's discussion of the sandalwood trade and appeared to betray the civilizing potential of commerce. Far from improving islanders, commerce produced instead "a very unfavourable effect upon their character."[32] Inglis, whom Erskine had taken to his new station at Aneityum in 1850, agreed that "so far from commerce exerting a beneficial influence and proving a handmaid to the gospel in the New Hebrides, it has proved a hindrance, and has degraded, if that be possible, the already debased inhabitants of these islands."[33]

Such descriptions, taken together over decades, are very much at odds with naval instructions to promote and protect British commerce; there were no qualifications about "legitimacy." After the repeal of the Corn Laws in 1846, the era of free trade began in earnest, and naval captains were probably politically inclined to support it. Fremantle was a Tory who served as Private Secretary to the Secretary of War during the Peel administration. Many Peelites supported the free trade movement, and Fremantle would give a speech about its virtues to a bemused gathering of Samoan chiefs in 1856.[34] Erskine entered Parliament as a Liberal in 1865.[35] The connection between the Royal Navy and free trade was one of the cornerstones of British expansion in the nineteenth century, and only strong feelings of humanitarianism could have prompted naval officers to attack trade as a source of corruption.

How did so much tension about the role of commerce arise? Humanitarianism's roots in the African antislavery movement had given trade a moral dimension; by attempting to persuade Britons that legitimate trade was more profitable than slavery, a liberal political economy arose to counter the old, mercantilist attitudes that had helped sustain slavery.[36] During the rise of free trade, the association between economic liberalism and humanitarianism became stronger and more problematic at the same time. In West Africa, where humanitarians hoped to establish a trade in palm oil and other tropical products as an alternative to slave dealing, there were a series of disappointments. In 1840 a naval expedition left Britain under the direction of Fowell Buxton's African Association, hoping to negotiate trade agreements with Niger River peoples and establish a model farm to teach agricultural skills. Instead, it was a disaster: local leaders were skeptical about the new proposals, the model farm had to be abandoned, and a large number of the expedition's personnel, all volunteers, died of fever.[37] Among the casualties was William Marshall, the young assistant surgeon whose humanitarian account of New Zealand had so impressed the Select Committee on Aborigines. Instead of a carefully guided trade, complemented by missionary activities, free trade produced an escalating exchange of liquor and firearms for palm oil, ivory, and gold. After the failure of the Niger Expedition, humanitarians found it difficult to sustain their hopes for commerce as a civilizing agent.[38] A powerful symbol of these failed hopes lay in the cargo hold of HMS *Daphne* as Captain Fanshawe left Valparaiso for the Pacific islands in 1849. "I have got on board a box containing the miserable remains of the presents that were sent out with the Niger expedition," he wrote, noting that the box had already made one or two tours of the islands, and "all but the most trashy articles are disposed of." The only tangible remains of Buxton's high-minded dreams were a few velvet caps, some pipe cleaners, and a tawdry pair of scarlet trousers.[39]

Pacific missionaries had some praise for humane traders like James Paddon. Within a few weeks of his arrival on Aneityum, Geddie wrote of the *Julia Percy*'s offer to take two teachers to Mare, the opportunity to send mail to Sydney aboard the *Jane*, and receipt of mail by the *Hirondelle*.[40] However, both mission and naval reports preferred to emphasize the depredations of other, less scrupulous traders whose relations with islanders were considered illegitimate and requiring supervision, if not suppression. The *Quarterly Review* observed in 1859 that the colonial trade in Melanesia "bore a far greater resemblance to a system of piracy than to legitimate commerce." The only hope for the "unhappy and helpless islanders" was the constant publication of trade depredations, so that more missionaries might come to the Pacific islands to rescue their oppressed inhabitants.[41] The dichotomy between islander victimization and trade villainy was the only palatable way humanitarians could explain the wayward effects of commerce on civilization. It was much easier to perceive British traders as obstructing benevolence for well-understood motives of greed or vice; much less appealing was the alternative explanation of islander choices based on an indigenous agenda outside mission understanding or control.

The retaliation theory was aimed mainly at traders, but humanitarians also blamed beachcombers for increasing the level of violence in the islands. The government of New South Wales had encouraged a trade in flax and timber with New Zealand since the 1790s; British and American whalers and sealers began arriving in New Zealand waters at the same time. The Bay of Islands was a commodious harbor that soon featured its own beach community at Kororareka; and as contact grew between Maori and *pakeha*, so did misunderstanding and violence. When nearby Maori murdered the crew of the trading vessel *Boyd* at Whangaroa Harbor in 1809, concerned observers regarded the incident as evidence of the revenge the Maori exacted for the brutalities of New Zealand's beachcombers and called for the creation of a mission to New Zealand.[42] The mission went ahead under Samuel Marsden in 1814, but as explorer and surveyor Ernest Dieffenbach explained, it was a mistake to blame white residents for provoking or instigating violence. Their small numbers and the control exerted over them by the Maori families into which they married gave them "neither the power to do much harm" nor the will to jeopardize their patronage.[43] It was a similar story with Charlie Savage, shipwrecked in the sandalwooder *Eliza* at Fiji in 1808. Savage's subsequent career in the service of the chiefs of Bau appeared frequently in mission and naval writings as evidence of the way immoral white men disrupted island societies with their muskets, ammunition, and European military tactics.[44] Preferring to emphasize white villainy rather than analyze the adaptability of island societies or the shrewdness of their leaders, humanitarians permitted men like Savage to cast a long shadow.

The Royal Navy often investigated missionary complaints about the negative influence of beachcombers on islanders; some of the best-documented of these involve Tonga, an island group whose chiefs had sponsored white men before the arrival of the first LMS missionaries in 1797. The early accounts of the castaway William Mariner and the renegade missionary George Vason drew attention to the important role white men played as various chiefs contended for the great Tongan titles during the early nineteenth century.[45] British observers often assumed that these white men played a larger role than they had. In 1830, Captain Waldegrave investigated attacks made by Finau 'Ulukalala on the British vessels *Rambler* and *Elizabeth*.[46] Holding a position of honor at Finau's court was an Englishman called Brown who, with William Mariner, had been one of the few survivors of the shipwrecked *Port au Prince* in 1806. The captain initially charged Brown "with being the advisor of Finow" in the attempt to seize the vessels, but after discussion with Finau himself it became clear that both ships' captains had attempted to cheat and insult the chief.[47] Waldegrave's report acknowledged the current problems of poor discipline and bad faith aboard some British merchant vessels, but it also revealed the extent to which he attributed agency to white men rather than islanders. "The majority of these English are so abandoned . . . that they ought for the safety of the Trade and character of our country to be removed," he reported, adding that, although he suspected Brown of organizing the attacks made on *Rambler* and *Elizabeth*, the operation "was so clumsily planned that I acquit him of it."[48] Presumably only Tongan planning could have produced such an ineffective operation. On the same visit, Waldegrave endeared himself to the mission by arresting an Englishman called Harris, who had been undermining the efforts of missionary John Thomas at the court of Finau, chief of Ha'apai. Learning that his tormentor was bound for Sydney, Thomas was grateful beyond bounds: "The King and his people were very much afraid, and seem to think that religion is of more importance now than they were willing to believe. I feel thankful that I was born in Britain and I feel it an honour that I belong to such a Sovereign who has such Officers."[49]

Similar dynamics surrounded the death of Captain Croker at Tongatapu in 1840. Seconded by the Methodist missionaries, the chiefs Josiah Tupou (sometimes spelled Tubou) and George Tāufa'āhau told Croker that two Englishmen were aiding the Ha'a Havea rebellion at Pea.[50] During his negotiations at the fort, the captain demanded the surrender of these two men, James and George, as the first condition of peace. James, known as "Jimmy the Devil," already had a reputation as a troublemaker.[51] It seems to have begun in Fiji, where he lived

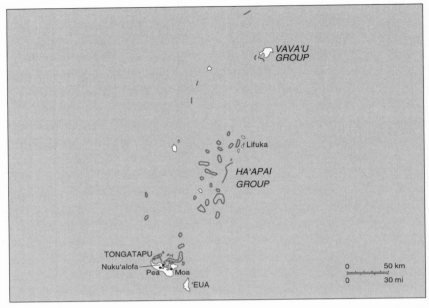

Map 2. Tonga

from about 1824 to 1830, before being "forced by the whites on pain of death to leave," owing to his violent and unscrupulous conduct. Recalling his subsequent activities at Pea, Jimmy claimed he had "decided the defence of the Tongan fort" against Captain Croker's attack in 1840. The Pea people all bragged about their triumph over the Royal Navy,[52] but *Favorite*'s officers held the Englishmen responsible for the effectiveness of Pea's defenses. In conference with the superintendent of Methodist missions at Sydney, Lieutenant Dunlop declared that not only had Jimmy and George helped repel Croker's assault, they had designed the Pea fortress itself.[53]

It is easy to see how Jimmy's character complemented the naval view of "troublesome persons." However, although the Tongan chiefs catered to humanitarian prejudice when they described the two Englishmen at Pea as "the principal instigators and supporters of the heathen in their rebellion,"[54] the two men had probably played little more than a supporting role. The Pea fort was of traditional Tongan type, surrounded by a large ditch twelve feet deep and forty feet wide. Within the ditch was a thick mud wall surmounted by a wooden fence, to which the Pea leader Lualala added improvements such as hollow logs for musketmen to shoot through.[55] Croker had confronted a formidable fortress of Tongan design, squandered his firepower by drawing the guns too close, and lost his life in a burst of suicidal zeal.

As the number of European residents expanded, especially at the larger beach communities like Levuka in Fiji, humanitarian generalizations about white depravity grew with it. There were undoubtedly many feckless and violent men among the collection of deserters, marooned sailors, and escaped convicts who made their way to Fiji from the beginning of the nineteenth century, but since their existence depended on the hospitality and protection of the local people, they were hardly free to do as they liked. After Fiji's brief sandalwood boom collapsed in the early nineteenth century, it was the sale in China of smoked bêche-de-mer, or sea slug, that sustained the white community of Levuka. Unlike sandalwood, the bêche-de-mer trade required shore stations of some permanence to clean and treat the catch, and such stations required provisioning, ship repair, and piloting services. They also required patronage if they were to survive the vicissitudes of Fijian politics, and the powerful district of Bau recognized the mutual benefit of collaboration with Levuka's white residents.

By 1844 the community had a population of about two hundred, mostly British or American men, Fijian women, and their children. There were unruly elements, but on the whole Levuka seemed industrious, especially during the

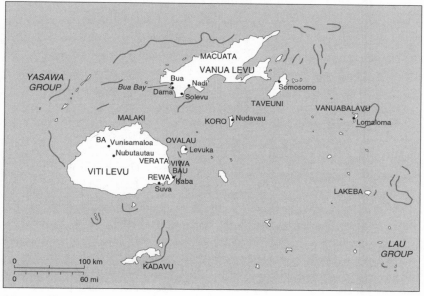

Map 3. Fiji

bêche-de-mer "season," building houses, shops, and small sailing vessels during the lull of the hurricane months.[56] However, missionaries like Walter Lawry, who visited Fiji in 1847, clung to images of drunken, depraved white men in their reports. Lawry called for strong measures to control misbehaving whites, saying, "We know that the Gospel needs not the aid of great guns; but there are times when refractory white men may be restrained by the presence of a British authority." "Many of the whites on these islands are men of abandoned characters," he continued, "whose bad example has had a pernicious influence on the natives."[57] In 1855 Captain Fremantle also claimed that the "moral example" of Fiji's resident whites" is conflicting to the efforts of the Missionaries. . . . It is their object to keep the native in darkness as long as they can, to perpetuate his ignorance of the real value of an empty bottle, a glass bead, or a yard of calico."[58]

It was therefore no surprise that if the Royal Navy could be persuaded to investigate the murder or robbery of traders at all, captains went out of their way to conciliate Fijians. Captain Crozier came to Lakeba in November 1836 to question the survivors of a recent shipwreck. The *Active* had wrecked off Lakeba and the crew was hospitably received there. When four men left in her boat to seek assistance, they were killed by other Fijians who were on their way to Lakeba. Crozier, taking missionaries David Cargill and William Cross as interpreters, went to the town of Levuka to question the murder suspect.[59] During the investigation, the chief of Lakeba persuaded the captain to punish him rather than risk civil war by punishing the suspects, who were guests from another area.[60] Cargill and Cross encouraged Crozier to set an example of benevolence instead of might, and the captain accepted a promise of good behavior in lieu of punishment. Two years later, Captain Bethune investigated an attack on the trade schooner *Sir David Ogilby* during which the master and a seaman had been killed by the people of Verata on Viti Levu. Bethune concluded that there had been no misconduct on the part of the *Ogilby*'s crew and that the young chief who had lost his life in the attack had been "of an enterprizing disposition, jealous of the power of his superior, and who probably imagined that by gaining possession of the trade in the vessel, he would be in a position to usurp his authority." Bethune warned the Verata people against attacking any other vessels in the future, and his lenience "was received with great satisfaction" by the Fijians; one wonders what other traders thought of it.[61]

By 1849, the Royal Navy had overlooked so many attacks on white men in Fiji that the comments of Mary Wallis, the wife of an American trader, probably reflected a frustration that many others felt. While Captain Erskine was demonstrating his ship's guns for a Fijian chief's entertainment in 1849, she remarked that none "of the places rendered memorable by the massacre of white men are to be visited or punished"; and during HMS *Daphne's* visit later that year she "did not learn that any notice is taken of the frequent massacres that have occurred among the islands."[62] Mrs. Wallis clearly expected Britain's navy to support Fiji's commercial community in general; American naval visits were rare. However, far from protecting traders and other residents, the Royal Navy ignored them at best and villified them at worst.

Few issues were as provocative as relationships between white men and island women. Neo-chivalric notions of their purpose in the islands inclined Victorian naval captains to adopt an extravagantly protective attitude toward the women in cases like this. On his pioneering cruise of Melanesia in 1849, Erskine decreed that no island woman could visit the ship unless escorted by her father or her husband, declaring that the sexual liaisons "which have been related as of daily and hourly occurrence in former years . . . could not now possibly occur on board of a British ship of war."[63] He was probably referring both to the well-known published descriptions of sexual contact during British and French voyages of the eighteenth century and to more recent incidents such as the visit of HMS *Cornwallis* to Honolulu in 1826, when over four hundred women boarded the ship on its arrival.[64] In 1871, an even more pointed sense of delicacy prevented Captain Markham from rescuing two island women who had been kidnaped by labor recruiters. He explained to them that he could not permit unescorted females aboard his ship, and when their canoe overturned as they pursued the departing HMS *Rosario,* he left them to their fate rather than compromise his rule. However, Markham's sensibilities allowed him to rescue the kidnaped wife of a Nukapu chief, because members of the woman's family had come along on the expedition.[65] The important thing was to maintain a public image of irreproachable virtue.

What junior officers and sailors did was sometimes another matter; on *Havannah's* 1850 cruise Lieutenant Swainson used the surgeon's office to have sex with several island women and enjoyed the opportunity for sex with young girls provided by a Fijian chief whose home he visited.[66] Aboard the survey vessel *Herald* at the Solomon Islands in 1854, naturalist John MacGillivray watched a father force his screaming young daughter into a canoe and hand her over to *Herald's* sailors in return for an axe. In a subsequent description of island women's sexual promiscuity, MacGillivray merely remarked that this particular "prostitute," though still obviously a child, had more "customers" than the rest of the females who came aboard during *Herald's* stay at the Solomons.[67] Incidents like these, involving a range of supposedly forbidden sexual contacts including the rape of children, remind us that naval captains wrote their reports while cut off from their crews by the traditional isolation of their position and perhaps also by selective vision.

Long-term attachments between white men and island women were considered even more threatening than brief encounters.[68] In 1850, missionary James Calvert wrote to Captain Erskine to complain that white men were trading muskets for female slaves in Fiji. Despite strong legal objections, the Colonial Office permitted Governor FitzRoy of New South Wales to issue an antislavery proclamation threatening British subjects in Fiji with prosecution. Calvert and his supporters were later forced to drop the issue after one of the British residents at Levuka, the main European settlement in Fiji, wrote to FitzRoy in protest. Captain Sir Everard Home, who delivered the proclamation to Fiji in 1852, reported that Levuka was trying to establish a system of self-policing. Not only was there no evidence of slavery, but he recommended the appointment of a British consul to offset the excessive influence of missionaries with the British government. It was the humanitarian support of a senior naval officer and other officials that had allowed Calvert's allegations to influence government decisions. A powerful conjunction of issues appeared to demand benevolent intervention: the victimization of helpless island women and the ruthless immorality of white beachcombers.

This was the first time since the Treaty of Waitangi that the British government had attempted to extend its jurisdiction in the Pacific islands, and the humanitarian rationalizations behind it deserve analysis. Behind the accusations of slavery lay generalized assumptions about the status of women in Fiji. Several missionaries had observed that Fijian men routinely made a *tabua* offering of a whale's tooth, and later a musket, when asking a woman's parents or her chief for permission to marry her.[69] Missionaries themselves offered muskets, if that was the compensation demanded, in order to save Fijian widows from strangulation. The *tabua* represented a costly offering, but missionaries chose to see it as evidence that Fijian women were not valued by their own society. Polygyny, which was almost universal in high-ranking Fijian families, reinforced images of savage male lusts and female victimization.[70] In lower-rank marriages, where women performed a great deal of manual labor, the slavery image was reinforced. As one missionary biographer noted, "the dignity of womanhood had to be taught."[71]

This explanation viewed the brutalization of women as a traditional, if deplorable, aspect of indigenous society; but when white men accommodated themselves to Fijian-style marriages, the fury of humanitarians knew no bounds. *Tabua* might constitute a marriage pledge for Fijians, but when offered by a white man who should know better, it was regarded as enslavement. Fiji's missionaries could write in positive terms about Levuka's mixed-race families —even Calvert noted the large number who asked missionaries to marry them and who swelled the ranks of Levuka's chapel[72]—but they could not accept as properly British the white men whose families were so different from British norms. Calvert's colleague Williams was referring to the *tabua* when he declared that "there is no truth in the assertion that the natives sell their women among themselves. Whatever there has been like this, has been taught them by white men."[73] Fijians were held blameless; their unthinking savage ways had been corrupted by knowingly savage Englishmen. Levuka resident William Nimmo claimed that he and his compatriots conformed to Fijian traditions because they had no choice: whether they wanted a woman as a sexual partner or a domestic servant, *tabua* was the price demanded by her relatives.[74]

For Calvert's friend Erskine, however, the situation was clear. An antislavery campaigner since his junior officer days in the West Indies, Erskine accepted Calvert's allegations without question, remembering conversations they had had on the subject during *Havannah*'s visits to Fiji. He was probably influenced, too, by the claims of other naval observers, particularly those of the U.S. Exploring Expedition's commander, Lieutenant Wilkes, whose charts of Fiji he had relied on. Wilkes had listened eagerly to the yarns of beachcomber Paddy Connell, a man whose promiscuity and brutality eventually led to his expulsion from Levuka. For Wilkes, however, Connell's stories of female slavery were evidence of the way many white men were imitating savage Fijian practices.[75] As for William Nimmo, the man who would protest about Calvert's campaign against Levuka, the missionary had destroyed his credibility with Erskine by telling the captain about Nimmo's trade in liquor.[76] It is not surprising, therefore, that Erskine urged Governor FitzRoy to act on Calvert's request without further investigation.

FitzRoy's legal advisors warned him that Calvert's accusations contained no evidence of slavery as defined by current British legislation, but the governor realized the political sensitivity of the issue and forwarded the matter to the Colonial Office. There it was dealt with by the humanitarian Lord Grey, who bullied his own crown law officers into endorsing an antislavery proclamation for Fiji. British subjects would learn that their personal lives were "highly injurious to the British name and character" and liable to prosecution "with the utmost rigor of the law."[77] By now Calvert had sent word of his campaign and its results to London, where Britain's championship of Fijian women became one of the highlights of the 1853 general meeting of the Methodist Missionary Society. Queen Victoria sent Governor FitzRoy her personal congratulations.[78]

When Captain Home took the proclamation to Fiji in 1852, it provoked a chorus of criticism from Levuka's white residents. Home himself seemed embarrassed by the absence of any evidence of slaveholding and by the self-conscious respectability that many of the men were trying to create. The community had been expelling undesirables like Paddy Connell for some time, and Home helped them by agreeing to remove a man accused of theft.[79] He supported their request for consular representation, although it would be six years before the British government appointed the first consul to Fiji. In his letter of protest to FitzRoy, William Nimmo claimed that the families of Levuka were the backbone of the Methodist chapel there and that relationships with white men were a blessing for Fijian women "by bringing them from the horrors of Heathenism and Cannibalism to the enjoyment of a somewhat civilized life and the happiness of Preached Gospel."[80] Disturbed by discrepancies between these representations and the original allegations, FitzRoy and the Colonial Office chose to draw a veil over the whole episode, and Fiji's missionaries did not mention it in their published mission histories.

Humanitarian prejudice against traders found its consummate expression in comparisons between benign islanders and "savage" white men. The observations of Royal Navy officers, so often involved in the restraining of white men outside the mission stations, were particularly pointed. Watching the Tongan chief Josiah Tupou at prayer in 1830, Midshipman Orlebar of the *Seringapatam* reflected "on the lesson here given by a half-taught savage, and some painful sensations arose from my neglect of a duty which ought to me to be much more sacred."[81] To Lieutenant Walpole of HMS *Collingwood* at Samoa, it seemed that "these gentle people in their relations towards each other are less savage than many with white skins and clothed in fine linen."[82] For Fremantle, at Samoa in 1855, every white resident in Apia—trader, beachcomber, and criminal alike— was a "coarse and infidel importation which pollutes [these] otherwise beautiful and fertile Islands."[83] "I confess my sympathies after my cruize are all in favor of the semi-civilized natives & against the European Intruders," he admitted. "They are nearly all Christians, and as such shew an example worthy of imitation by those living amongst them, who brand them with the name of Savages, whereas the terms might more appropriately be reversed."[84] Missionaries agreed. From Aneityum, John Geddie reported that "it is hard to say whether these savages are most degraded or the white men who encourage their revolting deeds."[85] For humanitarians, "savagery" was a moral state from which a Pacific islander could be raised and to which a white man could just as easily descend. This viewpoint was uncompromising. Islanders, new to Christian morality and steeped in barbarism, could be forgiven much; white men who sinned had fallen from grace and betrayed their superior heritage. Here, as usual, were assumptions about the nature of progress and civilization, and about British superiority, in which cultural relativism could play no part.

Historians of south Pacific beach communities have emphasized the difference between the early period of culture contact, where isolated beachcombers or small groups of Europeans lived under the protection and restrictions imposed by their island hosts, and the later period, when trade contacts intensified, beach communities grew, and issues of land ownership arose.[86] These studies have driven home the point that islanders were much more in control of the former situation; race relations would deteriorate at places like Levuka only after the white community grew large enough to assert itself. From the humanitarian point of view, however, these white men were all alike. The damage they did to vulnerable islanders was only a matter of degree. Perceiving islanders as dependent children, naval observers could not accept evidence of islander agency in the plunder of shipwrecked vessels or even in marriages between island women and white men. Convictions about islander "improvability" required an equal and opposite belief in white depravity; observations inconsistent with the image of backward primitives had to be blamed on Europeans. Missionaries offered civilization's benefits, even the gift of eternal life; but other white men introduced only civilization's evils.

3

Protective Supremacy?

ALTHOUGH Cook's voyages had opened up the possibility of a British south Pacific, the British government "showed no disposition . . . to turn this primacy of influence into political ascendancy."[1] Despite the activities of its missionaries and traders, and the possession of a natural base for expansion in the Australian colonies, Britain acquired south Pacific territory only once before the 1870s, with the Treaty of Waitangi. But the naval captains who patrolled the islands were frustrated by an ambivalent administration that invoked the idea of a British supremacy of influence only to reject definitive measures that might bring unwelcome responsibilities or upset diplomatic relations with other Powers. Even after creation of the Australian Division in 1848, captains were left to themselves to develop an approach to their complicated island duties. These points have been made before, but so far there has been no detailed examination of the way the imperialism of naval officers was shaped by their humanitarianism; the absence of government policy did not necessarily mean the absence of a sense of imperial mission. We also need a fuller exploration of the tense relationship between the Royal Navy and British consuls in the islands. Captains shared their paternalist relationship with islanders very reluctantly with others, and only with men they defined as respectable and honorable. Most missionaries fell into this category, but traders—and trading consuls—did not. This dynamic enhanced the naval self-image of knight-errantry, and it also alienated them from the only other British officials in the Pacific islands.

When the Admiralty ordered regular patrols in 1829, it merely noted that captains should "countenance and encourage the British Intercourse and Trade with the Society and Friendly Islands."² Station commanders in chief tried to create more detailed instructions, but these only tended to emphasize the importance of the captain's own discretion. They also revealed the complex process by which British interests were defined and priorities for protection were assigned. In 1838 Rear Admiral Owen ordered Captain Durrell Desausmarez of HMS *Zebra* to visit as many island groups as he was able to after consultation with the Governor of New South Wales. The captain's first priority was "to cultivate by all means proper the friendly disposition of the Natives and their Chiefs and to keep our relations with them on an amicable footing."³ The original Admiralty order made no mention of islanders, and Owen seems to have drawn this instruction from the existing standing orders relating to India. These standing orders, of which every captain had a copy, urged officers to refrain from interfering in local politics, even if requested to do so, and to demonstrate respect for indigenous society by conforming "strictly to the established Regulations & Customs of the Place" and by taking care that no offense be given "to the peculiar habits, religious ceremonies, or even to, what may appear to be the absurd prejudices of the Inhabitants."⁴ Only the vaguest reference was made in these instructions to the "countenance and encouragement" of British trade. After a brief reference to the original Admiralty directive, the order drew attention to the mistreatment of islanders by traders and other Europeans; Owen had received a copy of Waldegrave's 1830 report on the islands from Governor Darling of New South Wales and forwarded it to Desausmarez to emphasize the problems caused by British subjects outside mission stations. The instructions concluded with a description of the moral duties of naval patrols. Anticipating his captain's disgusted reaction to the depredations of escaped convicts, sailors, and traders in the islands, Owen reminded Desausmarez that his "own sound judgment" should be the foundation of his proceedings, adding: "You will remember that as on the one hand the misconduct of these people may be disgraceful to the British name and character as well as to the Christian religion and to Humanity so on the other you must take care that your desire to correct those evils and to secure the offenders shall not tend you to inflict intemperate severity or unjust restraint on unoffending individuals."⁵ Elements of these early instructions will be found throughout this study. Naval captains, who were shocked by the behavior of their fellow Britons and who tended to view European-islander interaction in moral terms, would often find it difficult to restrain their disapproval of the "evils" they witnessed. It was "the Christian religion" and "humanity" that they served and the islanders whom they protected.

At times naval officers grew understandably confused about the British government's intentions. Captain Vancouver had obtained the cession of the Sandwich Islands during his third visit in 1794, but his actions were unauthorized, and British influence in the group languished; the missionaries Vancouver recommended arrived from the United States rather than from Britain. New South Wales took a greater interest and, in response to a request by King Kamehameha, sent out a purpose-built schooner for his use in 1822. Delighted by the gift, Kamehameha renewed the cession offer by writing directly to George IV of Britain and reminding him of the bond between their fathers that Vancouver's negotiations had established.[6] Instead of a British protectorate, Honolulu got consul Richard Charlton, a retired merchant captain who arrived in 1825. This "rough, obtuse, foul-mouthed and choleric" man was a great disappointment to the American missionaries, whose own representative John Jones was little better than Charlton.[7] Had the missionaries been British, visiting Royal Navy officers might have taken greater exception to Charlton; as it was, they tended—with one dramatic exception—to concentrate their efforts where a British presence was more clearly established. Despatched to Honolulu in 1824 with the bodies of King Kamehameha and Queen Kamamalu, Captain Byron had carried instructions warning him against reopening the issue of Vancouver's cession agreement.[8]

The American missionaries began to make progress under Kamehameha's successor Kauikeaouli but made the mistake of antagonizing their French counterparts and associating themselves too closely with the business of government. Captain Laplace of the French frigate *L'Artemise* appeared in 1839 with threats of bombardment unless Kauikeaouli guaranteed religious freedom for Catholics and posted a bond of $20,000. Meanwhile, Charlton's debaucheries and bankruptcies were bringing consular operations to a halt, and the consul left for England in 1842 in hopes of thwarting American influence in the Sandwich Islands and sorting out his complicated personal affairs. He appointed Alexander Simpson his deputy, and Simpson, chief trader of the Hudson's Bay Company's Sandwich Islands operation and a supporter of British rule across the north Pacific, made strenuous but unsuccessful efforts to interest the British government in his imperial schemes.[9] He did manage to get a message to the commander in chief of the Pacific Station, however, which implied that the very lives of British subjects in Honolulu were at risk from the Americans and the French.

Full of zeal to protect his countrymen, Captain Lord George Paulet arrived with HMS *Carysfort* in February 1843 and threatened to bombard Honolulu unless Kauikeaouli recognized Simpson as consul, settled the grievances of British subjects to their satisfaction, and paid large sums in compensation to various British claimants including Simpson. Kauikeaouli resisted many of these demands and was unable to meet others; faced with the potential bankruptcy of his country, he saw no other alternative than to offer the Sandwich Islands once again to Britain. Paulet seized the moment, forty-nine years to the day after Vancouver had done the same, and ran up the British ensign. Risking his commission and the fortune he hoped to make carrying gold between ports in South America, the captain labored over the creation of a provisional law code and the resolution of disputes at Honolulu. However, Paulet's imperial initiatives were as unwelcome as Vancouver's had been. Admiral Sir Richard Thomas sailed for Honolulu and reinstated the islands' independence in July. *"Ua mau ke ea o ka aina i ka pono,"* said Kauikeaouli after the ceremonies were over: "The life of the land is preserved in righteousness."[10]

Meanwhile, the eviction in 1842 of French Roman Catholic missionaries by an alliance of Tahitian leaders and British Protestant missionaries had thrown Britain and France into a potentially explosive confrontation and forced the Foreign Office to issue its first comprehensive statement about British relations with Pacific islanders. As in the Sandwich Islands, there had been cessions of Tahiti that the British government chose to ignore. In 1825 Pomare II had written to King George IV asking for British protection and the right to fly the British flag; Foreign Secretary Canning's reply denied both requests but expressed hopes for the Christianization and civilization of Tahiti, along with an offer of "such assurances of protection as this country can afford to a friendly Power, in so remote a quarter."[11] Written in the spirit of the sovereignty principle, this despatch took the rare step of referring to Tahiti as a "Power," a designation usually reserved for European countries or the United States. Over the next few years naval visitors like Gambier and Waldegrave showed their support for British missions at Tahiti, and in 1839, when confrontations began with the newly arrived Catholic missionaries, the Foreign Office asked the Admiralty to ensure "moral support" for Queen Pomare in her dealings with the French.[12] Three years later, Foreign Secretary Aberdeen made it clear to the Tahitians and their missionary allies that the British government had no intention of ruling the island or any of the Society group and made the closest thing to a statement of policy to date. Urging the Royal Navy to continue respecting the sovereignty of island leaders, he encouraged them to resolve disputes through island-based authorities rather than by the use of force. He also declared that the British government wished to prevent other countries from exercising "a greater degree of influence than that possessed by Great Britain."[13] This confident directive was a prime example of "vigorous pronouncements unsupported by substantial force."[14] Aberdeen had no intention of jeopardizing the current *entente* with France. His government's navy, however, took a typically large view of its responsibilities.

Shortly after receiving a copy of Aberdeen's letter at Sydney, Captain Toup Nicolas of HMS *Vindictive* heard that a French warship had forced Pomare to cede Tahiti to France. Nicolas was confident that such a move was contrary to Aberdeen's "policy" of British supremacy, and he was encouraged by British consul George Pritchard, who had just arrived in Sydney after being expelled from Tahiti. The *Vindictive* sailed in January 1843, and Nicolas declared that since British "national honour was pledged," he was clearing his ship for action against the French.[15] Unfortunately for him, Aberdeen had already resolved the issue with the French minister Guizot, and Rear Admiral Thomas ordered *Vindictive* back to base.[16] When Nicolas learned that the British government had accepted the French occupation, he lamented the loss of Britain's moral credibility in the Pacific. It is easy to understand his frustration; he thought he had been following Aberdeen's own instructions, only to find himself reprimanded for "taking upon himself, without express orders from his Government, to prejudice the course which they may see fit to pursue."[17] This criticism, later withdrawn, unfairly assumed that naval officers had been kept informed of the government's "course." Aberdeen had in fact remarked to Guizot, "Is it not deplorable that you and I, two ministers of peace, should be condemned to quarrel about a set of half naked savages at the other end of the world?"[18] and agreed to overlook the ill-treatment of Consul Pritchard in return for an agreement guaranteeing the independence of the other Society islands.[19] British missionaries denounced this "betrayal" throughout the south Pacific, but naval officers appeared subdued by the turmoil of the 1840s: the death of Croker in Tonga, Paulet's Sandwich Islands "protectorate," and Nicolas' attempt to thwart the French at Tahiti. There would be no other similar imperial adventures until 1873, when Captain John Moresby decided to claim southeastern New Guinea for Britain.

Moresby took HMS *Basilisk* on what appears to have been a personal crusade. He was supposed to be patrolling the Queensland coast, looking for labor vessels and monitoring the employment of islanders at the pearlshell stations, but during his previous cruises in 1871 and 1872, he had become friends with Lord Normanby, governor of Queensland. Normanby and the magnates of Brisbane had convinced the captain that New Guinea was Queensland's natural area of influence and expressed concern about rumored French and German interest there. "I stored up every word," recalled Moresby, "hoping to turn it to good account as opportunity offered." That opportunity came during a preliminary survey of Torres Strait and the New Guinea coast in 1873. When Moresby's new orders failed to arrive as scheduled, he exercised his discretion and set out on a more extensive survey, filled with pride in his naval heritage and determined "to secure for England the honour due to the Motherland of Cook, Dampier, and Owen Stanley, by filling in the last great blank in their work."[20]

After exploring and surveying the southeastern tip of New Guinea, naming the commodious harbor at Port Moresby after his father, Moresby prepared to claim the area for Britain. "We made the best disposition we could to give some little éclat to the ceremony" by using a capped coconut tree as a flagstaff and pro-claiming the possession, by right of discovery, of the mainland and islands in the Port Moresby area on 24 April 1873.[21] It is not often that we can examine radically different accounts of flag-raising ceremonies, but Lieutenant Francis Hayter did not like his captain and confided to his journal about a ceremony that he regarded as self-indulgent theater. Moresby had arranged a group of marines and sailors to present arms and fire a salute after he read his proclamation. As Hayter recalled: "On John emerging from the Bush which he did in a way creditable to any Provincial Stage, we presented arms and the Bugler (who we had to conceal behind a bush as he was one of the digging party and all covered with mud) sounded the salute . . . spoiled by the Marines who, I believe, fired at the wrong time on purpose, because they didn't like being put on the left of the line." The glories of empire were lost on these men, Hayter believed, and only the prospect of splicing the main brace gave any gusto to the three cheers for Her Majesty.[22] After leaving Port Moresby, the captain imposed strict disci-pline on his crew, especially with regard to religious observances. "Dead nuts on prayers," as Hayter described him, Moresby decided that at a given moment every morning, the bugler would sound "Still" and every man on the ship would kneel for five minutes of devotion.[23] This did not improve the crew's attitude toward their unexpectedly lengthy cruise.

Moresby got a hero's welcome at Brisbane, but both Commodore Stirling and the British government repudiated his actions. Stirling was irritated to find that Moresby had written privately to Sir Alexander Milne at the Admiralty to ask (and receive) permission to take *Basilisk* home via New Guinea in order to do further surveying.[24] Stirling's successor, Commodore James Goodenough, was more sympathetic about Moresby's quest for empire, although he deplored what he called Moresby's "usual want of tact" in bringing controversy upon himself.[25] These were ironic comments indeed from a man who would force

Britain's hand over the colonization of Fiji, exceeding his instructions and riding roughshod over local political sensibilities.

The British government might have been indifferent to naval hopes for greater intervention in the south Pacific, but in the 1840s the ambitious Governor George Grey of New Zealand had plans of his own. Methodist mission superintendent Walter Lawry drew Grey's attention to Tonga in 1847, angry that the Royal Navy was neglecting these islands in favor of better-known places to the east. Lawry also encouraged one of Tonga's leading Christian chiefs, George Tāufaʻāhau, to submit a petition through Governor Grey, asking for a British protectorate in Tonga.[26] Grey asked Captain Maxwell of HMS *Dido* to report, and when he supported the petition, the governor agreed to make recommendations to the Colonial Office. Grey's aim was "Christianization and Civilization"; he applied the same principles to his relations with Pacific islanders that he had pursued as Governor of South Australia and was implementing in New Zealand.[27] Like his British naval allies, Grey believed that islanders were capable of adopting British legal and political institutions if they were properly guided in the process.

George Tāufaʻāhau of Tonga seemed proof of Grey's faith in the "improvability" of Pacific islanders, and the governor hoped to supervise the chief's progress at first hand. Forwarding Maxwell's 1847 report as evidence for the desirability of a Tongan "protectorate," Grey added that he hoped to visit Tongan leaders soon to "advise with them upon their present state." He also recommended British rule for Fiji because of "the evils which bad European characters are entailing upon those islands" and to protect the activities of British missionaries.[28] Since the missionaries at both Tonga and Fiji were Methodist, it is no surprise to find Superintendent Lawry reporting, "I am acting here silently, but I hope powerfully on the Governor, and thro' him, upon the Home Government on this question."[29]

Grey's recommendations begged the question of how he expected the British government to rule these islands. Tonga's 1844 petition, for example, almost certainly fell short of Grey's interpretation of it; written in response to the French occupation of Tahiti, it reminded Queen Victoria of Tonga's history as "a separate and independent kingdom," appealing to her to "afford us protection from our enemies."[30] Grey read this as a desire "to cede the sovereignty of their country to the British Crown," a dubious extrapolation. Words like "occupation" and "protectorate" occurred frequently in British correspondence about islanders, sometimes in translation and apparently without fixed meaning, making it difficult to analyze the intentions of those whose ideas are being described. A number of such petitions came to the Foreign Office from the islands during the 1840s and 1850s, when concern about the growing influence of France was at its height. The problem of definition was academic—the British government had no intention of ruling the islands in any case—but it is important to note that naval captains and their supporters used such expressions freely, without the implications such terms acquired in the later nineteenth century. Grey would say only that islanders throughout the South Pacific wished "to be brought under Great Britain, in the same manner that the New Zealand Islands have been."[31] He, of all people, knew how controversial a step that would be.

The Colonial Office equivocated, telling Grey that it was considering the appointment of additional consuls to provide "instructions and assistance to the Native Authorities towards the Establishment of a regular Government." Grey was not permitted to visit the islands himself, and one official noted that "it is impossible not to recoil at first from the idea of attempting to found a new Empire in the Pacific."[32] Perhaps the governor knew that it was pointless to recommend protectorates and decided to pursue a new tack recommending regular patrols by naval captains on longer commissions. He hoped that Captain Maxwell, "no fitter person could be found," might be returned to the south Pacific "to neglect no opportunity of attaching the Natives to British interests, or of promoting their welfare by his advice and assistance in the adjustment of their internal affairs, by recommending the formation of Courts suited to their present state of civilization, and for the adjustment of disputes between themselves and Europeans, by acting as mediator for the prevention of their now frequent wars, and by other similar measures."[33] This was an astute prediction of the extensive intervention naval captains would be making in the islands, but Grey wanted their role formalized and backed by instructions from the British government.

Colonial Secretary Lord Grey, delighted by a proposal that had neither territorial nor financial implications, wrote to the Foreign Office and Admiralty recommending "the delegation so far as may be practicable of [consular] duties to some Naval Officer."[34] Unfortunately, although the Admiralty itself was concerned about the growing French presence in the south Pacific, it was opposed to having its officers take on such a wide range of additional duties when there was already a British consul, George Pritchard, who had been transferred to Samoa after the Tahiti affair.[35] The Admiralty preferred to carry out its own plan to regulate island visits through the new Australian Division, thus countering the French naval base at Tahiti without creating expensive new commitments.

It told the Colonial Office that it had "very grave objections to combining consular powers with the ordinary duties of a naval officer."[36] Captains, if they wished to make political recommendations, would have to continue doing so through the usual channels.

The French decision to occupy New Caledonia in 1853 was of limited consequence in either Paris or London: the new colony consisted of little more than a penal institution.[37] Once occupied, the small French settlement at New Caledonia quickly became dependent on emigration and trade from the Australian colonies.[38] Even Governor Denison of New South Wales admitted that "any risk which may accrue to these Colonies or to the Trade of England in these seas by the establishment of French superiority in New Caledonia . . . I am disposed to consider as very trifling."[39] However, after returning to Britain in 1851, Erskine wrote privately to James Calvert: "I wish with all my heart these French Priests, who do unmixed evil to the cause of religion and civilization, were out of the Islands; but in the present state of our politics where such an apprehension exists of giving offence to France in the most trifling matters, it is not easy to deal with them, and we must be content to hope that the truth of our doctrine will find its way, even with the wild Feejeeans."[40] Just before leaving Sydney, Erskine had explained to the Colonial Secretary, Edward Deas Thompson, "I think the matter one of great importance to these Colonies, & intend to tell them so at home, if they will listen to me."[41] Though briefly roused under Lord Auckland's leadership, the Admiralty had returned to its neglect of the Pacific. Erskine told Thompson that it was ignoring all requests for greater naval support in the south Pacific, even though the Australian gold rush meant that ships sometimes lay at anchor for months, unable to find crews. The captain could not even get a hearing for his proposals, concluding bitterly that no one at the Admiralty seemed to see "that a great empire in the south is worth a sloop of war."[42]

Although captains like Erskine were primarily concerned with protecting "Christianization and Civilization," the advent of steamship communication and increased trans-Pacific shipping during the gold rush gave them an additional motive. The need for coal, watering, repair, and reprovisioning depots brought the New South Wales commercial community into the fray; it wanted Britain to ensure that strategic islands would not fall into other hands. Erskine's friend Robert Towns led the "steam communication" lobby in New South Wales, supported by Governor Denison, while in London Erskine and Captain John Lort Stokes, who had used a steam vessel during his New Zealand survey, considered steamship routes a vital aspect of Britain's interest in the south Pacific. Meanwhile, Fremantle's reports drew attention to the need for "call stations" in the Pacific islands once a steam postal service was established between California and Australia. He noted that the Samoan, Tongan, and Fijian groups "lie nearly in a track for such Mail steamers & good Harbours are to be found on each Group."[43]

When it became clear that the British government was resigned to the French occupation of New Caledonia, outraged naval captains redoubled their expansionist efforts.[44] Fremantle's reports were full of recommendations for "protectorates" and calls for an increase in British consular representation in the Pacific islands. He contrasted British naval operations with those that he believed were threatening "Christianization and Civilization." In January 1854 the Foreign Office asked Fremantle for more information about French activities, giving the captain an ideal opportunity to promote his interpretation of events. He reported under confidential seal that the annexation of New Caledonia had produced "universal alarm" throughout the south Pacific islands.[45] Consul Pritchard had been no help; one of his sons sold the former British consulate site at Apia to Roman Catholic missionaries, who were building a large cathedral on it. The Samoans were confused and worried, Fremantle said, because they interpreted the Pritchard family's activities as a sign that Britain was abandoning Samoa to France.[46] There was also the matter of the American navy. American warships rarely ventured west of the Sandwich Islands before the 1850s, but the expansion of American trade in the southwest during the 1840s demanded attention, and American commercial agents pleaded for naval support.[47] When Commodore William Mervine took command of the USN Pacific Squadron in August 1854, American commerce in the islands gained an eager champion. Mervine was anxious to compensate for the neglect of American interests in the southwest Pacific, and his orders to Captain Theodorus Bailey of USS *St. Mary's* in 1855 were typical. The "especial object" of Bailey's visit to Fiji was "to demand and insist upon reparation for wrongs committed upon the property of American Citizens by the Natives of those Islands, and to take such other steps as will in your opinion best afford protection in future to the large Whaling and Commercial interests of our Citizens in that quarter."[48]

Commercial interests preoccupied most American captains under Mervine's command, and this explains why their activities so antagonized their British counterparts. The Wilkes expedition had already provoked the wrath of British humanitarians: Maxwell reported from Samoa in 1847 that Wilkes' abortive reprisals there had "naturally caused great distrust and suspicion in the Native mind, which has not yet altogether subsided," and he had to work hard to gain their "confidence regarding British Men of War."[49] Bishop Selwyn, who became *Dido*'s chaplain in order to take his first tour of the islands with Maxwell, remarked that "the advocates of Physical Force as the only correction of the vices of barbarians would learn a useful lesson in Samoa. A notorious murderer whom the American squadron tried to catch is still at large in Savai'i."[50]

When Commodore Mervine visited Samoa himself in 1856, his behavior alienated the British missionaries. He insisted on sending watering and leave parties ashore each Sunday, over the objections of Samoans who were holding their church services nearby. By the third week of his visit, he began holding target practice in Apia harbor at the moment they began their worship. "Surely the great Christian Government of the United States do not sustain their Navy and send forth their ships of war for such purposes as these!" wrote the missionaries, who added that Mervine's investigation of complaints against Samoans had been aggressive and, they believed, entirely unfair.[51] Captain Fremantle agreed:

> The French & American men of war do not treat these poor people well, they shew them no consideration, and it is seldom that a vessel passes without inflicting some severe chastisement, or imposing some heavy fine, and I am sorry to say that in a great measure these arbitrary & harsh proceedings are prompted by a feeling of jealousy, because the English people are so much more liked & respected, and on account of the paramount influence which the self-denial and perseverance of the English Missionaries have obtained.[52]

On his return to Sydney in 1855, Fremantle worked with James Calvert, Governor Denison, and that self-appointed expert on the Pacific islands Charles St. Julian on a program of British intervention that would safeguard the humanitarian gains of previous decades and prevent the further erosion of British influence. St. Julian, an energetic and eccentric man, was a reporter for the *Sydney Morning Herald*, author of various publications on Polynesia, and the Sandwich Islands government's commissioner to the Pacific islands.[53] Just before Fremantle's arrival as Senior Officer in 1854, St. Julian had made a series of proposals, including recommendations for the appointment of additional British consuls to the islands.[54] He added that "the advice and assistance of naval commanders and consular officers should, when sought for, be so far afforded as to aid the native rulers in legislating and governing upon sound principles" and that "*some* foreign power . . . *must* step in sooner or later. It is not a question as to whether *any* of the Great Powers shall attain the supreme influence in these regions, but *which* of them shall acquire this position." St. Julian offered the concept of "protective supremacy" as the best form of British rule in the islands, although he was quick to add that French annexations in Melanesia probably made direct rule a better alternative. Although the British government was still opposed to territorial acquisition in the Pacific, it was quite prepared to revive the consular proposals rebuffed by the Admiralty almost a decade earlier. A complicated series of recommendations and reactions followed, and a battle emerged between naval officers and their supporters in New South Wales, who wanted naval consuls to supervise British "protectorates," and the British government, which preferred to extend the existing consular system.

There is evidence that Lord Clarendon's own benevolent sympathies inspired support for increased British involvement of a sort. While waiting for Fremantle's report, Clarendon wrote to the Treasury, forwarding copies of St. Julian's paper and asking for information on Britain's commercial activity in the south Pacific. Emphasizing the need for the "guidance and protection of judicious Consular Officers," who would be "highly conducive to the advancement of civilisation" in the islands, Clarendon's recommendations echoed the protective concerns of captains like Fremantle. Clarendon suggested that "some form of Protective Supremacy" was required and asked the Treasury to fund additional consulates.[55]

Unfortunately for Fremantle, his other recommendations were too radical even for the sympathetic Clarendon. First, the captain's interpretation of "protective supremacy" was clearly some form of direct rule or, as the Admiralty put it, British "occupation."[56] Claiming that "the British Flag might be hoisted at Apia without asking a single question," Fremantle had declared that "the British name and British character are well known amongst them, and appreciated by the Natives, who may also be said to entertain and cherish a downright loyal feeling towards her Most Gracious Majesty."[57] In Samoa, he continued, British rule would be a "happy deliverance," not only from the French threat, but from "internal discord": naval officers had struggled for decades with Samoan resistance to centralized government.[58] In Fiji, the leading chief Cakobau was under pressure from white residents and their supporters in the American navy, especially with regard to the "American Debt" (Chapter 4 will discuss this in detail). Fremantle believed that British protection was essential to Cakobau's survival as "King of Fiji." The captain also stressed the need to protect islanders from expansionist threats from Tonga. Tonga had reached "an advanced stage of self-government" and was now showing "indications of ambition & independence" in its aggressive involvement in Fijian affairs. Concerned that the Tongan government was no longer dependent on British support (see Chapter 4) and claiming that earlier Tongan offers of cession would probably not now be repeated, Fremantle advised Britain to rule Tonga anyway and obtain "the acquiescence of King George" afterward.[59] Such recommendations were bound to be unpalatable in London.

The second unwelcome feature of Fremantle's reports was his attempt to ensure naval supremacy in any new British regime in the islands. Although the captain assumed that naval captains could not act as consuls themselves, he recommended that a ship be specifically assigned to island duties, in order to "establish and maintain the possession of the three groups." A consul or "Resident Commissioner" could be appointed to Samoa, Tonga, and Fiji but would be "subordinate to the Captain of the Ship who might be constituted as Governor General."[60] The Foreign Office rejected this suggestion out of hand, on the strength of Admiralty objections to similar suggestions in the 1840s, but Clarendon's remarks indicate that he was in favor of the idea, agreeing with Fremantle that the purpose of such an appointment would be "principally to aid in advancing the progressive civilization of the Islanders, and as an effective method of maintaining & furthering British Interests, especially by introducing a uniform system of policy in dealing with the Natives."[61] Shared emphasis on "civilization of the Islanders," rather than encouragement of trade, and a mutual recognition that a consular office backed by naval resources would provide a more "effective method" than the current consular system gave Clarendon's vision of British protectiveness much in common with the earlier, rejected suggestions of Governor Grey.

The real problem with many of these recommendations was the call for British "supremacy." A vague concept, this could be interpreted as direct rule by enthusiasts like Fremantle and St. Julian or as "guidance and protection" by the more cautious Lord Clarendon. The Foreign Secretary, despite his private misgivings about France and the United States, was bound to prefer the least controversial interpretation in order to maintain the status quo between European Powers. The Foreign Office composed a memorandum in which it rehearsed a number of familiar objections to what it called "the occupation of Islands in the South Pacific by the British." It also pointed out that the navigators of other countries had been visiting these places, opening up the possibility of territorial claims based on the principle of discovery. The Foreign Office described a situation of "conflicting claims to the Sovereignty" of various islands,[62] but we know from the petitions coming from the islands themselves that islanders were not offering their sovereignty. Islanders and British officials were failing to understand one another's intentions, and because the concept of protectorates had yet to develop, the government viewed offers of cession as requests for occupation. It is worth pointing out that the word "annexation" rarely appeared in the correspondence of this period. This word described the forcible conquest of a piece of territory and its subsequent colonization, something that was rarely considered before the end of the nineteenth century and was usually dismissed in any case. The British government was preoccupied with island sovereignty precisely because colonization by force was out of the question. There were various other options such as colonization by the doctrine of *terra nullius,* as with New South Wales, or by treaty of cession, as in New Zealand.[63] However, Britain had allowed its right by discovery to lapse, notably in the Sandwich Islands and Tahiti, and never repeated the New South Wales procedure. I will take up the problem of treaties and other legal mechanisms later. For now, it is important to note how central the issue of sovereignty still was to the British administration's understanding of the Pacific islands.

There were other, less direct reasons why the British government shunned greater commitments in the south Pacific at mid-century. Inquiry into the 1853 cession of Sarawak to Sir James Brooke (a former naval officer) produced instructions discouraging naval support for schemes of territorial aggrandizement.[64] In 1854, the United States seemed about to annex the Sandwich Islands, but Clarendon worked hard to maintain "the status quo in the Sandwich Islands."[65] The Indian Mutiny and a change of ministry came in 1857, and shortly after that Gladstone made it clear to Admiral Stokes that he would

> hesitate to admit, even to my excellent friend the Bishop of New Zealand, the propriety of any indefinite or wide extension of our Protectorate, by acts or by a policy of ours, to tribes not within our dominions, while I regard the further extension of those dominions by fresh assumptions with misgiving and even with dread. There is no country upon earth so charged with responsibilities as we are; and I am by no means sure that we are not more ready to undertake than ready to meet them.[66]

Stokes replied that Britain was leaving the southwest Pacific "waste and unchristianized," an argument that would weigh with a man of Gladstone's piety. Gladstone, however, recognized the ambiguity of Britain's civilizing mission in the Pacific: the difference between self-assigned responsibility for islanders and the ability to translate that responsibility into political and financial policy.

Given the government's reluctance to intervene directly, naval officers might have been expected to work closely with the sole British representative in the area, Consul George Pritchard at Samoa. Unfortunately Pritchard was jealous of his official privileges, and his commercial dealings alienated his fellow missionaries to the extent that they refused his reinstatement as an LMS preacher in 1849.[67] Apia's British residents, however, were delighted to find an eager champion in their new consul. Pritchard had visited Samoa with the missionary John Williams in 1839, trying unsuccessfully to encourage the creation of a legal code for the protection of European property.[68] After taking up residence in Apia, his despatches to the Foreign Office were full of concern for the "rights" of the European community: during a series of battles on Upolu in 1844–1845, Europeans felt threatened and Pritchard pleaded for a warship to "exact redress" for damage done to their property.[69] Preoccupied by Maori uprisings in New Zealand, the Royal Navy had not visited Samoa for two years after delivering Pritchard to his new post in 1845. Responding to directions from the Foreign Office, Admiral George Seymour despatched HMS *Juno* from the Pacific Station in 1847, but Pritchard's expectations of punishment and vengeance put him on a collision course with the humane Captain Blake. A manipulative and alarmist man, Pritchard presented an ideal target for humanitarians: his contempt for Samoans and defense of resident Europeans were diametrically opposed to their approach. British missionaries and naval officers expected to work with a consul who shared their benevolent, protective image of islanders and their condemnation of unruly beach communities. A pattern of opposition to Pritchard emerged as his behavior continued to be at odds with humanitarian ideals.

When Blake arrived, Pritchard had a long list of grievances, many his own, for which he demanded satisfaction. Blake received these cautiously, having learned at once that Samoans had "exalted notions of a man-of-war," based on Pritchard's repeated threats of naval retribution, and that the consul himself would "hear neither explanation, palliation, nor other version than his own, but with unbending pertinacity holding to his own judgments, infallible and absolute, he would at once, without remorse, proceed to execution, and visit with the last measure of severity, alleged delinquencies, which since I have taken pains and studied to examine them, I confess appear to me to admit in some instances of doubt."[70] The captain proceeded carefully, attempting to reassure Samoans while investigating the grievances as impartially as he could. Of these, the most useful example is the matter of the Salelologa fine for damages sustained by a European resident, Henry Epps, during the civil conflict on Upolu.

Pritchard told Blake that Captain Home had levied a fine of 150 pigs on the people of the Safotulafai and Salelologa districts in 1844; whereas the former had paid their part, the latter had not. When Blake's investigations revealed that Epps

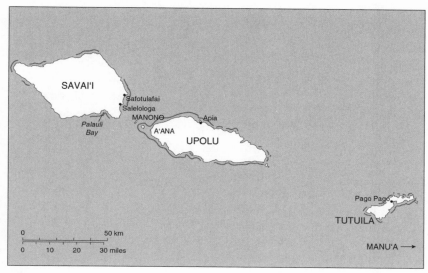

Map 4. Samoa

"took a part in the war, and therefore shared the fate that might be expected in the wars of savages,"[71] Pritchard became vague about the origin of the fine, saying it had been levied by "some authority then in Samoa" (probably himself) who had appealed to Home for support. Blake sent his first lieutenant directly to Salelologa, where he, Pritchard, and an interpreter conferred with the chiefs. Turning the tables on Blake's invitation to make restitution "in accordance with your own custom when you have done injury to another people,"[72] the Salelologa leadership demanded due process according to British justice: "It was their wish there should be an investigation, and if proof could be brought against any one person, they were willing to pay. They understood that it was justice to inquire into a case before a decision took place. How could the man-of-war hear from England, or any other place, that they were guilty?"[73] After hasty consultation with Pritchard, Epps dropped the charges. Not only had Blake refused to demand payment without investigation, he provided the Salelologa people with an opportunity to demolish the case.

Blake's own opinion of Samoans was shaped by the dignity their chiefs showed on occasions like this. Reporting to Admiral Seymour, he praised Samoan "independence," their understanding of quid pro quo, and their "law, or custom, of the whole body, being accountable and responsible for the acts of individuals," which be believed was "a salutary provision and restraint."[74]

These qualities contrasted sharply with what he viewed as Pritchard's "rigid or too stringent line of conduct." Before leaving the islands, the captain rebuked the consul, claiming he was inspired to do so by his admiration for Samoans themselves: "the remarkable acuteness and quickness of perception in these people, their very tenacious ideas of property, and their strongly rooted feelings of attachment to Samoa their country."[75] There were probably other considerations as well. Blake had also come to Samoa bearing impressions of island conditions gathered during previous service in the south Pacific. Investigating the massacre of islanders at Ngatik in 1837 by the crew of the trader *Lambton* (whose master, Hart, was already accused of hanging a chief at Ascension), Blake reported that Hart and his men killed islanders because of trading frustrations. Calling Hart's crew "a strong armed gang of Renegade European Seamen," Blake lamented the deaths of "mere savages whose only defence against fire arms rested in their Native Clubs and Slings."[76] Preconceptions about the offensive character and behavior of European traders and humanitarian sympathy for victimized islanders probably affected Blake's perception of his duty in Samoa.

Captain Maxwell visited Samoa later in 1847 from the East Indies Station. He sympathized with the consul at first, believing that Pritchard's low standing with Samoans had resulted from the fact that he had never been officially presented to them. After taking Pritchard on a tour of Samoa and investigating his complaints, Maxwell began to change his attitude. One case involved an English resident's cattle killed by local Samoans because they had torn up village plantations. Maxwell had been amazed to see "a troop of 8 or 10 wild young horses galloping through" Apia, noting that Europeans did nothing to control the stock they introduced to the island. The captain concluded that cattle and horses "must be a very great nuisance" to Samoans "and in most cases a positive injury to them." By the end of his Samoan visit, Maxwell's sympathies had transferred from Pritchard to Captain Blake, and he told the consul that, even though he did not have a record of Blake's proceedings, he "found no reason to differ from what I understood had been his opinion on them."[77]

The following year, Samoans made an equally favorable impression on Captain Erskine. The captain admired the refined oratory and consensus-based government of Samoa, declaring that "it was impossible . . . not to be struck with the decorous, and even highly-polished, manners exhibited here, as at the smaller meetings in Tutuila. The business of this large assembly, where many different opinions prevailed on an important subject, was conducted in a way which would have done credit to the British House of Lords or Commons."[78]

When Pritchard complained again to the Foreign Office about the lack of naval support for his complaints, Erskine assured the Admiralty that Samoa had been "more frequently visited by Men of War, than any others in the Pacific," and Samoans were "in a tolerable state of civilization & perfectly well disposed to British Subjects."[79] The positive impression Samoans had made on their naval visitors was operating against the interests of Consul Pritchard.

There was one apparent exception to this united front against Pritchard: Captain Worth of HMS *Calypso*, who blockaded the Manono people at Pritchard's request in order to recover an indemnity for European property damaged during the civil conflict on Upolu. This was actually a compromise solution designed to deflect some of the consul's other grievances against Samoans. Worth's report has not survived, but Lieutenant Conway Shipley, who published an account of the episode after his return to England, suggests that the wardroom's opinion of Pritchard (and his American counterpart) was not flattering: "the two Consuls, who talked very well, were retailing musquets, powder, and shot to both parties," with Pritchard "haggling whether to give three or four bullets for a duck." Pritchard had given Worth a list of claims for property damage, including a supposed mission building. Shipley tells us that Worth "could not view all these matters in quite so strong a light as the residents" and refused to pursue most of the complaints, hoping that action in the matter of the mission building would help protect British missionaries and mollify the consul.[80] Behind the scenes, the captain complained about the kind of British official his orders forced him to support. After a private talk with Worth, Seymour's successor, Rear Admiral Hornby, told the Foreign Office:

> Though it does not appear in any of Captain Worth's Papers, I have reason to think from conversation with that Officer, that it would be judicious to restrain Mr. Pritchard from carrying on the *threefold occupations of Consul, Missionary and Shopkeeper*, which he now does at his Residence at the Navigators Islands, thereby bringing himself in disagreeable contact with Foreigners and Natives, and lowering his Consular Office in their eyes.[81]

Opposition to Pritchard became more strenuous when it became clear that he was dealing in liquor as well as armaments. Having supported missionaries throughout the islands in their attempt to limit, if not ban, trade in liquor, Captain Home was appalled to see that Pritchard and his sons were selling alcohol from the consulate itself. Home had a particular interest in developments at Apia; it had been his recommendation that resulted in Pritchard's appointment. It now appeared that the consul Home had hoped would be a catalyst for civilization was encouraging the corruption of Samoans instead. "The place called the Consulate is of a description quite unfit for a respectable Englishman to live in or for the English Flag to fly in front of," Home reported.[82] In a private letter to Pritchard, responding to the usual complaints about damaged property, Home berated the consul for failing to support Samoan attempts to control the sale of liquor and recommended that he follow a more humanitarian policy so that "by kind treatment and conciliatory manners shewn to the natives by the Europeans settled amongst them there will be no longer any repetition of the acts complained of."[83]

The fact that Home confined his criticism to private or internal correspondence raises an important point. Naval officers did their best at first to shore up Pritchard's public dignity. Although it must have been clear to Samoans that Pritchard's threats were not being carried out, they were urged by a succession of captains to respect the consular office and assured that it existed for their protection. Noting that Erskine and Worth had both explained the consul's mandate to Samoan chiefs, Home wrote an open letter of his own explaining the "line of conduct" they should follow. It stated that the Royal Navy would ensure "that English subjects as well as the natives are not ill used," without indicating whether similar instructions were being given to resident Europeans as well. Home urged the chiefs to guarantee the safety of foreign persons and property, declaring that if they failed they would be treated "as heathens and savages and be made to pay for the damage."[84] Pritchard was irritated by the contradiction between this confident stance and the navy's obvious lack of support in specific cases, and by the repeated lectures on humanitarianism.[85] The conflict was about to end. Exasperated by the consul's obstinacy and sympathizing with Samoan complaints about him, naval officers abandoned their public support for him.

Captain Fremantle's visit in *Juno* was Pritchard's undoing. Fremantle arrived in October 1855 with a copy of Erskine's published journal in his hand, reporting that he could add nothing to his predecessor's exemplary description of the islands and clearly in sympathy with Erskine's positive impression of Samoans. At Apia he noted that Pritchard and Aaron van Camp, the American agent, were exploiting the ongoing civil war for their own commercial benefit, while encouraging the division of Apia into mutually hostile British and American camps.[86] Apia's residents had formed a Foreign Residents' Society in 1854 to create a united front against the power of Samoan chiefs.[87] By 1855 there was an atmosphere of anarchy at Apia that made Fremantle welcome the arrival of

HMS *Dido* and Captain Morshead, an old schoolfellow of his. The two men quickly agreed that the British consulate was a disgrace, and Morshead reported that "should any Vessel be trading with fraudulent intentions or loosely worded articles, or defective papers, they can now depend on having every thing arranged here, with some of the external forms of justice, as any oath or affidavit can be procured instantly, & witnessed before a consul with his seal attached to it, to give it an apparent validity."[88]

The first case Pritchard brought to the two captains' attention was a dispute concerning the British schooner *Crescent*. The Manono people has seized the vessel when a shipment of ordnance purchased from Pritchard failed to arrive. Pritchard attempted to portray this as a case of piracy, demanding that Fremantle intimidate the Manono into giving up the schooner. The captain preferred to investigate first, and his report reveals the degree of influence Samoans themselves exercised on his judgment. The Manono chiefs asked Fremantle for "protection on their own parts from the exceptionable acts of the Consul," and after investigation Fremantle concluded "that the extenuating circumstances admitted of the most favorable and broadest construction." Openly defying Pritchard, he demanded that the consul refund the money for the guns, and the Manono people duly released the *Crescent*. It was then discovered that a bale of printed cotton was missing from her cargo, and Fremantle asked the Manono to pay for it, which they did. The captain refused to enforce Pritchard's demand for additional compensation for the seizure of the vessel, blaming the whole business on "the very unprudent conduct on the part of HM's Consul by mixing himself up in the international disputes of the natives by the sale of the Guns, & by retaining the sum paid for them after it was known that they had fallen into the wrong hands."

Like previous naval visitors, Fremantle admired the "good intellects," "great form and etiquette," and "moral and true Christian" nature of the Samoans at Apia and was not surprised that they resented the complaints and threats of the European community and its consular representatives. Fremantle felt it was hypocritical to tell a Samoan chief that he "must be thankful for the compliment of having a Consul sent to him and to treat him with respect and consideration, when in reality and upon tolerably just grounds he entertains sentiments directly the reverse." Although the captain pitied Pritchard the man, he believed that his appointment had been counterproductive and recommended his dismissal with an allowance.[89] The Samoan chiefs of Upolu, meanwhile, had petitioned Queen Victoria to remove Pritchard "because of the many things which are crooked in his conduct." Sending a copy of the petition to Governor Denison of New

South Wales, they asked him to replace Pritchard with John C. Williams, son of the missionary John Williams, who was "well fitted for us in Samoa."[90] Fremantle's report echoed their recommendation.

Williams already enjoyed humanitarian endorsement. In 1848 Captain Maxwell had hinted that the bilingual Williams, who already held the office of American commercial agent in the absence of a suitable American candidate, "would readily exchange his present appointment for one in the Service of his own country." There was no one "more fit to fill the appointment" of consul or commercial agent, he continued, because Williams "is very popular with the Samoans having lived among them since his boyhood, and they seem to regard and respect him."[91] Governor Denison forwarded the Samoan petition to the Foreign Office, advising them to await Fremantle's report, which, when it arrived, completed an unanswerable case against Pritchard. When Fremantle returned to Samoa in 1856, he found that Pritchard had resigned before he could be dismissed; John Williams, now acting consul, was formally appointed in 1857. George Pritchard's son William was made the first British consul to Fiji in 1858, also on Captain Fremantle's recommendation. Unfortunately, it would not be long before the two new consuls fell out with their naval patrons and with the missionaries. As I will show in later chapters, the more a consul developed a relationship with the traders and other British residents whose interests he was supposed to represent, the more he found himself isolated by humanitarians who preferred to emphasize the protection of islanders. Given the humanitarian campaign for greater consular representation in the islands, this hostility seems baffling, but it was directly related to the fear of "white savagery" that I explored earlier. Consulates could blur the vital distinction between respectability and nonrespectability too easily. What naval officers and their mission supporters were seeking in the islands was apparently a greater formal British presence. At the same time, they resisted the arrival of other players on a stage where they preferred to perform alone.[92]

4

Kingmaking

ATTEMPTS to introduce or develop centralized government in the islands became central to the program of "Christianization and Civilization," especially where a stratified social system already existed, as in the Society Islands or Tonga. In places like New Zealand or Samoa, where sociopolitical units were locally based and less hierarchical, ideas about unified rulership had no indigenous counterpart. The concept of Maori or Samoan "nationhood" arose after European contact, but its problematic relationship with island traditions doomed early attempts at unification to failure.[1] Behind the rhetoric of protection and improvement lay a complicated process of negotiation with island leaders, and the Royal Navy's extensive involvement with this process gives us an opportunity to analyze it in detail.

Collaboration with ambitious political figures is a common theme of empire, but the story here is not only one of the consolidation of power for mutual gain. There were contradictions, as usual, at the heart of the British approach itself. In Tonga and Fiji, where British influence was unchallenged for a relatively long period, the humanitarian relationship with kingmaking lasted long enough for its tensions to emerge clearly. These two cases are usually considered very different in terms of their outcome. Tonga developed a kingship through an effective combination of indigenous politics and borrowed practices. Fiji's aspiring king, Cakobau, led an increasingly precarious existence until his authority was guaranteed by colonial rule. However, these two situations also have a great deal in common. In both island groups, British support for kingmaking was deeply ambivalent, reflecting tension between the generalized concept of indigenous sovereignty and the knowledge that British involvement had influenced the outcome. Naval officers and the British government paid island leaders a very double-edged respect, as if they could not fully accept island monarchies as "real."

Given Captain Cook's involvement with Tahitian politics, one might expect to find his successors embroiled in the kingdom Pomare II managed to create in Tahiti with the help of the LMS. But there was such a scarcity of naval visits during the crucial 1820s, when Pomare II finally consolidated rulership of all Tahiti, that both the chiefs and their missionary advisors were inclining toward American influence when Captain Waldegrave visited them in HMS *Seringapatam* in 1830.[2] By that time, the young Pomare III had died after a brief reign and had been succeeded by his regent Aimatta, now Queen Pomare. Although the Royal Navy had much to do with her struggle with conflicting European interests in Tahiti, France in particular, the Tahitian monarchy was already in place. Elsewhere in the south Pacific, naval officers had a more direct involvement in the creation and succession of island rulers.

The tensions inherent in British kingmaking were apparent by the 1820s in Hawai'i. HMS *Blonde* visited Honolulu in 1825, bringing home the bodies of the king and queen who had died of measles during a visit to England. The absence and untimely death of the king had consolidated the ambitious plans of his sister Kaahumanu, who converted to Christianity immediately after his departure and created a national flag that included the Union Jack.[3] She had already achieved the abolition of *kapu*, the set of prohibitions that defined and controlled Sandwich Island society, and the king's death made her regent of his young brother Kauikeaouli. Lord Byron's visit in the *Blonde* was an opportunity to reinforce her political authority and her relationship with Britain. An impressive series of ceremonies ensued, beginning with the state funeral of the king and the queen. Byron and his officers attended in full dress, providing a guard of honor, salutes, and gun carriages for the caskets. The captain had brought a present for the new Kamehameha III from George IV: a full dress Windsor uniform with royal insignia, complete down to the initials "GR" on the solid gold buttons. Having dressed the young king as a miniature image of his English patron, saluting him before the assembled chiefs (to Kaahumanu's delight), Byron patted him on the head and "bade him to be a good boy, attend well to his studies, and mind all his kind friends the Missionaries said to him."[4] The captain had dressed Kamehameha in the trappings of a British monarch but could not treat him like one. Nor could he treat him with the dignity appropriate for a chief: whether formally *kapu* or otherwise, to touch the head of such a high-ranking individual was a shocking breach of etiquette. Perhaps, to Byron, the young king seemed like a boy playing dress-up in his father's clothes, needing the encouragement and admonitions of a friendly uncle. In Tonga and Fiji we will not see such a graphic demonstration of British condescension; for one thing, George Tāufaʻāhau of Tonga and Cakobau of Fiji were grown men of impressive stature and bearing. But we will see outlines of the same story. After exhorting islanders to govern themselves and encouraging them to adopt the forms of British monarchy, Britain was not prepared to recognize the resulting governments fully.

The LMS abandoned its first mission to Tonga in 1800 after a series of disappointments, including the defection of George Vason, who "went native." The Methodists made the next attempt in the 1820s with a series of native teachers from the Society Islands, followed by British missionaries in 1826. At this time Tongan politics were dominated by the rulers, *tuʻi*, of the Haʻapai and Vavaʻu island groups, and the large island of Tongatapu.[5] The missionaries quickly found favor with one of these: the Tuʻi Kanokupolu of Tongatapu, Aleamotuʻa, who was baptized "Josiah" in 1830. Josiah urged his fellow chiefs to consider the benefits of the new religion, and both Tāufaʻāhau of Haʻapai (baptized "George" after George III of Britain) and Finau of Vavaʻu converted in 1831. By the time Captain Bethune of HMS *Conway* visited Vavaʻu in January 1838, George had succeeded to Finau's title. Naval support for missionaries now became support for "King George" in his ambition to rule all of Tonga. Bethune wrote to the *tuʻi*, assuring him of "the anxious desire of my Government to maintain the friendly relations which have now happily existed for so long a period, between your Majesty's dominions and Great Britain."[6] This greeting, which could have been exchanged with a European monarch, shows how formally George's "kingship" seemed to be endorsed by his British naval visitors.

Like most naval captains, Bethune relied on mission stations for information about Tongan politics and responded to mission support for George's ambitions. George's father had been the Tuʻi Kanokupolu, and he had every reason to hope to inherit the rulership of Tongatapu after the ailing Josiah's death. The trouble was that an alliance of chiefs on Tongatapu, known as the Haʻa Havea, had opposed George's father and made it clear that they would also resist the son. The small mission community at Nukuʻalofa reacted by fortifying their settlement and denouncing the Haʻa Havea people as the enemies of Christianity. The missionaries saw a double significance in the growing conflict: the struggle of Christianity against heathenism and unjust rebellion against rightful rule. Matters came to a head in 1837, when an allied force under Josiah and George confronted the Haʻa Havea and defeated them after what the missionaries called a "holy war."[7] Bethune's arrival the following year and his support for the Christian chiefs seemed providential to the missionaries. John Thomas wrote: "We are always thankful for the visits of H.B.M. Ships of War. . . . The cause of our common Christianity is promoted by their visits to the stations we occupy."[8] "Our common Christianity" would continue to be a compelling reason for naval interference on Tongatapu, one for which Commander Walter Croker of HMS *Favorite* was prepared to sacrifice both his professional reputation and his life.

Analysis of Croker's activities benefits from comparison with those of Charles Wilkes, commander of the U.S. Exploring Expedition. Wilkes arrived in April 1840, just two months before Croker, but his perceptions of the Tongan political situation were radically different. Realizing that the conflict on Tonga-tapu was really about resistance to "King George" rather than to Josiah or to Christianity, Wilkes tried his hand at peacemaking.[9] He concluded that the war "was in great measure a religious contest, growing out of the zeal the mission-aries have to propagate the gospel," combined with George's opportunistic ambition to be the first overall ruler of Tonga.[10] Wilkes left Tonga under a cloud of mutual recriminations, making it difficult to determine exactly what happened during his negotiations.[11] However, the difference between Wilkes' dispassionate appraisal of the political maneuvering he observed and Bethune's uncritical acceptance is clear. Croker would confirm the British tradition of support for George, but his fate also revealed a dangerous disjunction between idealized British motives and Pacific island responses. Croker's romantic zeal killed him, just as it would kill another naval captain, Commodore James Goodenough, thirty-five years later.

Reaching Tongatapu in June of 1840, Croker quickly became embroiled in its civil conflict. Josiah and the missionaries informed him that "rebellion against the King and government" was becoming more violent and asked for his assistance as mediator.[12] They appealed to Britain as their natural protector, declaring: "We have a Flag here, and at Vavau, which we respect because they were given to us by Commanders of English Men of War . . . England will have a bad name in the world if you will not help us in our distress now after our so earnestly entreating your friendly aid in humbling the rebels . . . against the King, the Laws and the religion of Jesus Christ."[13] Croker found this trinity of motives irre-sistible. Captain Waldegrave or Bethune, one of whom must have presented the flags, had given the Tongans a symbol whose significance they were fully able to appreciate and exploit.

Croker agreed to arbitrate but prepared for battle too, ordering guns to be landed and carried, with ammunition, within striking distance of the Haʻa Havea fortress at Pea. On 24 June, Croker and his two lieutenants mustered their forces, eighteen marines and sixty-four seamen, in the mission yard: a powerful symbol of the relationship between missions and the "arm of flesh" they so often scorned in theory. By moving to the fort from the mission station, Croker was siding with the Christian party rather than providing disinterested arbitration.[14] At Pea, Croker insisted that the Haʻa Havea must respect the Christian community under the umbrella of "King Josiah's" authority and dismantle all their fortifications on Tongatapu.[15] After deliberation, the Pea people agreed to make peace "but did not wish to see King George's face for a long time"[16] and asked for more time to discuss the peace terms with their allies outside the fort. It seems clear that the old feud between the Haʻa Havea and George was the source of conflict; religious differences were playing only a secondary part. However, Croker had been swayed by the Christian view that "the Ground of [Pea's] rebellion is their hatred to the Gospel, and their desire for War," a description designed to appeal to his support for the missionaries.[17] He broke off negotiations and returned to his forces to do battle.

Croker's choice of tactics was disastrous. He moved the guns within one hundred yards—musket range—of the fort. Having wasted his superior firepower, Croker decided to make a heroic charge, and, drawing his sword, he shouted, "Come, blue jackets, follow me," and flung himself against the fortress gate.[18] He and two of the men at the guns were killed almost at once. In the disorganized mêlée that followed, other members of *Favorite*'s crew were wounded, and the guns were abandoned in their exposed location. Lieutenant Dunlop, at the rear with George's reinforcements, rallied the British group long enough to organize the evacuation of the killed and wounded back to the ship.[19] On the following day, Gunner's Mate John New and George Freathy, captain of the forecastle, were buried at sea and Croker, in the mission compound. Dunlop wanted to negotiate for the guns, but the chiefs and missionaries "said it would be certain death for any one to attempt communicating with the people in the Fort."[20] *Favorite* left Tongatapu that evening, evacuating Tucker, Rabone, and their families to Vavaʻu before returning to Sydney.

The few historians who discuss this episode do so only briefly, citing it as evidence of missionary meddling in Tongan politics and dismissing Croker as a naive accessory.[21] The evidence suggests that the situation was much more complicated than this and requires us to put Croker's own motives under scrutiny. Croker's tragic mishandling of his peacemaking mission was rooted in his personal enthusiasm for the mission cause and a dramatic sense of chivalry. Josiah and George had invited the captain to join in the campaign to "strengthen the Church of Jesus Christ by saving the lives of the Christians and their Missionaries,"[22] and Croker agreed unreservedly. Not only did he put the lives of his crew at risk, but he boasted that the Christian cause was more important to him than his professional career. He might even have had a hunger for martyrdom; before the "battle" he asked missionaries to bury him at their chapel in Nuku'alofa, rather than at sea.[23]

Tonga's missionaries quickly distanced themselves from Croker after his death, revealing a typical ambivalence about naval support. John Thomas marveled that many more were not killed, since "their ill fated Captain had taken them so close to the fort that their large guns were of no service, and the heathens had every advantage."[24] Francis Wilson was less diplomatic. Lamenting the "rashness and imprudence" of Croker's actions, he said that those who were on the spot "can only account for his conduct by supposing him to have been the subject of mental aberration at the time."[25] Later, when the New South Wales press criticized the missionaries' encouragement of the unfortunate captain, the superintendent of Methodist missions rushed to defend his colleagues. He interviewed *Favorite*'s officers himself at Sydney, relieved to find them "in agreement about the blamelessness of the missionaries."[26] Croker, whom the Tongan missionaries had invited to chair their district meeting, was now denounced as a madman. His fellow officers found the whole business embarrassing; their superior, Captain Joseph Nias, assured the Admiralty that Croker "had no directions from me to pursue the course detailed in . . . *Favorite*'s proceedings prior to this dire calamity," and the Admiralty made no comment on his report.[27] Commander Thomas Sulivan, who took *Favorite* back to Tonga in 1842 to retrieve the captured guns, declared that he intended "to say as little about the late Commander Croker as possible."[28] The Ha'a Havea turned over the ordnance without hesitation; they had found a new way to infuriate George and his Methodist supporters by inviting French Roman Catholic priests to join them at Pea.

Later naval visitors continued to be impressed by George's ambition and joined the missionaries in creating the trappings of European monarchy about him. Sulivan reported that George was "the most enlightened Chief I have seen in these Seas" and, despite the conflict on Tongatapu, referred to him as "the principal chief of this place."[29] An even more vigorous supporter arrived in 1844, when Captain Home made his first south Pacific cruise as captain of the *North Star*. Home's personal admiration for George inspired him to create an aura of dynasty about his family. The chief's wife, baptized Charlotte to his George, had just given birth to their first son and accepted Home's advice "to name him George after his royal father."[30] George, "dignified and extremely grave," impressed Home, who reported that the *tu'i* was "doing all in his power to Civilize his subjects."[31]

By 1847 and Captain Maxwell's visit in *Dido*, George had succeeded Josiah as Tu'i Kanokupolu, adding Josiah's titular name of Tupou to his own. He had also attracted the interest of Governor George Grey of New Zealand. Providing Maxwell with a cargo of gifts, including some specially selected for the "king," Grey encouraged the captain to spend more time at Tonga than at Samoa, "the inhabitants of which have neither such strong claims upon us as those of Tonga, and have not made any similar friendly advances."[32] George Tupou had captured Grey's imagination, and the governor wanted the Royal Navy to encourage his protégé by doing everything possible to "produce a favourable impression upon the inhabitants of the Friendly Islands."[33]

Captain Maxwell's visit was a landmark in George's relationship with Britain. The captain did more than join the ranks of the chief's admirers: he also supported a petition for British "protection" in Tonga and helped reinforce the connection with New Zealand. Acknowledging George as "the sovereign chief of Tonga," despite the continuing hostility of the Ha'a Havea chiefs, Maxwell was pleased to observe the extent of Christianization in Tonga—roughly two-thirds of the population had converted—and to see that missionaries were "consulted on all occasions by those chiefs who have embraced Christianity, who usually follow their advice, and King George is one of their most zealous and instructed disciples."[34] Grey continued his correspondence with the chief and offered to educate his son in New Zealand. In a poignant letter, Grey explained that he had no children, "my only little boy having died," and promised that he and Lady Grey would take the boy into their home.[35]

It must have gratified George to have established such an influential connection, and he used it to develop his plans for a Tongan legal code. He had promulgated a series of laws in Ha'apai in 1838, based on a combination of traditional and Christian prohibitions, and extended it to Vava'u and Tongatapu once he acquired authority there. He devised a more comprehensive, written code in 1850 after consultation with Grey and his Chief Justice, William Martin: its central theme was the divine origin of his kingship and his subjects' obedience.[36]

Anxious to uphold the *tu'i*'s authority, Maxwell's successor Captain Erskine "waited on King George" at Vava'u, "the residence of the King of the whole group," at the beginning of August 1849. Adopting the same royal language as his predecessor, Erskine reported to London that "the whole of this group . . . stare at present under the dominion of George Tubou, who unites in his person the dignities of King of Vavau and Habai, and that of Tui Kanakabolu, which gives him the sovereignty of Tonga, to which latter he succeeded on the death of Josiah Tubou."[37] Erskine was impressed to find "regular Government" under George's rule, based on the exercise of power through "Governors at the islands where he is not actually present . . . with laws for the punishment of offenders."[38] The captain gave him a guard of honor during his visit to *Havannah*, and a departing salute of thirteen guns, "an attention which has been shown to him by several British ships-of-war, and which he is said to prize, as an acknowledgment of his sovereign authority."[39] The most important thing, concluded Erskine, was "securing the succession of George's son, the only means of keeping these numerous islands united and prosperous," and to that end he recommended (without success) the appointment of a resident consul.

Governor Grey and his naval allies were behaving as if George was the undisputed ruler of all Tonga, but by the time of Captain Home's second visit in August 1852, the civil conflict there had grown more serious. The leader of the Ha'a Havea resistance, Tu'i Tonga, underlined his connections with France by converting to Roman Catholicism in 1851.[40] For the Methodist chiefs and their missionary advisors, this was a sinister development, and Home arrived just as George was massing his forces for an attack on Pea. Within sight of the fort, the chief entertained his guest with war dances and conferred with him afterward at the nearby mission station, nearly duplicating the conditions of Croker's meeting twelve years earlier. Home was already aware of his predecessor Erskine's concern that the Ha'a Havea people were more than mere "rebels"; the Tu'i Tonga had his own claim to power, albeit a shaky one, and should George die before his son came of age, Erskine had worried that "disputes will certainly arise as to the sovereignty of the different islands, and civil war be the consequence."[41] Home was equally determined to see George as "king" of Tonga but emphasized that his dedication to the cause stemmed from the British tradition of support, not from George's indigenous qualifications. One of Tonga's Catholic missionaries, Chevron, tried to explain to the captain that at the moment George was still outranked by the Tu'i Tonga. Home's reply was revealing:

> The Chief of Nukualofa, George Tuboo was universally acknowledged as the King of the Friendly Islands; that Josiah Tuboo his predecessor had offered the sovereignty of the Islands to Queen Victoria, that they might enjoy the protection of Her Majesty but the offer had been refused in a letter addressed to

George Tuboo from the Secretary of State by the Queen's Command. Had Tuboo been only one Chief among several, he could have offered only his own portion to Great Britain, or acted in concert with the rest; but the act was entirely his own, and he has also been acknowledged King of the Friendly Islands by other nations.[42]

Missionary Richard Amos, interpreting, recalled that Home used even stronger language while explaining his interview with Chevron to George. Referring to the letter of support for "King George Tuboo," Home mentioned that he had copies of this and all the other relevant correspondence, supplied to him by Sir George Grey, and that it was these documents that authorized him to support the king's government.[43] He recognized George's kingship because the title was acknowledged in British official correspondence, or, as he put it, "he knew [George] as the King of Tonga because the Queen of England says he is, and not because *he* says he is."[44] This was an extraordinary piece of circular reasoning. The British government's knowledge of Tāufa'āhau came almost entirely from naval reports or the despatches of Governor Grey of New Zealand, and Home's own reports from 1844 were among the Foreign Office's earliest official accounts of Tonga. Home was, in effect, endorsing his own conception of Tongan politics; he should have said that George Tupou was king because he, Home, had defined him that way eight years previously.

The timing of Home's second visit was one of the most fortuitous coincidences of George's campaign. The captain advised the Catholic missionaries to flee "the protection of a Chief in open rebellion against his lawful sovereign," and after several days Pea agreed to submit.[45] There is no doubt that Home's visit to Tonga gave George the advantage he needed to force the surrender. The Catholic missionaries there had apparently promised that France would come to their aid,[46] and one of them had recently left for Tahiti, promising to return in a warship. When the *Calliope* was first sighted from Pea, its inhabitants assumed she was the promised French support. It is not surprising that the reappearance, instead, of their enemy's old friend Captain Home would have demoralized George's besieged rivals. Home's timing, though accidental, had been effective.[47] Records of the Catholic mission indicate that Protestant Tongans "taunted the Catholics . . . to summon France to their aid."[48] In the Protestant mission stations "all was joy and many were in high hopes peace would be made."[49] It was indeed the end of resistance to George Tupou and the beginning of a new era for Tonga as Home raised his glass to the man who was now, beyond doubt, King George Tupou of Tonga: "Glory as a Christian Prince attends your clemency to those who have fallen into your power. Grateful should they be to God that they are subjects of so just and so merciful a King."[50] After Home's departure George deliberately avoided further conflict with Tongan Catholics, and the Tu'i Tonga lived under his protection until his death in 1865, when George abolished the title.

The reconstruction of George as a heroic Christian monarch seemed complete; had not Captain Home praised him as "the Alfred the Great of the Friendly Islands"?[51] However, the missionaries grew to resent the independence that drove the king's ambition. In 1853 he visited Sydney, where he began a long correspondence with the journalist and aspiring diplomat Charles St. Julian, whose advice on the Pacific islands was sought by many people but whose Catholicism horrified Tonga's Methodists. Even when the king took a more acceptable advisor, Methodist missionary Shirley Baker, in 1860, the other missionaries quickly began accusing Baker of exercising undue influence. Their colleagues in Fiji were horrified when the king threatened to visit Fiji in person to collect payment for the Tongan warriors who fought in defense of Cakobau in the 1850s.[52] "Now he was their patron rather than the reverse," and they resented it.[53]

The record states that the British navy provided twenty-one-gun honors for King George from 1865 onward, although we do not know how Captain Home chose to commemorate George's victory in 1852. By 1876 Commodore Hoskins was wondering why the British government still refused to recognize a flag and government that the Royal Navy had been saluting for years.[54] The king himself had been trying in vain to negotiate a treaty of friendship with Britain, and even after the promulgation of Tonga's first constitution in 1875, it would be another four years before Britain recognized his government and its independence. Tonga's monarchy was the most straightforward of indigenous sovereignties in the southwest Pacific, but even here Britain's missionaries and officials had an ambiguous response to the centralized rule they helped to create. Islanders perceived as childlike dependents were one thing; confident rulers with ideas of their own were quite another.

In Fiji, as in Tonga, British humanitarians found an ambitious island leader eager to enhance his power. Britain's mission and naval contacts with Fiji began in earnest in the 1840s, coinciding with a dramatic increase in the importance of the *vanua* (district) of Bau, its military leader Tānoa, and Tānoa's son Cakobau.[55] Fiji's missionaries recognized the value of a close relationship with Cakobau, who, if he converted, might facilitate the extension of Christian influence in Fiji. For his part, Cakobau aspired to the rulership of Fiji as "Tui

Viti," something without traditional precedent. As Bau's political fortunes declined in the 1850s, Cakobau converted to Christianity at last and began relying on outside support—from Britain and Tonga—to maintain his status. However, since his "Tui Viti" title was obviously invented, the British government would reject Cakobau's offers of cession until 1874, thus embroiling itself in a self-generated dilemma. An alliance of missionaries and naval officers had begun defining a protective role in Fiji decades before the issue of British rule arose, sponsoring political centralization through a "Tui Viti," in hopes of reforming Fijian society. But when cession investigations later discredited the Tui Viti title, they also exposed the weakness of Cakobau's "kingship" and of the humanitarian representations that helped create and sustain it.

British Methodist missionaries had established a foothold at Lakeba in the eastern Lau island group in 1835. From Lakeba, an area of considerable Tongan influence and a logical starting point for the Fijian mission, Fiji's first white missionaries, William Cross and David Cargill, had been looking out for the best potential base in the populous central island of Viti Levu. In 1838 Tānoa, the *vūnivalu* or military leader of Bau,[56] had recently returned to power with the help of his son Cakobau. Cross and Cargill did not yet appreciate the complexities of Fijian politics, and because of the bloody purges the two men observed that year at Bau in the wake of Tānoa's return to power, Rewa seemed a more sensible place to begin God's work in Viti Levu. Tui Dreketi, the Rewan leader, was delighted to enjoy the prestige of resident white men at the expense of his Bauan rivals. However, Bau's subsequent rise to power would make the missionaries regret their choice.

Nineteenth-century Fijian politics were complicated and volatile, based on alliance, counteralliance, and intrigue. Their most notable feature was the unprecedented rise of the Bau district during the late 1840s and its equally spectacular decline during the following decade.[57] Briefly, from 1843 to 1845, the first of a series of conflicts between the large *vanua* of Bau and Rewa resulted in a decisive victory for Bau. Through a series of battles and the betrayal of the town of Rewa from within, Bau was able to impose a puppet governor on Rewa in 1845. A lull ensued until 1852, when the renewal of hostilities saw the tide turn in Rewa's favor. Meanwhile, British missionaries and naval visitors between 1848 and 1852 saw Cakobau at the height of his influence, and the observations they made about his status would outlast the reality.

The usual hopes for "Christianization and Civilization" appeared in British accounts of Cakobau's influence, and his political position was deliberately enhanced by humanitarian observers in the hope that such a powerful man might eventually rule all of Fiji. As Captain Erskine put it in 1849: "The adoption of Christianity, and the concentration of power in the hands of one individual, will (it is to be hoped) tend to improve this state of affairs; and it cannot be doubted that a show of sympathy with their interests on the part of our Government, would materially advance these desirable objects."[58] British support for Cakobau took various familiar forms, including attempts to increase his prestige. A proud and ambitious man, Cakobau appreciated the value of such distinctions and grew accustomed to them.[59] By the mid-nineteenth century, however, shifting alliances and the increasing involvement of Tonga began to threaten his position, something that his British patrons ignored at first and then tried to counter. Three cession proposals were made at this time—in 1855, 1858, and 1874—which involved varying degrees of official inquiry, and in each case the issue of Cakobau's kingship was critical. Did he or did he not possess the authority to cede territory to Britain? Like George Tupou of Tonga, Cakobau found that British representatives struggled to reconcile their own tradition of support for him with their knowledge of his position's controversial status in indigenous terms.

Mission and naval reports from the 1840s painted an optimistic picture of Cakobau's status and authority, often giving him European aristocratic or political designations. Visiting Fiji in 1847, Methodist superintendent Walter Lawry "went over to the imperial city of Bau," where he met "the *élite* of Feejee."[60] Captain Worth's report of HMS *Calypso*'s visit in 1848 described Bau's political preeminence in unequivocal terms: "There are five or six independent districts on this island, scarcely at all connected with Bau, but they are not by any means so powerful as the Bau kingdom, nor are the people equal to the Bau men in intelligence, and energy of character."[61] Cakobau struck Worth and his officers as dignified and confident, "a splendidly-made noble looking man" who "honoured us with a visit."[62] Worth and his colleagues were looking for a monarch and found one. Missionary James Calvert reported to London in 1849 that "we are in constant intercourse with Lord Feejee, whose renown & influence extends less or more to every part of Feejee,"[63] while Captain Erskine, visiting the same year, found Cakobau "looking every inch a king." The captain reported "the greater part of them [the Chiefs of Fiji] acknowledging a kind of dependence on the Chief of Bau, (or Ambow,) a small island on the coast of Viti Levu, which forms his capital, and may be considered that of all the Feejees."[64] Moreover, Cakobau had "within a few years taken the title of Tui Viti, or King of Feejees. He is a person of considerable energy and better disposition than ordinary, being very kind to the white residents generally, and (although not professing Christianity) particularly so to the missionaries, whose principal station is at another small island, Vewa, (or Biva,) a mile or two distant from Bau."[65]

It is unclear exactly when the title "Tui Viti" first came into use, but there is evidence to suggest that Cakobau had not so much "taken the title of Tui Viti" as had it thrust upon him. After an exchange of letters with the missionaries at Fiji, the British Consul General at Tahiti, General Miller, wrote to "Tui Viti" in 1844.[66] This had a cumulative effect when, in 1849, Erskine endorsed the title by explaining that Cakobau "had been addressed [thus] by General Miller."[67] This self-referential use of royal designations parallels the British response to "King George" of Tonga, whom Captain Home declared to be ruler of the entire island group "because Queen Victoria says he is." In this case images of a centralizing Fiji owed more to humanitarian hopes than to island reality. Cakobau was happy to use the title, but his power—as long as he could maintain it—was still based squarely on a precarious pattern of military conquest and political alliance.

British naval officers deliberately enhanced Cakobau's prestige in order to help missionaries like James Calvert obtain permission for a station at Bau. Captain Erskine invited Cakobau aboard *Havannah* several times for meals, entertainment, and a demonstration of the ship's guns. Captain Jenner, a friend of Erskine's, presented Cakobau with a full dress uniform of the Guards, "which exceeded in magnificence anything he had ever seen before, and was put on with great satisfaction."[68] Calvert, as translator, reminded Cakobau of the honor done him by "the quantity of powder and shot expended in his honour and for his amusement," and Erskine reported to the Admiralty that Cakobau was "quite capable of valuing the opinion of other countries."[69] Cakobau had requested a personal letter from Erskine, which was delivered in 1850 by *Havannah*'s tender, the *Bramble*. It praised his "increasing authority," exhorting him to use it to help civilize his people.[70] During *Bramble*'s visit Cakobau renewed his acquaintance with many of the ship's company and was delighted when the schooner anchored at Bau. He was received and sent ashore with a seven-gun salute, "with which he seemed much pleased."[71] This pattern of conspicuous attention, paid to no other Fijian leader, was repeated during subsequent naval visits.

Before Cakobau's conversion in 1854, missionaries had made little progress in Fiji and often found themselves helpless amid violent civil war; at few other places in the southwest Pacific were British missionaries so vulnerable. Tui K'ila'ila and Tui Cakau of Somosomo had enticed missionaries to Vanua Levu in 1840. They subsequently ignored them, and the mission was abandoned in 1845. New stations were established at Nadi and Bua Bay in 1847, sites of the brief Fijian sandalwood boom forty years earlier, but again the missionaries were disappointed in their hopes for a chiefly convert; only a small number of disaffected local people embraced the new faith.[72] The nature of Vanua Levu politics, as elsewhere in Fiji, featured a network of kinship and tributary obligations that connected villages and districts within *vanua*. Conversion to Christianity and subsequent refusal to pay traditional tribute involved the mission settlements in a series of civil wars. Captain Erskine was determined to end this political conflict at a stroke, using the authority of "King" Cakobau of Bau. During discussions with the chief in 1849, Captain Erskine had contrasted the hostility toward missionaries on Vanua Levu with the protection afforded them in areas under Cakobau's control. He told Cakobau that he intended to visit Bua and Nadi, and the chief, anxious to reassure his visitor, informed Erskine "that there was now no danger of any harm happening to the missionaries, declaring that he would take care of Bua himself."[73] Erskine's flattery had obtained the desired promise of protection, but Cakobau's ability to control such a distant, turbulent area was doubtful. At Bua, Erskine warned Tui Bua's family of the consequences of continued threats to the mission station: "I took occasion, in speaking to this Chief of the lately contemplated outrage, to explain to him Tui Viti's promise to me, that he would take care to permit nothing of the kind in future; and as few in these islands are desirous of exciting the displeasure of Bau, I believe this would be most efficacious in checking them."[74] "Assurances of good intentions were earnestly repeated,"[75] and Erskine left Fiji convinced that if there was any more trouble on Vanua Levu, Cakobau would be able to deal with it. Hearing the following year from Lieutenant Pollard of hms *Bramble* that the Bua and Nadi stations were still threatened, Erskine wrote to Cakobau from Sydney, making it clear that he would be held responsible as Tui Viti for the safety of the missionaries. Believing that it was a straightforward matter in which Cakobau was simply failing to exert himself, Erskine threatened him with a diminution of prestige: "I should be very sorry to be obliged to use the power which you well know we possess against any persons in Feejee, and my doing so would certainly have the effect of weakening your power and authority, which, as long as it is properly exercised, I should rather wish to strengthen."[76] This letter presented Cakobau with a dilemma: in exchange for a desirable recognition of his power, he was required to exercise influence on Vanua Levu, which he did not possess. Many areas in the west of the island were renouncing former obligations to Bau, and Cakobau's promised protection for missionaries meant nothing: attacks on their settlements continued. Although Cakobau had come to "think that the support of naval officers might contribute to his prestige, to the ceremonial acknowledgment of his position as first among the other high chiefs who were his equals, and even more,"[77] he simply did not have the kind of political control missionaries and their naval patrons expected him to exercise. Erskine had made a serious miscalculation, distracted by his own hopes.

The resumption of open warfare between Bau and Rewa in 1852 reversed the situation of the late 1840s, and Cakobau suffered a series of humiliating defeats, aggravated by the defection of former tributary areas such as those on western Vanua Levu. Concerned missionaries and naval officers found Cakobau threatened by the realities of Fijian politics, and, beginning with Captain Home's visit in 1852, naval visitors began distorting Cakobau's position to maintain his status as "Tui Viti." Home maintained the impression of Cakobau's power in his reports, even though he knew that Bau's political position was threatened: "Tui Vete the principal Chief of the Feejees is at war with his near relation Ratungarra which has lasted twelve years; the cause of it they do not know; the object is to see which can get the upper hand. The people are tired of it and many are leaving Tui Vete and strengthening the Chief of Rewa that an end may be put to it, and he has now the advantage."[78] Despite this advantage, the captain still referred to Bau as "the capital" of Fiji.[79]

The situation was now complicated by King George of Tonga. In 1853, Cakobau had attempted to compensate for a series of military reverses in the Bau-Rewa conflict by attacking the peninsula of Kaba at the mouth of the Rewa River. Several of his leading warriors were killed, and Cakobau himself was forced to flee. Shortly afterward Bau was destroyed by fire, and the Bauan tributary villages on the island of Ovalau, ruled by Tui Levuka, openly rebelled against him. Completely demoralized, Cakobau received a letter in April 1854 from George, who had been following his military reverses with interest. It promised Tongan assistance, but at a price: "It is good you should be humble; it will be well for you and your land. I wish, Thakombau, you would *lotu* [convert]. When I visit you we will talk about it; for I desire that Bau and the Fiji friends may stand well. But it will be well for you, Thakombau, to think wisely in these days."[80] Cakobau relented, seeing in conversion a chance to confound his enemies while gaining powerful allies, and on 30 April 1854 he formally accepted Christianity. Later that year, Captain Denham of HMS *Herald* held an inquiry at which Cakobau and his enemies were invited to air their grievances and make peace, but no one other than Cakobau and the missionaries came. The captain began to suspect that Bau had little real authority in areas outside its direct control, but he still tried to smooth relations with Rewa and Levuka's white residents for Bau's benefit.[81]

This would itself have far-reaching effects. Commander Edward Boutwell of the USS *John Adams* arrived to investigate American claims against Cakobau just after Denham had left Fiji. He would impose an indemnity of U.S. $45,000 on the chief, an exaggerated sum that became known as the "American Debt." In support of his official report, Boutwell appended a copy of Denham's invitation to David Whippy to meet "the king of Bau (Tui Viti)" with the other white residents of Levuka.[82] There were other views of Cakobau, however, and one of his most acerbic observers was Denham's naturalist, John MacGillivray. MacGillivray was cynical about the "diplomatic propensities" of his captain, claiming that the white residents were "quite a match for this 'King of the Cannibal islands.'" He also reported that Cakobau's enemies were using the meetings aboard *Herald* as an opportunity to cement their alliances against Bau.[83] MacGillivray found his captain's support for "Tui Viti" risible. When Cakobau came aboard *Herald* on November 9 for a conference, Denham used the excuse of the Prince of Wales' birthday to greet Cakobau with a twenty-one-gun salute:

> The motive was very apparent, the poor Prince, who had never before been so honored, still less our own Queen, was made a cover for causing the officers to appear in cocked hats and other gewgaws, and by dint of noise endeavour to make the Fijians believe that we were a regular Man of War, when about to receive a breechless savage lately a cannibal. The principle of legitimacy was never carried out more absurdly than in the present instance when the individual in question, chief of Mbau, anotating to himself the title of King of Fiji (Tui Viti) is supported by Captain Denham, and all others are designated as rebels.[84]

"The principle of legitimacy" was the cornerstone of the humanitarian approach to islanders: the belief that island leaders should be treated respectfully in order to encourage their acculturation. In Fiji, as in Tonga, humanitarians went to great lengths to support the authority of a Christianized leader with "civilizing" potential. MacGillivray's observations remind us that not all British observers of Fiji accepted this view of events.

Fortunately for Cakobau, his enemy Tui Dreketi was also ill, and Cakobau rallied after the Rewan leader died in January 1855. Other enemies had gathered in the meantime, and the "Tui Viti" claim was still difficult to sustain. The latest challenge came from Ovalau, where the newly converted Tui Levuka led a deputation of the Lavoni people from the interior and representatives of both American and British residents to request British rule for Ovalau. This was a triumph of diplomacy for the chief, who had reconciled his traditional Lavoni enemies and capitalized on the resentment of Bau in Ovalau's white community. He had also successfully manipulated the preoccupations of the missionaries, who interpreted his cession offer in light of their almost hysterical prejudice against Ovalau's new French Roman Catholic missionaries.[85] Denham was touched by the "demonstration of attachment" but forced himself to "calm them down, & control my own impulse" until he could consult Captain Stephen Fremantle, his Senior Officer.[86]

Tui Levuka's seizure of the initiative in this offer of cession is striking evidence of Bau's declining influence. He had underestimated Denham's determination to maintain Cakobau's status as Tui Levuka's overlord, however. After noting the Ovalau cession in his journal, Denham remarked that "as they [on Ovalau] were in degree subordinate to Tui Viji (King of Fiji) the matter would have to be referred to him."[87] They had not been subordinate for at least two years, but having asked Denham to intervene on Ovalau as a representative of the British government, Tui Levuka had to abide by the captain's choice of strategy. Denham took advantage of the situation to shore up Cakobau's position and "parried the point as first depending on a peacemaking with Tui Viti."[88] This peacemaking required far more of Tui Levuka than Cakobau's consent to the cession: it required him to return Ovalau to Bau's dominion, the very thing he had rebelled against.

At this point, Tongan involvement in Fiji intersected with British naval activity there. Cakobau hastened to Levuka from Bau to meet Tui Levuka aboard the *Herald*, "escorted" by George of Tonga, who was "on a visit" with forty war canoes and three thousand warriors.[89] Given the recent history of George's relations with Cakobau, it is not surprising that aboard *Herald*, with the Tongan king by his side, Cakobau "accepted the palm"[90] from Tui Levuka. He would be well rewarded in the short term, when Tongan military reinforcement enabled him to overwhelm his Fijian enemies at the battle of Kaba in April 1855. Meanwhile, anxious that initiative was slipping from his grasp, mindful of warnings from George and a succession of naval officers about the importance of British goodwill, Cakobau approved the cession of Ovalau, "declaring his desire to join, if not *lead* in the example."[91] Once again, the Royal Navy had created an opportunity for Cakobau to commit himself further to the "Tui Viti" claim within his relationship with Britain. To observing French missionaries, who had recently arrived at Levuka, the whole business smacked of collusion between Denham and his translator James Calvert. Denham had asked the Frenchmen to witness the proceedings (much to Calvert's chagrin), and they complained later that Calvert had mistranslated Cakobau's response to the cession proposal, leaving out the chief's proviso that "I don't give the earth."[92] As we have seen, the words "protection," "sovereignty," and "cession" had complicated meanings in English, making their translation across cultural and linguistic divides extremely problematic. From Denham's point of view, things were relatively straightforward: Cakobau had become a Christian ruler, potentially king of a British "protectorate," and to emphasize the importance of the occasion, Denham sailed the *Herald* to Bau, the first time that a Royal Navy ship had ever anchored there.

Unfortunately for Cakobau, the "Tui Viti" title would prove a poisoned chalice. Unlike George of Tonga, Cakobau had no traditional mechanism to reinforce his claim to kingship, and he grew increasingly dependent on outside support against his many rivals. The situation was complicated further by the presence, from 1858, of a British consul at Fiji. As we will see in Chapter 9, naval and missionary support for "Tui Viti" would wax and wane depending on the degree of approval granted to Cakobau's white advisors. As so often was the case, hopes for islanders and suspicion of other white men went hand in hand.

5

The Sandalwood Crusade

As late as the mid-nineteenth century, British explorers in Melanesia believed they traveled "untrodden paths where novelty, where ignorance; and a thick veil of obscurity hangs."[1] The fleeting contacts made by European explorers in the eighteenth century—Carteret, Bougainville, Cook, and d'Entrecasteaux—had revealed a dangerous place for Europeans: treacherous to navigate and inhabited by suspicious, often violent people. When the French explorer La Pérouse disappeared after leaving Sydney for the Solomon Islands in 1788, Melanesia's grim reputation seemed confirmed. In an episode that became the most famous of its kind in the Pacific, the missionary pioneer John Williams was killed on Eromanga in 1839. His death became a plea for Melanesia's salvation in missionary journals everywhere, but mission progress was slow and costly. It was 1848 before the Presbyterian John Geddie settled successfully on Aneityum, taking advantage of the presence of a sandalwood station that had accustomed the islanders to living alongside Europeans. LMS missionaries found an easier foothold in the Loyalty Islands, where chiefly authority was greater and languages fewer than in other island groups; by the 1860s the whole population of Mare, Lifu, and Uvea had converted to either Protestant or Catholic Christianity.[2]

Sandalwooders, too, risked life and limb to ply their trade. Melanesian sandalwood was probably first exploited in 1825 by Peter Dillon, who took word of it to Tahiti.[3] There, Dillon's friend Samuel Henry mounted the first documented sandalwood trading voyage to Melanesia in 1829. Other ships followed, mostly American, and after the East India Company's trade monopoly ended in 1834, colonial traders from the Australian colonies were able to participate in their

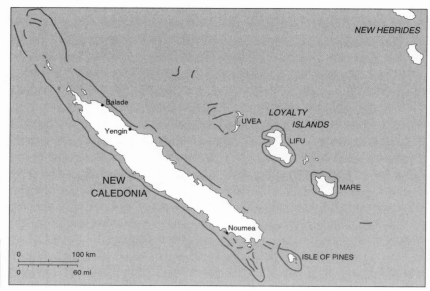

Map 5. New Caledonia

own right. Soon the trade spread to the Loyalty Islands, the Isle of Pines, and New Caledonia. Like its earlier counterparts in the Sandwich Islands, Marquesas, and Fiji, the Melanesian sandalwood boom peaked quickly, and the trade was nearly extinct by 1860. Fluctuating prices in China meant that its returns were uncertain even when supplies were plentiful. Nevertheless, the success of businessmen like shipping magnate Robert Towns, who sometimes cleared up to a thousand pounds' profit each year, was enough to draw men to the trade despite its dangers.[4]

The Royal Navy lagged behind both traders and missionaries. Melanesia's waters were among the most dangerous in the world for larger vessels; few reliable charts of their reefs and shoals existed, and naval pioneers like Captain Erskine were forced to use the charts compiled and published by the sandalwooders.[5] Conflicts in China and New Zealand in the 1840s drew most available naval ships away from the islands at the very time that the colonial trade was establishing itself. Also, the publication of Cook's and Belcher's accounts of Tanna and other "savage" islands played a significant role. Since both were widely read by later captains, it is no surprise to find that in 1847 Captain Maxwell believed that the Isle of Pines was too dangerous to visit. Bishop Selwyn, who volunteered as Maxwell's chaplain in order to acquaint himself with the islands, was determined to investigate the island despite the captain's qualms. At Tanna he met the sandalwood trader James Paddon, who found it odd that a man-of-war was afraid to encounter islanders he had worked with peacefully for years.[6]

As British missionaries and naval officers began expanding their Melanesian activities in the late 1840s, they applied two familiar sets of assumptions to their observations of the sandalwood trade: that traders usually mistreated islanders and that islanders retaliated by indiscriminately robbing or murdering the next white men to visit. This perceived cycle of violence and retribution, which Dorothy Shineberg has named "the retaliation theory," reinforced the push to Christianize Melanesia and prompted recommendations for the control of trade until islanders were equipped to participate as equals. Meanwhile, stories about the massacre of crews in Melanesia began to spread, apparently endorsing the humanitarian view of violence in the sandalwood trade. In 1844, the *Nautical Magazine* ran a humanitarian article by "Tasman," who declared that he had been "led into this train of thought" by reading about trade violence in the colonial papers. He chose to publish his views in the *Nautical Magazine*, because "there is no surer medium through which a notice can gain general publicity among seamen."[7]

A particularly sensational story about Éfaté would take on a life of its own. Three vessels from Tahiti, captained by Europeans, took on a Tongan work crew and moved through the New Hebrides collecting sandalwood in 1842. At Éfaté, the Tongans quarreled with the local people and shot about sixty of them; when eight others hid in a nearby cave, the Tongans suffocated them by lighting fires at the entrance.[8] Both LMS missionaries and Captain Erskine investigated the matter, concluding that this was a classic example of sandalwood brutality.[9] They also suppressed the issue of Tongan involvement: by 1856 missionary William Gill's version claimed that one hundred thirty Éfatese had died in the cave, including "the aged, and women, and children," suffocated by "the white men."[10] Another exaggerated account followed in 1861, in a pamphlet describing the difficulties facing Christian missions in Melanesia.[11] The story's most exalted appearance came in 1872, when Erskine, now a member of Parliament, used its grisly tale of "two or three hundred" butchered islanders to underline the importance of the proposed Pacific Islanders Protection Act.[12]

Because they accepted such a simplified explanation for trade violence, with white behavior at the center of attention, humanitarians believed that the solution to the problem was equally straightforward. Bishop Hinds had once mused that "savages are influenced not so much by instruction, reasoning and exhortation, as by the impression of personal character,"[13] and men like Erskine tried to set an example of humane tolerance in their encounters with Melanesians. Erskine began his 1849 voyage determined "that no act of hostility towards any of the native inhabitants should originate with us during the cruize, but that a system of forbearance and conciliation towards them should be the rule to be observed on our part."[14] John Inglis, who traveled to his mission in 1850 as Erskine's guest, remembered the captain's handling of a potential dispute about coconuts at Aneityum. Aggrieved Aneityumese came to the mission station with complaints about sailors raiding their trees, and Inglis took the matter to Erskine. The captain insisted that his crewmen pay for the coconuts with tobacco, explaining that "the success of the expedition depended on their maintaining peaceful relations" in contrast to "other expeditions" (sandalwood voyages) that had been "complete failures owing to the seamen stealing from the natives, getting into collisions with them, and lives being lost on both sides."[15]

The importance of personal example and the need to accelerate the pace of Christianization had motivated Bishop Selwyn to establish a training program for young Melanesian men at St. John's College in New Zealand.[16] Rather than sending Polynesian teachers to Melanesia, as the LMS was doing, Selwyn preferred to bring young Melanesian men to New Zealand for several months'

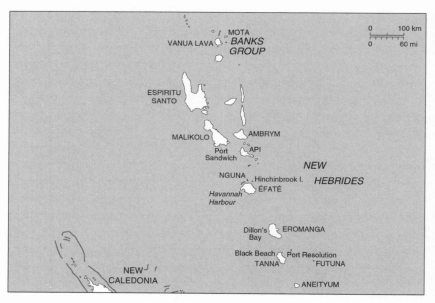

Map 6. New Hebrides/Banks Islands

training in English, scripture, and Western lifestyle; after their training, the young men were taken back to their homes, often on Royal Navy ships. These students might begin their education in the spirit of adventure and curiosity, but Selwyn hoped they would return each year for further training and choose to become missionaries to their own people. The scheme was never particularly successful: even by the 1870s the Melanesian Mission, under Selwyn's successor, Bishop John Patteson, had made little progress.[17] The attempt to show humane restraint in dealing with islanders and the mission college were based on the assumption that Melanesian islanders were like blank slates. Because they appeared to lack any political organization, British observers assumed that they lacked spirituality or any other cultural reference system that could give their actions motive and meaning. Humanitarian attempts to "improve" them had little influence, because Melanesians did, in fact, have strong religious and social beliefs and did not see advantages in Christianization.[18] Unwilling or unable to accept this possibility, humanitarians claimed that other white men had corrupted the islanders. If Melanesians were defined as the passive reflectors of European behavior, then the brutality of sandalwood traders must be to blame for islanders' resistance to more benevolent examples.

Humanitarians believed that trade violence was shrouded in secrecy and increased their efforts to publicize sandalwood "atrocities." Erskine regretted that greater publicity had never been given to the humane activities of captains Bethune, Maxwell, and Home other than "a few straggling notices in the 'Nautical Magazine' " and made a point of publishing as much as possible about his own observations of island conditions.[19] During his 1849 visit to the Noumea area of New Caledonia, investigating the site of an earlier sandalwood incident, he received promises of good behavior from "the Chiefs" he questioned. However, he warned the Admiralty that "whether they will be enabled to keep their word will of course depend upon the way they may be treated; but the occasional visit of a ship of war, and publicity in general on all matters connected with these people, would certainly be the best means of ensuring it."[20] LMS missionary George Turner, apparently unaware that the sandalwood trade was declining for economic reasons, claimed that the publicity of sandalwood crimes by Erskine and his mission allies was the reason for the infrequency of "atrocities" by the 1860s. The *Quarterly Review* took a similar view in a review of Erskine's book, declaring that only humanitarian publicity and example had prevented the sandalwood trade from "being little else than a series of unjustifiable aggressions by one party, and murderous retaliations by the other."[21]

Trading could certainly be violent—the published memoirs of sandalwooder

Andrew Cheyne contain vivid descriptions of attempts to ambush and seize his vessel—but there is no evidence that traders always used force or intimidation in their interaction with islanders.[22] After all, sandalwooders depended on island labor to gather, clean, and store the wood for collection, and large stations like Paddon's on Aneityum employed a number of islanders on a more or less permanent basis.[23] Although traders were prepared for attack, knowing that islanders could react unpredictably for reasons of their own, it was not in the interest of trade to commit indiscriminate violence. Shipowner Robert Towns always cautioned his captains to avoid antagonizing islanders, warning them that he would "sooner abandon the Trade altogether" than employ anyone who attempted "any act of cruelty or hostility towards the Natives."[24] Cheyne warned his readers: "As the success of your voyage depends entirely on keeping on peaceable terms with the natives of the different islands you may visit, you should take care not to be the first aggressor. Therefore, take nothing from them without payment, not even a cocoa-nut, nor so much as a bundle of grass." This message was hardly at odds with the humanitarian approach. Where Cheyne's perceptions differed was with regard to islanders themselves. His frequent references to "savages" would not have endeared him to more benevolent readers, but other aspects of his account of trade practice would have been even more unpalatable. After the exhortation to honesty quoted above, Cheyne added that traders would "have to submit to many insults," a reference to the fact that Melanesians knew how to drive a hard bargain and sometimes tried to intimidate their visitors. Cheyne also knew that the best of intentions could not always bridge the cultural divide. Speaking of another sandalwooder, Captain Ebrill of the *Star,* he noted that although Ebrill "bore an excellent character for kindness and humanity to the natives," he was killed and his ship seized at the Isle of Pines for no apparent reason.[25] Humanitarians manipulated information about the *Star* massacre to conclude that its crew had provoked an attack, but other sources suggest that it was the missionary teachers Ebrill brought with him that were undesirable in islander eyes.[26] Ebrill himself was skeptical about stories of trade depredations in the islands; at New Caledonia in November 1850, he investigated the circumstances of a recent attack on one of the boats belonging to the sandalwooder *Vanguard.* "It may be said, that the crew must have given some provocation . . . but in this instance, there was none given, which I can vouch for"; he knew from personal experience that the *Vanguard's* master treated islanders "with liberality and kindness."[27]

Sandalwooders could also be their own worst enemies. In 1857, Captain William Loring of HMS *Iris* went to Tanna to investigate the murder of two crewmen belonging to the sandalwooder *New Forest*. Investigating at the Governor of New South Wales' request, Loring had received assurances from merchant Robert Towns, owner of the *New Forest*, that he would have the full cooperation of Towns' agents in the islands.[28] Towns believed the Royal Navy needed more encouragement to investigate the murder of traders and wrote to one of his agents, Underwood, to say that Loring's visit was "the first step in the right direction," adding that the captain was "a first rate fellow" and hoping "you will do all you can to please him."[29] Towns wrote in a similar vein to three other men in his employment and to missionaries Geddie and Inglis for help in finding suitable interpreters for the investigation.[30]

Loring met two of Towns' men, Henry and Underwood, at Aneityum but "could not obtain much assistance," and after inquiring at Tanna, he found it impossible to identify those responsible for the murder. He also learned that the *New Forest* had recently taken aboard at Black Beach seven Tannese laborers who never returned to their island; when the vessel returned to the same place without them, her boat's crew might have been attacked to avenge the men who were presumed dead. Loring decided to warn the Tannese of "serious consequences" should there be any further aggression against white men, hoping that his prompt investigation would prove their actions were being monitored and make them "more careful in future."[31] On his return to Aneityum, the captain's opinion of sandalwood traders fell further when, to his astonishment, he met George Clerk, who had been chief mate of the *New Forest* at the time of the murders. Clerk had been on Aneityum ever since, and the captain was furious that he had not come forward to help, wondering how much more "may have been withheld from me in the same spirit of disingenuousness which was marked by the withholding from me the knowledge of the presence of the Chief Mate."[32] Geddie, ever ready to criticize traders, declared: "If the Tannese are a savage people their cruelty is far exceeded by the barbarities of white men."[33]

Towns was furious when he learned of his agents' furtive behavior. Writing to Paddon in 1858, he still praised Loring as "a fine fellow" but warned Paddon that although the captain was "inclined to protect you on your legitimate trade . . . I fear he has been to some Extent prejudiced against Sandalwooders." He added, sarcastically, that should Paddon encounter first mate George Clerk, "the man that was mate of the *New Forest* when Captn Loring was there and wanted information," he should "give him a Hearty Welcome you well know he deserves it."[34] But the damage was done. Loring's report to the governor was clearly in favor of the retaliation theory, and he "did not consider that I should be justified in treating the two men who came on board the ship as murderers, nor did

I think it right or advisable to fire, or to land, and commit indiscriminate slaughter and destruction on the Natives. . . . It is possible, and indeed probable, that
provocation may have been given, either on a former occasion by them, or by
some other persons."[35] Loring's perceptions influenced the governor's own attitude about the incident. Writing privately before the *Iris* sailed, the governor
had suggested that "the attack was entirely unprovoked and it would therefore
be very desirable for the sake of the security of the vessels trading among the
Islands that such a murderous attack should not be allowed to pass unpunished."[36] Denison changed his tone after receiving Loring's report and agreed
that "it appears probable that the removal of the Natives may have been the
original cause of the attack made upon the unoffending parties."[37] A reluctance
to help Loring had done nothing for the sandalwood trade's reputation.

Humanitarian assumptions about motives for violence, like those about the
nature of trade practices, tended to ignore the issue of islander agency. There
were many possible motives for conflict with sandalwood traders: the desire
for European goods or ships, jealousy of trade that favored traditional rivals,
reaction against the appearance of disease, and simple misunderstanding.[38]
Observations about Melanesians, designed to stress their vulnerability, actually
obscured the vitality of their cultures. The Melanesian side of the story is difficult to recover for the early nineteenth century, although analysis of oral traditions is proving useful.[39] The traders' perspective is more accessible and sheds
valuable light on the dangers of an entirely paternalistic interpretation of trade
violence.

Two of Erskine's crusades were cases in point. In 1850, the captain arranged
the prosecution of John Lewis, a Towns agent, for the murder of three Mare
islanders. Lewis was acquitted, largely because he insisted that he had acted in
self defense when the islanders tried to take his ship *Will o' the Wisp.* When
another Towns vessel, the *Lucy Ann,* was cut off and its whole crew killed in
1851 by the same people on Mare, Erskine used the episode in his book as a classic example of retaliation. Recalling the disappointment of Lewis' acquittal,
Erskine noted that his "slaughter of these three [Mare] men, however, was not
without its fruits," claiming that the islanders took the *Lucy Ann* in retaliation
for the murder of their countrymen. This proved, he said, that the sandalwood
trade "had a very unfavourable effect upon their character."[40] There was another
possible explanation, however; both Lewis and Towns thought that the second
attack proved that the Mare people had always wanted to seize a European
ship.[41] Lewis' use of force to defend his ship might have forced the islanders to
wait until a better opportunity came along, and it was their own priorities—not

retaliation for European activity—that led to the *Lucy Ann*'s capture. Even British missionaries occasionally admitted that "desire for plunder" was a frequent motive in trade violence; the Samoan missionary George Turner noted privately in 1845 that people from the Isle of Pines were encouraging Loyalty Islanders "to take a vessel also, as a good speculation—a royal road to wealth."[42] Confident, sometimes defiant islanders were well known to those who lived and worked among them, but they were invisible to humanitarian eyes.

Not all Royal Navy officers were determined humanitarians: one of Erskine's own subordinates came to different conclusions while investigating the site of a massacre in New Caledonia. Although the story is about a bêche-de-mer trader, rather than a sandalwooder, it is worth noting for the light it sheds on differing interpretations of trade violence. Early in 1850, the *Sydney Morning Herald* published news of a Mr. Fitzgerald of Auckland, who had gone to the Balade area with twenty Fijian laborers to establish a bêche-de-mer station in 1849.[43] After a dispute with the local people, during which several islanders were killed, Fitzgerald abandoned the station and the Fijians. Although initial accounts of the affray were "very confused and cannot be depended upon," Erskine was convinced that the New Caledonians had been provoked. Not only had Mr. Fitzgerald set up an establishment in their territory "without any permission asked, or granted," but his people had destroyed coconut trees, failed to make appropriate payment for labor, and kidnaped women. The final insult came when one of the Balade chiefs was taken on board the *Mary* and "detained sometimes in Irons, and ill treated." It was then that the Balade people attacked the *Mary* and her crew. Erskine accused Fitzgerald and the commercial community at Sydney of trying to cover up the episode; "so carefully were all these circumstances concealed" that although Fitzgerald had already returned to Sydney, "nothing was allowed to transpire until I had sailed for New Zealand."[44] Erskine despatched the *Fly* under Captain Oliver to investigate all the scenes of recent trade violence in Melanesia; Oliver was to muster all the crews of trading vessels he encountered (a tactic reminiscent of the African Squadron), and where he could find more information about "outrages committed by British Subjects," he was to obtain evidence that could bring the offenders to court in Sydney.[45]

Oliver's report must have come as a disappointment. After meeting "Bonyone," Oliver was convinced that the chief's arrogant manner signified guilt.[46] Determined that "an example of severity is much wanted at this place," Oliver gave no presents and allowed no trade, "to show our abhorrence of their crimes."[47] Erskine made no comment on Oliver's findings in his report to the Admiralty, nor did he qualify the retaliatory explanation of the Fitzgerald incident he later included in his book. Oliver's instincts might have been more appropriate than Erskine's: the destruction and plunder of a Roman Catholic mission in 1847 may have whetted the Puma people's appetite for European goods.[48] During *Havannah*'s 1849 visit to the area, one of Erskine's own officers had been warned that the "1st time they get a chance they will cut off a boats or ships crew."[49]

Sometimes humanitarian observers actually fabricated evidence in order to sustain the retaliation theory. In 1852 at Tanna, Captain Home found a document left by the master of the barque *Eliza*. He read that four of the crew had been kidnaped and then rescued by the intervention of Samoan missionary teachers, who ransomed them for nine muskets and twelve pounds of gunpowder. After talking with the teachers, Home arbitrarily connected the attack on the *Eliza* with the earlier murder of "the principal Chief of the Islands," Gaskin, by sandalwooder Captain White of the *Deborah*.[50] Because he believed that the *Eliza*'s crew was attacked after White's "drunken affray," Home drew the attention of the New South Wales government to the problem of retaliatory violence in the sandalwood trade. Worried that White's crime would put all subsequent traders in danger, the New South Wales government issued a public notice warning ships' captains about the dangerous situation on Tanna.[51] John Geddie lamented "the cruelty of our own countrymen to these islanders," declaring, "The sooner the wood is exhausted the better for the cause of humanity and Christian missions."[52] Although White seems to have been genuinely vicious, and the murder of Gaskin was (and still is) bitterly resented by the Tannese, there is no evidence that they took indiscriminate revenge for it.[53] It was at about this time that Captain Paddon moved his sandalwood station from Aneityum to Port Resolution, with no opposition or difficulty, and a year later a visiting missionary remarked that "the foreigners residing in this bay seemed in no danger whatever and have, evidently, a considerable influence over the natives."[54] Nevertheless, telling the story of White in his 1853 book, Erskine claimed that the captain's "tyrannical and vindictive disposition" met an appropriate fate when he was clubbed to death by the Tannese. Though morally satisfying for humanitarian readers, this dramatic conclusion had no basis in fact.[55]

The need to trace islander behavior to previous European activity could go to absurd lengths. Trying to explain the murder of John Williams at Eromanga in 1839, missionary James Gordon blamed Captain Cook's firing on islanders at Traitor's Head in 1774, over sixty years earlier.[56] Even when others questioned the humanitarian assessment of trade violence, as in the Fitzgerald case at New

Caledonia, determined paternalists like Erskine simply refused to acknowledge dissenting opinions. Benevolent interpretations reinforced themselves through repetition in a publication campaign that united missionaries, naval officers, and organizations like the APS in Britain. Hoping to take their crusade one step farther, humanitarians began testing the British government's political will to intervene.

Assuming that traders were incapable of controlling their own behavior and islanders equally incapable of managing their own affairs, naval officers and missionaries invited their government to supervise, even suppress, the sandalwood trade. Speaking of Mare in the Loyalty group, where the cutter *Sisters* had been attacked in 1843, Captain Erskine concluded that "unless the trade shall be regulated by higher authority, it is to be carried on the principle of the right of the stronger party, by the white men."[57] One of the most obvious ways of controlling the trade was through more frequent naval patrols by benevolent Royal Navy captains, who, as Bishop Selwyn put it, "will enter into the spirit of the work."[58] Reciting a catalog of sandalwood crimes, the APS bulletin *Aborigines' Friend* declared:

> If, notwithstanding the immense importance of the South Seas as a field for mercantile speculation, the British Government refuse to place two or three armed cruisers on the station, by whose presence alone, or near vicinity, the bloody outrages of the traders may be suppressed, then we think it is imperative that they should at once forbid and put down a traffic, which, however valuable in a commercial point of view, is disgraceful to the British character, by reason of the foul crimes which have attended its carrying out from the commencement.[59]

The question of whether naval patrols were actually effective in suppressing "outrages" will be discussed later; for now, it is sufficient to note the way humanitarian publications in Britain were using the sandalwood trade to make sweeping recommendations for British intervention in Melanesia. Their suggestions bore a strong resemblance to those of Governor Grey and his naval allies, demonstrating the extent of shared humanitarian conceptions of the Pacific islands. The same pattern would develop in response to the developing labor trade in the 1860s and 1870s. Meanwhile, the need to patrol Australian waters during the gold rush of the 1850s dominated the Australian Division's small force, and a decade after the APS's call for increased naval resources, Loring was lamenting that "the presence of a Man of War constantly cruizing amongst these Islands is very much wanted to restrain the natural barbarism of the Inhabitants.

But it is still more wanted to restrain the lawless habits which have for some time prevailed amongst the White Traders and Adventurers, who consider themselves out of the reach of Legal Power."[60]

Other ideas for restraining sandalwooders included the appointment of a British consul to the New Hebrides. By the mid-1850s, Governor Denison of New South Wales was convinced that Melanesia was the south Pacific's greatest law and order problem, and he argued, as the APS had done, that increasing trade with the islanders made British supervision in the area of crucial importance.[61] This proposal got a sympathetic hearing from Foreign Secretary Clarendon, who agreed that islanders needed the "guidance and protection of judicious Consular Officers," who would be "highly conducive to the advancement of civilisation" in Melanesia.[62] Others at the Foreign Office had second thoughts, however. Although naval and mission reports had praised Protestant missionary success on Aneityum, suggesting it would make an ideal consular base, at least one Foreign Office official believed that Melanesians were all "confirmed Cannibals" and wondered "who would run the risk of being cooked for 350 [pounds] a year?"[63]

Frustrated, a coalition of Aneityumese chiefs with missionaries Geddie and Inglis approached Captain Loring in 1857 about the possibility of British protection for Aneityum. Loring did not have time to discuss the matter with the local people, but Geddie and Inglis assured him "that the Chiefs are very desirous to be received under the British protection or Sovereignty." The missionaries outlined Aneityum's economic potential and strategic location "in the track between California and Australia" and praised the "peaceable and industrious" Aneityumese. They claimed the islanders were afraid of French expansion from New Caledonia and hoped that an official relationship with Britain would "deter evil disposed foreigners from injuring unprotected natives."[64] As in all proposals involving British "protection or Sovereignty" during this period, the islanders' own intentions in this proposition are difficult to assess. Forwarding the Aneityumese offer of cession in his report to the Admiralty, the captain noted only that the islanders were "very well disposed" and deserved protection from the depredations of "lawless" white men.[65] The missionaries knew they had a friend in Loring, and when they abandoned their offer of cession in favor of a renewed campaign for the appointment of a British consul, they commended the captain and his fellow knights-errant for proving "a terror to the evil-doers that frequent these seas."[66]

The sandalwood crusade shows how like-minded missionaries, naval officers, and colonial officials could work together to create and reinforce paternalistic perceptions of island conditions in Melanesia. Their combined efforts produced something of a publicity triumph and certainly swamped the small number of trader publications on the subject. Nevertheless, they were unable to obtain the degree of official support they sought from London. As morally compelling as the humanitarian case might be, the British government had no intention of accepting proposals involving territorial expansion, especially in an area where France had established interests. While believing in the benefits of "Christianization and Civilization" for islanders, government officials could not agree that extensive (and expensive) imperial intervention was desirable. However, the issue of slavery was already rearing its head in Melanesia. The recruitment of Melanesian islanders in 1847 and 1848 for plantation work in Queensland provided another focus for protective impulses and further calls for greater British supervision of island conditions in the western Pacific.

In 1847, Governor Grey asked Captain Maxwell to investigate missionary reports of a clash between Rotuma islanders and the crew of a colonial trade vessel. Maxwell reported that Captain Kirsopp of the *Velocity* had been recruiting Melanesian laborers for his employer, Benjamin Boyd, and some of the men had attempted to escape when the ship called at Rotuma for supplies. Boyd, "half successful businessman and half scoundrel," had come to New South Wales in 1842 and soon became the biggest private landowner in the colony from his base in Twofold Bay.[67] His need for cheap labor grew accordingly, and in January 1847 he despatched the *Velocity* to hire Pacific islanders to work his properties. Although Boyd's instructions do not seem to have specified Melanesians, Kirsopp sailed to the Loyalty Islands, Tanna, and Aneityum to obtain laborers, who each put their mark to a five-year contract.[68] Their time in New South Wales was a disappointment to them; after winter arrived, many of the men ran away, and colonial opinion was roused, particularly after some of the islanders marched in a group to Sydney to demand redress.

Governor Grey, that self-appointed champion of Pacific islanders, was already pressing Governor Charles FitzRoy of New South Wales for an inquiry when he received further ammunition from Walter Lawry, the Methodist mission superintendent, in December 1847.[69] Lawry had recently visited Tonga, where a Tongan teacher had come back from Rotuma with stories about a massacre that had occurred there during the visit of the *Velocity*, now on her second recruiting trip. Apparently a group of Uveans recruited by Kirsopp had become suspicious and decided to jump ship at Rotuma. They were protected by a local chief, who refused to turn them over and was shot with several of his people when the captain tried to retrieve the Uveans by force.[70]

Grey wrote at once to Maxwell, enclosing Lawry's letter, and asked the captain to investigate the allegations at Rotuma, because they represented "a system of procuring labourers from the Islands near New Caledonia under circumstances which are open to grave suspicions and to strong objections."[71] Grey authorized Maxwell to take steps to bring the offenders to justice, if possible, warning him that others must be deterred from such recruiting or "great calamities" would result for Pacific islanders.[73] Already, Grey believed Kirsopp to be guilty of illicit labor recruiting, and he assumed that Pacific islanders would be helpless to protect themselves against such methods. At Rotuma, Maxwell confirmed that the chief "Mushevek" and several of his people had been killed by Kirsopp and his crew. He also discovered what Kirsopp's recruiting methods had been. The son of a high chief at Uvea was persuaded to visit Sydney with his attendants, and his father was promised a musket for every man he could get on board. This strategy showed a shrewd appreciation of Uvean society: Kirsopp was able to secure the recruitment of a group of men bound to follow their leader. When Maxwell questioned one of the Uveans, it seemed that no contract had been seen or signed, or money received.[73] By the time *Velocity* reached Rotuma, the men had been starved, beaten, and taunted about never returning to their island.[74] After the Uveans escaped from the ship, they placed themselves under the protection of the local chief, who paid with his life for his hospitality. In order to stress the victimization of the Uveans, Maxwell reported that "the power of the Chiefs is most despotic in those Islands," where common people could be disposed of at will; once a leader could be convinced to sail with the vessel, he could command others to attend him. Kirsopp's entry in the Rotuma shipping register had not helped him; he had stated that *Velocity*'s purpose was "Trading for Cannibals."[75] Maxwell concluded that the issue was not merely the terms and conditions of employment, but whether recruiting should be allowed to take place at all among such "primitive" islanders: "I cannot contemplate or believe that the British Government would sanction or tolerate any system that would attempt to take advantage of such a State of Society as a means of procuring labourers for New South Wales, or any other of our Colonies by hiring or purchasing the services of such unfortunate people from their Chiefs and afterward taking them out of their Country without their consent or agreement."[76] Maxwell was effectively denying islanders the right to accept labor contracts, since they might only be following the directions of "despotic" chiefs. Erskine's publication of the episode also stressed the vulnerability of Uvean islanders; he noted that the islanders' friendliness and "love of wandering" must have influenced Boyd's decision to recruit them by "inducing the chiefs."[77] Inglis called the *Velocity* one of the forerunners of the labor trade.[78] Even traders manipulated information about the *Vanguard*'s activities for their own purposes; Captain Bradley, a sandalwooder, brought word from Tanna that wives of some of Boyd's laborers had been killed when their men did not return. His article started a war of accusation and denial in the Sydney newspapers, in which he was accused of inventing the story to preserve his own labor supply in the islands.[79]

Speculation about indigenous motives also occurred during Erskine's investigation of the Fitzgerald incident in New Caledonia. Like the story of the massacre of Éfatese by Tongans, this story contained unpalatable evidence of islander agency. It seemed clear that Fitzgerald's Fijian laborers had helped to antagonize the Balade people, an unacceptable distraction from the issue of European misbehavior. Describing the incident to the Admiralty, Erskine leapt at once to the conclusion that Fitzgerald's Fijian laborers had been employed against their will, "most probably without the consent of the Chiefs or people." He learned from one of Fitzgerald's colleagues that the Fijians "were procured by Mr. Fitzgerald and his partner, a Mr. Williams, United States Consul at the Feejees," from the chief Cakonatau of Rewa. Erskine reminded the Admiralty that Cakonatau was "a man of great ability, but of most depraved Character," to whom his people were "in fact Slaves." This placed Cakonatau in the same category as the "despotic chiefs" who had supplied Boyd's laborers in 1847. Once again, helpless islanders had been taken advantage of, either by white recruiters or by their own leaders. Lest their Lordships miss the point, Erskine reminded them that they "have been informed by Capt. Maxwell, late of the Dido, of previous attempts to introduce among these Seas a modification of the Slave Trade, by buying from the Chiefs of the Loyalty Islands their influence in inducing their people to embark for New South Wales. . . . It is also a common practice among the Masters of Vessels to procure the Services of Natives of the different Islands for little or no Wages, abandoning them when it suits their own convenience." The "secretiveness" of sandalwood traders was evidence of their guilt, he believed, and the timing of the *Sydney Morning Herald*'s report was part of a conspiracy "with the object of attributing the blame of these outrages to neglect, or indifference, on the part of the Navy." The report proved the need for "the constant presence of a Vessel of War among these Islands," something Erskine's present small force was unable to provide.[80]

The humanitarian interpretation of trade violence misconstrued Melanesian behavior and publicized stereotyped interpretations that did little to advance knowledge about the area and its peoples. It also cast traders in a role of unqualified villainy, without taking account of differences between individuals, and between traders and the shipowners they worked for. The correspondence of merchant Robert Towns reveals that even he was susceptible to the retaliation theory with regard to his own employees. His instructions to Captain Jones of the *Elizabeth* in 1844, stated, "On no account allow the least freedom between the native women and your crew, such Indulgence I am quite sure has been the origin of most, if not all the misfortunes which have occurred on similar voyages."[81] He warned his traders against overconfidence but also believed "there has been too much cold blooded massacre among these Islands in former times which I have no doubt has goaded the Natives to many acts of diabolical Murder."[82] A humane man, he declared he "would sooner give up the trade altogether than risk the life of any one."[83] There was also Towns' friendship with a series of naval officers to consider. Throughout the 1850s he diversified his investments as the sandalwood trade declined, until by 1856 he became influential enough to become a life member of the Legislative Council of New South Wales and seek the approval of aristocratic naval visitors. During his rise to prominence, he cultivated Erskine and his successors, encouraging them to pursue wrongdoing among his island agents even when this led to a series of legal prosecutions. He regularly visited Home and Loring, and when in England in 1858, he enjoyed a reunion with Erskine to talk about colonial affairs and the need for an independent Australian naval station.[84]

However much they had in common when traders behaved badly, Towns discovered that his naval friends would not support him when it seemed clear that islanders had initiated violence. Towns had wanted Captain Home to investigate the attack by Mare islanders on the *Lucy Ann* in 1858. Full of confidence in his naval connections, Towns had told his London agent Robert Brooks:

> I expect the Men-of-War will go down & demand proper satisfaction. I have many claims on their assistance they have put me to considerable expence in the detention & trial of one of my Masters for having Shot three of the Natives belonging to the same tribe which are reported to have destroyed the 'Lucy Ann' & they appear well disposed to carry out the investigation. I am sorry Capt. Erskine is leaving in the 'Havannah' he would have seen me righted. I must now hope Sir Everard Home will act in his stead.[85]

As his published views demonstrate, Erskine would probably not have seen Towns "righted" and neither would Home. Towns wrote bitterly to a friend that "nothing has been done by Sir Everard in the case of the *Lucy Ann*. I did apply and expected they would have sent down to Chastise the Villains."[86] Home had just written to the Colonial Secretary in Sydney for legal advice about his ability to punish those responsible,[87] only to be told that the law officers felt powerless to give an opinion on a matter "entirely of Imperial Concern."[88] Although Governor Denison expressed his regret at this response, Home was powerless when Towns brought the *Lucy Ann* case before him.

The frustrations of men like Towns could not be ignored forever. As "outrages" increased with the number of ships trading in the islands, so did pressure for the Royal Navy to protect white traders as enthusiastically as it championed islanders. One particularly prominent case acted as a focus for discontent about naval lenience. In 1853 the British ship *Gazelle* had called at Woodlark Island (Murua) near New Guinea to bring supplies to a group of Italian missionaries there. The ship wrecked, and the islanders killed the passengers and the crew. British relatives of some of the victims began calling for retaliation, claiming that the Dutch at nearby Indonesia did not hesitate to take punitive action against islanders who murdered Dutch citizens.[89] The case dragged on as the correspondence shuttled between New South Wales and London; finally the *Gazelle* lobbyists took their concerns directly to the Admiralty and Colonial Office. At the Colonial Office, the Duke of Newcastle had few qualms about ordering bombardments to protect British interests and directed Captain Loring to make a punitive cruise to Woodlark. Newcastle warned the Admiralty that "the steps taken should be such as to impress upon the Natives that whilst Her Majesty's Officers will be extremely reluctant to resort to force, they are perfectly determined to do so in case the laws of humanity and honesty can be enforced by no other means."[90] Captains were expected to be "perfectly determined," despite their traditional dedication to the protection of islanders. Time seemed to be running out for measures of benevolence.

6

A House Divided

B Y mid-century, hopes for British "protective supremacy" in the Pacific islands had been quenched by the government's doubts about territorial expansion, but equally responsible were the contradictions of humanitarian benevolence itself. During the 1850s, especially in Melanesia, it became clear that protective paternalism could not accommodate the realities of trade violence. The behavior of both islanders and traders often failed to conform to the roles assigned to them in mission and naval reports. British law, too, failed the humanitarians who placed such faith in it. These inconsistencies stretched benevolence to the breaking point as humanitarians found themselves unable to provide justice for those they sought to protect. We must therefore question concepts not often examined in the south Pacific context, especially "British authority," "policing," and "commodore justice."[1] These phrases imply the existence of jurisdiction, laws to enforce, and a system of effective sanctions, none of which existed with reference to islanders, and all of which were of questionable application to British subjects living outside British territory. This situation was part of the problematic legal history of British expansion everywhere and warns historians against taking contemporary statements about justice, authority, and control at face value. Instead, we need to scrutinize the way British naval officers and other observers occluded the complexities of European-islander relations and the way they struggled—and failed—to harness British and international law to their moral crusade. This struggle produced some remarkable tensions: consuls and naval officers attempted to exercise an authority that was often illegal, while regarding themselves as forces of law and order. In the absence of clear legal guidelines, moral representations became the source of that perceived authority. The language of imperial benevolence provided a framework for action and for interpreting the actions of others.

It is well known that the British authorities were primarily concerned with controlling the behavior of their own subjects in the Pacific islands. The Governor of New South Wales appointed missionaries as justices of the peace in Tahiti and New Zealand at the beginning of the nineteenth century, and Britain passed the Murders Abroad Act in 1817,[2] to permit Royal Navy officers to arrest British seamen suspected of murder or manslaughter in New Zealand or the Pacific islands. When these measures proved ineffective, the Australian Courts Act of 1828 attempted to transfer responsibility to New South Wales by permitting such men to be tried at Sydney.[3] Escaped convicts could always be recaptured on the authority of the Governor of New South Wales alone. These measures encouraged collaboration with Pacific islanders. Royal Navy officers encouraged chiefs to identify European troublemakers and to authorize their removal: a system ideally suited to the humanitarian agenda. As Captain Bethune put it in 1838: "I believe that many cases of property taken, boats cut off, &c. have arisen in consequence of the Foreigners citing the natives to plunder. . . . The Natives are becoming tired of their friends, and would doubtless aid in [our] Crusade. It would be advisable to convey the lot to Sydney, where, if rogues, they could be identified."[4] Bethune's crusade applied this method enthusiastically, adopting an elaborate disguise to fool the beachcombers into thinking his frigate was a trading vessel and then imprisoning everyone found without written identification.[5] Earlier, Captain Waldegrave had arrested four "troublesome persons" at Tonga with the approval of his commander in chief, who believed it was part of a captain's duty to "carry off from time to time the runaway Convicts and other Vagabonds" from the islands.[6] In 1852, while capturing two escaped convicts at Fiji, Captain Home arrested a third man simply because he had been keeping company with the others.[7] Commanders in chief sometimes worried that these summary proceedings were legally suspect. After reading Captain Waldegrave's report, Rear Admiral Owen warned his captains against treating "unoffending individuals" with "intemperate severity or unjust restraint."[8] A lawsuit for wrongful imprisonment against Captain Lambert in 1834 reminded the Royal Navy that, despite the pleas of shipping magnates in London, it did not have the authority to interfere with disciplinary matters in the merchant service, except in cases of mutiny.[9] In the wake of Bethune's 1838 "crusade," his admiral hoped that "some means could be adopted for the removal of these worthless characters, but I am not aware of any one having the power to do so, and certainly not in the summary way proposed by Captain Bethune."[10]

There was another problem: officers committed to the concept of island sovereignty were at a loss when island leaders refused to turn "these worthless characters" in. Naval reports about the need to protect islanders from white men overshadowed evidence suggesting that the two groups often found ways to live together amicably. Although there were many white men living in the islands whose behavior was unacceptable by contemporary British standards, they did not necessarily dominate or "corrupt" islanders to the extent that naval captains claimed. Whether individually or in the developing beach communities of Apia or Levuka, European men usually lived with their island families in extended networks of mutual obligation and support.[11] White men provided a variety of services for local chiefs in return for the patronage and sustenance on which their lives depended, and those who could not justify their keep did not survive. However distasteful these terms of "adoption" might have seemed to some British observers, they did not necessarily constitute the exploitation of islanders. Erskine's account of the Tannese civil war, for example, emphasized the part played by an Englishman called Stephens but also noted that his involvement was "no more than a duty he owed to the chief under whose protection he was living" and that hostilities resumed after Stephens' departure.[12] Men like Stephens participated in island life on indigenous terms, assisting island leaders rather than overshadowing them.

These leaders were often reluctant to let such useful people go. At New Zealand in 1831, Captain Desausmarez was unable to apprehend "any of the Convicts or other ill disposed persons said to infest the Bay of Islands," not only because every white man in the area fled to the interior when the ship hove in sight, but because the Bay of Islands chiefs would not retrieve them even when offered rewards.[13] Similar problems continued through the 1850s. In 1852, Home could only secure the escaped convicts he sought by taking two Fijian chiefs hostage, following the advice of David Whippy, who would have known how reluctant Fijians would be to relinquish valuable sources of information and goods.[14] At Samoa in 1855, Fremantle was unable to capture certain white men on the island whose "habits are prejudicial to morality and the growth of civilization," because they were being "protected and rather encouraged by the Chiefs."[15] The "problem" with Samoa's white residents seemed to be greater for the Royal Navy and British missionaries than for Samoans themselves, who Fremantle admitted found their European associates "both useful and profitable."[16]

Meanwhile, the government of New South Wales was uncertain about exercising its statutory right to hear cases involving the Pacific islands. At Tonga in 1834, Captain Blackwood of the *Imogene* found two crew members from the *Lady Rowena*, a British whaler that had recently visited New Britain. They told him that their captain, Russell, had shot some of the islanders there without provocation. Blackwood was certain that Russell's actions were "so harsh and unjustifiable, and so little warranted by any Act of the Natives towards him, his people, or his Ship, that I have thought it my duty to put the Government of this Colony in possession of these depositions in order that it may act as the circumstances of the case may require."[17] The two deponents were held for questioning while Governor Bourke wrote to the Colonial Office for advice. Bourke did not seem to realize the powers of his own Supreme Court, but the British government confirmed that under the Australian Courts Act, New South Wales had jurisdiction over offenses committed on the sea in various places, including any "island, Country or Place, situated in the Indian or Pacific Oceans & not subject to any European State," if the offense was committed by masters, crew, or British subjects on board British vessels.[18] Russell's attack might "amount in law to Murder, for which he might be brought to trial in any of the Colonies in that part of the Globe," if it could be proved that his ship was not under threat of attack.[19] Coming up with such proof was tricky; the depositions included observations that canoes coming off to trade with the *Lady Rowena* were full of warriors "armed with spears which they were flourishing about."[20] The solicitor recommended further investigation after the *Lady Rowena* returned to Sydney, but evidence about what happened next has disappeared; it may be that the ship never returned to New South Wales. This case, though inconclusive, saw the colony move toward greater involvement in island affairs; there would be no question about "sending home" for advice in future cases.[21] The case was also a benchmark for humanitarian assumptions about European misbehavior. Reinforced by missionary accounts, the story of Russell's brutality confirmed preconceived notions about an overwhelming law and order problem in the islands.[22]

The Russell case involved British deponents, but there were serious questions about whether non-Christian islanders could take oaths on the Bible to act as witnesses or to bring actions of their own. This was a general problem in the nineteenth-century empire; only colonies with earlier origins, such as India, had mechanisms in place for permitting other forms of swearing-in.[23] The APS was concerned enough to make the issue of indigenous testimony its top priority, hoping "to obtain justice for the natives by an improved administration of law."[24] Its leader in this movement was Saxe Bannister, a former Attorney General of New South Wales dismissed in 1826 for interfering with the government's handling of criminal cases involving Aborigines. Bannister had visited the Cape Colony in south Africa and had a long-standing interest in colonial-Indian relations in Canada; drawing on this background and his humanitarianism, he published a number of books proposing sweeping legal reforms in the area of British-Aboriginal relations.[25] His recommendations were familiar ones: the need for treaties, magisterial authority for British consuls with Royal Navy support, and the encouragement of centralized authority within indigenous groups. More dramatic was the proposed reform of British evidence law to permit unsworn testimony by indigenous people. Drawing on testimony to the Select Committee on Aborigines, Bannister concluded that the requirement to testify under a Christian oath unjustly disadvantaged non-Christian peoples, especially those whose societies lacked recognizable legal systems. If such people could not testify, they could not seek redress: a clear violation of their rights as British subjects.[26] In 1843, largely owing to APS influence, the British Parliament produced a Colonial Evidence Act,[27] permitting colonies to overturn British law in order to admit unsworn testimony.

Unfortunately, New South Wales did not create appropriate enabling legislation for decades, ruling out the testimony of non-Christian islanders and Aborigines alike. Even Christian islanders encountered problems, as in the 1869 trial *R. v. Hovell and Rangi,* when crew members from the *Young Australian* were tried for murder. This case, famous in the history of the south Pacific labor trade, largely hinged on the testimony of a Rotuman youth named Josiah who, though Christian, expressed confusion as to whether the courtroom's English Bible was the same as a Rotuman version that contained only the New Testament. The defendants were convicted but not sentenced to death. Public pressure to further mitigate their sentences led Attorney General James Martin to wonder whether the Rotuman witness' oath had been unsound. Responding to Governor Belmore's request for advice, the Colonial Office insisted that the sentences had to stand; to dilute the effect of the conviction any further would discredit the attempt to encourage islanders to seek British justice for offenses committed against them by British subjects.[28]

In the meantime, there remained the question of how to capture British suspects for trial. I have already noted the 1848 Foreign Office directive that encouraged Royal Navy officers to look to island governments for the means of redress. Deciding what sort of approach was appropriate, especially when indigenous leadership appeared to be absent or took an unrecognizable form, was left entirely to each captain's discretion. Captain Erskine sought clarification from the government of New South Wales after returning from his first island cruise in 1849. The attorney general confirmed that any suspect who had served on a British vessel was liable to prosecution but warned that "general reputation would be insufficient ground for apprehending him, nor having Evidence, but if the Captain of a Man of War (or indeed the Master of any Vessel) could at the same time bring legal evidence here to offer against him," he could arrest him for trial.[29] This was an appropriate caution, since "general reputation," usually transmitted by missionaries, often influenced naval opinion.

The John Lewis case seemed a perfect opportunity for Erskine to invoke British justice and test the colonial legal process. During his 1850 cruise, Erskine heard that Lewis, a sandalwood agent for Robert Towns, had murdered three men on the island of Mare in the Loyalty group. After reading Lieutenant Pollard's report on the case, Erskine decided that it encapsulated all that was wrong with British trade in the islands, and the sandalwood trade in particular, revealing the true "spirit of the Sydney traders": uncivilized and brutal.[30] He pressed the New South Wales government to prosecute, and Lewis was arrested after returning to Sydney in May 1851. The Lewis case was a landmark: the first prosecution of a British subject for the killing of a Pacific islander. It was also an example of the way humanitarian sensibilities reinforced images of islanders as the passive victims of European violence, while discounting traders' own accounts of such encounters. Questioned by Pollard at Lifu, Lewis made no attempt to deny what had happened. He explained, in a statement he later signed, that while gathering wood at Mare, he heard about a plot to seize his schooner *Will o' the Wisp* at a nearby harbor. Wondering whether this was an attempt at intimidation by the rival sandalwood trader who lived there, Lewis proceeded to the harbor, where three Mare men swam out to his ship and threatened him. They refused to go ashore and then Lewis, seeing them beckon to an armed crowd gathering on the beach, shot them and fled.[31] During the trial, Pollard relied on the retaliation theory to explain Lewis' story. He admitted that trade in Melanesia was dangerous, saying that "the natives at Mare are cannibals & that they had killed several Englishmen," but added that "in many instances provocation had in some degree been given."[32] He excused the threatening behavior of the Mare islanders on this basis, failing to address the legal points at issue: whether Lewis had been negligent or whether he had acted in self-defense. Lewis' lawyer avoided the complexities of Pacific trading by drawing a bizarre but effective analogy, describing Lewis' position as that of a man in England who resolved to continue a journey despite warnings about highwaymen on the road. He emphasized the testimony of members of Lewis' crew that the islanders on the beach appeared to be preparing an attack while an onshore breeze was carrying the *Will o' the Wisp* toward them. Lewis was acquitted, to Erskine's outrage, in apparent proof that the citizens of Sydney did not consider "the murder of a savage a blameable action."[33] The legal point was actually whether the jury believed there was reasonable doubt that the murders were committed in self-defense, but Erskine's humanitarianism rejected the possibility of islander initiatives where there had been no previous European provocation. For Erskine, Lewis' guilt was "proven" when his other brig, the *Lucy Ann,* was captured and all hands murdered by the same group of Mare islanders later in 1851.[34] Because this second incident could be interpreted as a retaliatory attack, it fit the humanitarian formula in a way that Lewis' account of the *Will o' the Wisp* could not.

Captain Home continued the campaign for more effective legal protection for islanders. In January 1852 the Sydney police superintendent received information from a sandalwooder, Captain Mansfield of the brig *Eliza,* that Captain White had murdered the chief "Gaskin" at Tanna in 1851, apparently in a drunken rage.[35] The inspector general, forwarding Mansfield's statement to Governor Gipps, worried that White's crime would prompt retaliation against other traders and suggested that a warning be posted.[36] There matters rested until Home's visit to Tanna later that year, when, hearing about the incident from the LMS teachers there, he asked for an opinion on the case from the colonial law officers.[37] Their reply was not encouraging. There was no proof of the crime that would stand up in court, since neither the LMS teachers nor Mansfield "had any personal knowledge of the facts, nor is it shewn how they acquired their information, or from whom we might expect to obtain Evidence in support of proceedings."[38]

The 1854 trial of sandalwood trader John Ross for the murder of a Lifu boy showed that even when a conviction could be obtained, sentencing would not necessarily meet humanitarian expectations. Ross, captain of the *Black Dog,* claimed he hanged the boy to prevent an attack on his ship, but his actions were too extreme to sustain the plea of self-defense. Evidence given at the trial suggests that the boy was killed in retaliation for the death of another sandalwooder, Peter Martin, who had been left in charge of the shore station at Lifu. Obliged to return a guilty verdict, the jury recommended mercy because of the "critical position" Ross had been in and his previous good behavior, but the case was important enough to be referred to the whole court "that there might be a clear exposition of the law in writing."[39] Since New Caledonia, the Loyalty

Islands, and the Isle of Pines were now under French rule, there was some question about whether the Australian Courts Act would still apply. The court met to affirm that it did, since the murder was committed by the captain of a British vessel, aboard that vessel. As in the Lewis case, the court declared that the case should be treated "as if it had been committed on British land."[40] Ross' sentence reveals that the judge was more than prepared to allow for the "critical position" of sandalwood traders in Melanesia, and his leniency must have disappointed humanitarian observers. Ross, originally sentenced to death, served only a two-year commuted sentence in the relative comfort of Paramatta jail.[41]

Even this commuted sentence was too much for the Sydney trading community, whose reaction to Ross' conviction was published in *Empire* newspaper: "It is quite clear that the trade must be abandoned, or some protection afforded to these traders, for such are the trying positions and difficulties under which the masters are so frequently placed, that it is impossible for them to protect themselves without the most vigorous measures."[42] Traders were frustrated that more attention was paid to islanders than to the lives and property of British subjects or to the complex, often dangerous conditions of island trading. Amid the jumble of raw nerves and conflicting interests involved in the sandalwood trade, few players conformed to the characters assigned them in naval reports. By restricting themselves to moral absolutes, naval officers and their mission supporters often misunderstood the nature of trade violence. For example, if Mare islanders had actually been plotting to seize a European ship and its goods, as Lewis and Towns suspected, then Erskine had prosecuted a man who had been within an inch of becoming a victim himself, leaving the Mare people free to pursue another vessel. In their eagerness to champion "helpless natives," humanitarians denied islanders their own motives and the ability to assert themselves.

Even when the case against a British subject seemed clear, so did the legal obstacles to prosecution. Robert Towns was shocked when he heard that another of his captains, John Oliver of the sandalwooder *Royal Sovereign*, had kidnaped two high-ranking men from New Caledonia in exchange for a large cargo of sandalwood in 1853. Oliver shot one of the captives himself, leaving the other one for a rival chief to dispose of. There also appeared to have been trouble about a woman Oliver took aboard the ship by force. Towns, who heard about the incident from another of his traders,[43] detained Oliver and his crew when they reached Sydney. Oliver duly appeared before the Water Police magistrate and was released on bail pending his trial. Towns then wrote to Captain Home for help with the prosecution, but his letter went astray under suspicious circumstances on the same day that Oliver, his wife, and most of the *Royal Sovereign*'s crew left Sydney.[44] The case collapsed when the lone naval ship on station could not be spared to pursue them.[45] This was just the sort of frustration that convinced Erskine, Home, and others that only naval vigilance stood between civilization and anarchy in the south Pacific:

> The difficulty of procuring sufficient evidence to convict the perpetrators of these offences . . . is so great and the opportunities of evasion so numerous and easy, that I have only to repeat the opinion I have before ventured to express to their Lordships that the constant presence of a Vessel of War among these Islands will be the only means by which Trade with them can be maintained without the constant recurrence of affays and bloodshed.[46]

New South Wales became unwilling to prosecute Britons for offshore offenses, even when a native mission teacher was murdered by a British subject in 1864. The solicitor general decided that it was not worth the effort of assembling a case, since the only witnesses were non-Christian islanders who would not be able to testify.[47] The crown law officers in Britain agreed, knowing that New South Wales had failed to implement the 1843 Colonial Evidence Act.

By the 1860s it was clear that the principle of island sovereignty had failed to produce a workable system for the punishment of British offenders, and legal difficulties made it impossible for New South Wales to take practical responsibility. The British government began considering magisterial powers for British consuls, an ironic development given its opposition to such powers in the past. Similar suggestions had been made about Busby, the British Resident in New Zealand before colonization, and naval officers in the 1840s. In 1858 consul William Pritchard in Fiji negotiated such powers with a consortium of leading chiefs who, he said, had urged him "to assume the management of political and commercial affairs."[48] Three years later he created "a court more equal to the requirements of the times than the consular court,"[49] to the horror of the Foreign Office, which believed this would "become very embarrassing."[50] The British government's position, reinforced by the decision to remove Pritchard after a missionary-influenced naval inquiry in 1862, effectively repudiated the right of Fiji's chiefs to create a legal process to deal with Europeans. As we have seen so often, concepts that the British government claimed to support in principle —indigenous sovereignty in this case—proved difficult to accept in practice.

If British law was difficult to apply to British subjects in the islands, it was impossible to impose on islanders. Whether they were considered to be citizens of sovereign states or not, Pacific islanders were neither British subjects nor subject to British law through treaty arrangements. In earlier years, naval reports circumvented the whole issue of islander offenses by dismissing cases of the murder or plunder of British subjects, justifying their tolerance by referring to islanders as impetuous, childlike savages who could not be expected to behave like civilized men and who needed protection while their Christianization and "improvement" was under way. Captains were unmoved by trade losses in the islands, even the loss of life, claiming that British entrepreneurs should go elsewhere if the area proved too dangerous. When they chose to investigate the murder of British subjects or theft of their property, they usually found ways to excuse the incidents. One common explanation referred to the primitive state of island society before Christianization. Investigating the ambush of the colonial schooner *Sir David Ogilby* at Fiji in 1838, Captain Bethune admitted that there had been no provocation offered to the Fijians who attacked the ship's crew, but he added that "unfortunately in the state of Civilization in which these People are, they may at some time be led away to commit similar outrages."[51] Bethune's use of the passive voice here recalls other, less veiled statements in which captains blamed white men for encouraging islanders to attack Europeans. From this point of view, traders seemed unreasonable in their demands for protection. In a private letter to the colonial secretary in May 1859, Loring agreed to send a ship to investigate the reported plunder of a shipwreck on Uvea but doubted "if she will be able to effect anything": "I am sorry to say that human nature is such that wrecks are plundered to this day in Ireland & England, not to say a word about Sydney Heads. How can we expect that Savages should hold their hands? It is one of the risks that Savage trading is accompanied by."[52] Earlier, Erskine had been ready to excuse "the plunder now and then complained of" at Samoa because it was based on outdated heathen custom: "In the few cases of wrecks which have lately happened, the people have all been well treated; and although in one or two instances attempts have been made to keep some of the property saved, it has always been given up on a proper demand being made to the Chiefs; and it should be remembered that here, as in all the Polynesian Islands, before the introduction of Christianity, wrecks were considered offerings made to the gods."[53]

With equal dexterity, captains also excused crimes committed by the Christianized islanders who, in turn, exploited the approval they enjoyed as converts recently emerging from "savagery." Captain Blake, investigating the plunder of the shipwrecked schooner *Breeze* at Samoa, was impressed when the chiefs "said that they had done it in ignorance" and offered to pay compensation.[54] "The candid acknowledgment and submission made by the chiefs and people of Saleimoa was remarkable," he reported.[55] In 1855, Samoans convinced Captain Fremantle that "the most friendly disposition & the utmost confidence is entertained towards the English"[56] and they profited from his goodwill as he investigated the long-standing *Adario* case. After they "pleaded guilty, palliating their conduct under the plea of ignorance & the imperfect civilization of the inferior classes," Fremantle levied a minimal fine "in consequence of the humble tone assumed by the chief."[57] In a private letter, he admitted that he "let them off very easy," because "they are generally very submissive and penitent."[58] Captains also used the retaliation theory to dismiss the need to prosecute islanders for murder or theft, while emphasizing British traders' responsibility for their own misfortunes. At Uvea in 1832, Captain George McMurdo of the *Zebra* explained the murder of crewmen aboard the British trading vessel *Oldham* as retaliation. Even after one of his own men was killed recapturing the vessel, McMurdo was determined to treat the islanders with forbearance for the sake of later visitors to the island, reporting that the affray had begun in revenge for the brutal behaviour of a half-Hawaiian man who had arrived at Uvea five years before. He had "called himself a European" and set up a small but tyrannical rule in competition with the island chiefs. When the *Oldham*'s captain seemed to side with this man by making drunken threats to kill the "king" of Uvea, the islanders decided to attack. It seemed obvious to McMurdo that "it was while smarting from the effects of this Man's tyranny, which compromised the European character, that the 'Oldham' arrived, and as the Captain and Crew commenced and pursued the same unjustifiable and lawless line of conduct, it ceased to be a matter of surprise that the Natives sought so severe a retaliation." Warned not to pursue revenge in the future, the Uveans apparently promised "faithful compliance with the usages of civilized Nations," whatever they might have meant by that, and McMurdo considered the investigation closed.[59]

In other cases captains demonstrated their ships' firepower, hoping that fear would enhance their moral exhortations. Most naval reports include references to "entertainment" for islanders, including target practice and exercising marines. Hoping these demonstrations would "have a good effect,"[60] captains assumed that the "fear and terror"[61] they inspired would be enough to ensure the peace of Europeans in the future. In 1838, Bethune "carefully avoided using threatening language" while in Fiji, but after "shewing them the resources of the Ship, left them to draw their own conclusions."[62] Erskine, peacemaking at Solevu in 1849, put on a firepower display "to amuse the Chief, and shew him at the same time that his town was in our power" and, for this reason alone, reported confidently that "I do not think there is any fear of an outrage towards white people being committed in that quarter."[63] Islanders must have been aware of the advantages of expressing their admiration and respect for British power, although some regarded it purely as entertainment. Erskine agreed to conduct a marines' exercise after a *fono* at Pago-pago, and the meeting broke up in chaos as excited Samoans rushed to the beach.[64] We will see later that even after experiencing bombardment, islanders did not necessarily react in the expected way.

Humanitarian captains preferred legal procedures to threats, and, searching for effective alternatives, they petitioned the crown law officers in Sydney and London. In 1838, the *Sir David Ogilby* had brought two Fijians to Sydney, accused of participating in the recent attack on that vessel, and Bethune asked for a legal opinion before going to Fiji to investigate.[65] The attorney general ordered the Fijians released, since "there is no Law to warrant an Apprehension and Trial of those savages. They must be treated as a separate nation and according to the Law of Nations." He suggested that Bethune try to make use of the Fijian justice system, if such existed, adding that "if they are mere savages without any Established Government it is difficult to suggest what course is best calculated for the security of the ships that Trade with them." He concluded with a familiar observation that "greater caution" should be observed by traders.[66] In 1846, the commander in chief of the East Indies Squadron asked the Admiralty for specific instructions about "redressing outrages committed upon British Subjects and property and protecting British Commerce,"[67] but Palmerston's reply—the 1848 directive—merely encouraged captains "to demand and exact redress from the ruling and responsible Chiefs," and such advice could only be followed on islands with a recognizable political structure where island leaders were convinced of the need to punish Britons.

Referring to the 1848 memorandum, Home asked the New South Wales law officers just how far he could apply pressure on "ruling and responsible chiefs" to obtain redress.[68] Violence against Europeans was "by no means uncommon in some of the Islands of the Pacific," he wrote, "and without a knowledge of the power which an Officer in Command of any of HM Ships legally possesses in such cases, the visits of Ships of War have not their full effect."[69] In a private note to the Colonial Secretary, he confided that the surveying vessel *Herald* was about to arrive, and since he did not know "the disposition of her Captain or of the Officers who will command the tender under her," he wanted "ground upon which I can give orders upon these matters." Home wanted legal backing for a humanitarian agenda, adding that the chief justice believed it was a point that had to be settled.[70] The law officers refused to hazard an opinion, saying they were not qualified to give it: "The point is entirely of Imperial Concern; and is such as should, we humbly conceive, be the subject of further instructions from the Lords of the Admiralty."[71] Their reason was that "the instructions would appear to point to the exhibition and perhaps to the actual use of warlike force . . . to which the Imperial instructions apply."[72] Presumably this meant they were unwilling to comment on the power of naval captains to employ their guns as an act of war, an Admiralty matter, but their reticence seems strange in light of previous "Imperial" reminders about the colony's legal responsibilities in the islands.

It seems puzzling, given the long history of treaty negotiation in West Africa and elsewhere, that the British government did not authorize naval captains to make similar agreements with Pacific islanders. Collaboration with African leaders on law and order issues was a familiar aspect of the British antislavery campaign.[73] Aberdeen's affirmation of indigenous sovereignty could have been the basis for Pacific treaties, but instead the Treaty of Waitangi remained the only agreement of its kind until the cession of Fiji in 1874; other treaties, like Paulet's of 1843 at the Sandwich Islands, were repudiated. I. C. Campbell has noted that Britain's reluctance to sign treaties in the south Pacific underlined the difference between its apparent acceptance of the doctrine of sovereignty and its reluctance to recognize the kind of political legitimacy implicit in the treaty-making process.[74] But by the 1840s the humanitarian position on treaties had itself become ambivalent. Members of the House of Commons Select Committee on Aborigines reported in 1837 that "savages" were incapable of understanding such agreements or coping with their consequences. The committee denounced most treaties as a mockery of justice within which "ignorant savages are often made amenable to a code of which they are absolutely ignorant." It concluded that "the safety and welfare of an uncivilized race require that their relations with their more cultivated neighbours should be diminished rather than multiplied."[75] Even when treaties were necessary, as in Africa, they were now "conceived as bonds between superiors and inferiors who recognized themselves as such."[76] There were still men like Saxe Bannister, who believed that treaties were the best way of protecting indigenous peoples, but there was no consensus on the issue. British governments of the day usually preferred to procrastinate on such matters and were happy to defer the question of new treaties in favor of the moral suasion being exercised (however ineffectually) by their consuls and naval representatives in the area. Unlike west Africa with its slave trade, the south Pacific had no political imperative—at least, not yet.

Financial claims were the most common European grievance against islanders, and it seemed logical for British officials to try negotiating compensation through island leaders. As with any attempt to communicate across cultural frontiers, fines and other economic sanctions did not necessarily convey the intended moral and legal messages. In 1848 Captain Worth sailed for Samoa with instructions to support Consul Pritchard. Worth's predecessor, Blake, had alienated the consul by disregarding most of the European community's grievances and openly siding with the Samoans. Pritchard found Worth more malleable and persuaded him to blockade the island of Manono as punishment for the destruction of European property during the ongoing civil war on Upolu and for the burning of a building used by the local LMS mission. The blockade continued until a fine was paid to the consul, who was satisfied that "these proceedings appear to have produced upon the minds of the Natives generally a very salutary effect. They now see that they will not be allowed to injure British persons and property with impunity. Had similar steps been taken by Captain Blake when here in H.M.S. 'Juno' these late depredations, it is believed, would not have been committed."[77]

The LMS mission's reaction was positive at first, turning to dismay as they realized the extent of Samoan resentment provoked by Worth's actions. Initially reporting his measures as "kind and judicious," preventing the need for "more severe measures," they later distanced themselves from the decision. Declaring that no formal claim had been made by the LMS for the "chapel's" destruction, missionary George Stallworthy wrote to London disclaiming responsiblity for actions "done entirely on the responsibility of HBM Consul and Capt. Worth." The missionaries were worried that the building was not widely known to be mission property. Manono's chiefs pointed out that the building was considered part of the rival A'ana district's holdings, and therefore a potential wartime target; the mission committee agreed, concluding that "under such circumstances it would be better to bear the loss of the Chapel than hazard a greater evil, viz, the disaffection if not positive hostility, of a great body of the people occasioned by enforcing a fine the justice of which they cannot see." The Samoan committee resolved not to receive the fine from Pritchard, who returned it to Manono "with an explanation and request that they be more careful with Mission property in future." The explanation was accepted, but the return of the fine was haughtily refused, and missionary George Pratt declared that the episode "caused us to stink as a Mission in the esteem of the natives."[78] Whatever lesson Worth and Pritchard hoped to teach the Manono people, it had not been that one!

There was also the problem of the collection of fines. The whole point was to inflict economic hardship, but naval officers were often unable to collect payments because of the shortage of ships and prior commitments in other parts of the Pacific. In 1859 the people of Wallis Island plundered a British trade vessel, the *Maria*, and Commander Vernon of HMS *Cordelia* had imposed a fine on them. Then the Maori Wars intervened, and it was three years before another warship visited Wallis. The fine (of coconut oil) had not yet been collected, and Commodore Burnett sent a warning to the Queen of Wallis that "it is my intention to exact the full amount so long wanting, and apparently so well considered by numerous Naval Officers."[79] Burnett's ships were committed in New Zealand, however, and the fine was apparently never paid.

Indigenous politics, too, could hamper the collection of fines. In 1865, Cakobau accompanied Captain Luce of HMS *Esk* to Savu Savu, where he claimed to have paramountcy, and gave his endorsement as "Tui Viti" to a fine assessed in compensation for European property destroyed. Although Luce was suspicious of Cakobau's status as king of Fiji, he had not realized how tenuous the chief's position really was in areas outside his immediate influence. This complicated situation worsened when the man who had demanded compensation seemed unwilling to collect it. In the end, Luce had to ask another chief for a guarantee of payment, if only to preserve some semblance of consistency in his own actions. Given the complainant's loss of interest in the matter, it is not clear what sort of lesson this process conveyed to Fijians. In other cases warfare intervened to delay payments. In 1872 Captain Montgomerie of HMS *Blanche* had fined both sides of the current civil conflict for damage to European property, but in 1873 Captain Douglas had to extend the due date because the war was still going on. Only in November 1873, nearly a year after the original fine, did all parties begin to collect the levy.[80]

In more serious cases, especially those involving the murder of white men, the ambiguities of "British authority" became even clearer. Especially notable was the muted response to missionary Thomas Baker's murder by Fijians from the interior of Viti Levu in 1867. At the request of acting British consul John Bates Thurston, Captain Charles Hope took HMS *Brisk* to investigate, instructed by his admiral to avoid inland punitive expeditions at all costs. Hope agreed with Thurston that Cakobau should act on his authority as "Supreme Chief of Viti Levu" and supervise a manhunt for the murderers, but once Hope's ship was out of sight, Cakobau "subsided into his previous state of apathy."[81] Himself a firm believer in indigenous sovereignty, Thurston attempted to stimulate the chief into action, eventually accompanying an expedition in April 1868 that not only failed to capture the murderers, but was routed by the hostile interior people. The Methodist mission in Fiji remained strangely quiet about Baker, remarking among themselves that he had pressed inland against the advice of the Fijians he had been visiting.[82] Thurston entertained hopes that the Royal Navy would return with authorization to pursue the matter, but the Foreign Office and the Admiralty decided that without any Fijian authority to collaborate with, it was pointless to proceed.[83] Thus the murder of a British missionary went not only unpunished, but virtually uninvestigated by the British authorities.

Ironies multiplied when the Foreign Office decided to reopen the question of consular jurisdiction just five years after dismissing Pritchard for trying to obtain it. The government had maintained that Pritchard's 1858 agreement was unsanctioned by British or international law.[84] However, Pritchard's replacement Captain Henry Jones noted that the United States had passed an act of Congress in 1860 authorizing its consuls and agents in the south Pacific to try civil cases for amounts under $1,000, and this jurisdiction applied whether or not there were treaties with the islands concerned.[85] Later correspondence made it clear that the United States found this authority impossible to enforce,[86] but at the time there seemed to be a precedent for establishing consular jurisdiction. For several years, right up to passage of the first Pacific Islanders Protection Act in 1872, the Foreign Office, the Treasury, and the Colonial Office argued about how to grant magisterial powers to its south Pacific consuls. Such powers had been granted elsewhere through treaties ratified by order in council under the Foreign Jurisdiction Act of 1843, but having repudiated the 1858 agreement with Pritchard, the Foreign Office had backed itself into a corner. As Jones continued to appeal for action on the matter, one official wondered why the government could make these arrangements so easily in west Africa, signing treaties with a number of chiefs if necessary, and balk at similar procedures in Fiji.[87] To another plea for increased authority written in 1867, Jones added that the system of obtaining laborers for Fiji's plantations "is evidently founded on slavery, if it be not actually such."[88] As I will show in the next chapter, the humanitarian zeal for antislavery campaigning would soon focus on the south Pacific, with profound implications for official British attitudes.

Other changes were in the air. By mid-century, the islands trade had become well established, and the Royal Navy could not simply dismiss the appeals of influential businessmen like Robert Towns of New South Wales. As "outrages" increased with the number of ships trading in the islands, British traders pressed their navy to protect them as enthusiastically as it protected islanders. The high-profile *Gazelle* case, which dragged on from 1856 to 1858, acted as a focus for discontent about naval lenience. Asked to take reprisals at Woodlark Island for the murder of the *Gazelle*'s shipwrecked crew and passengers, Captain Fremantle refused unless "distinct and decisive" legal direction was available for "the Officer in charge of so invidious a task."[89] Knowing how much time had already passed since the incident, Fremantle demanded "all suitable arrangements in the way of interpreting, and evidence for identifying the murderers" in order to avoid punishing the innocent.[90] The government had difficulty meeting the captain's demands and Fremantle dropped the case, pointing out that Woodlark was outside the Australian Division's limits in any case. As we know, friends of the *Gazelle* victims then took their concerns directly to London. Lord Palmerston had replaced Clarendon as Foreign Secretary, and instructions went out to Fremantle's successor, Captain Loring, demanding the bombardment of Woodlark Island in retaliation for the murders. There had been changes at the Colonial Office as well. In 1859, under pressure by colonial traders, Loring wrote to the Admiralty for instructions about the plundering of the *Maria*, explaining that he had tried to avoid violence by sending Commander Vernon in the *Cordelia* to levy a fine, which had not been paid. Governor Denison upheld the fine when the principal chief of Uvea wrote to him in protest, but Loring told the Admiralty that "probably this oil will not be paid unless the demand be backed up by the presence of a Man of War. And it now becomes a question whether under these circumstances it will be expedient to send a Man of War with orders to enforce the payment and to burn the Village and destroy property in case it be refused, bearing in mind that it is quite possible that such operations may be attended with loss of life."[91] Loring was not anxious to extend punitive action to cases of robbery as well as murder; while waiting for the Admiralty's response, he would only despatch a ship to inquire about payment, "with orders *not* to resort to any extreme measures."[92] The Admiralty deferred to the Colonial Office,[93] and it was the Duke of Newcastle who replied that, in the absence of any other effective means of enforcing payment, "it becomes inevitable to resort to stronger measures, and in the last resource even to those of burning Villages and destroying property."[94] The Royal Navy had helped create a vicious cycle in which it was now trapped. If islanders understood nothing but force, as the retaliation theory suggested, then nothing but force could be used against them. This might have been a more serious problem for the south Pacific philanthropists had not the emerging labor trade distracted attention from the problematics of the humanitarian position. By presenting labor recruiting as slavery, humanitarians were able to generate the political will that had been absent so long from Britain's relationship with Pacific islanders.

7

Antislavery Imperatives

B Y the time the labor trade issue arose in the late 1860s, British humanitarians had already developed a protective approach to Pacific islanders,
especially in Melanesia where Christianization was making such slow progress.[1]
The crusade against sandalwood traders had created a set of interpretations that
helped observers make sense of baffling, alien societies and their sometimes violent interaction with white men. However, sandalwood and other traders resented
the Royal Navy's prejudice against them and were demanding more vigorous
support. The Foreign Office and the Admiralty obliged with instructions requiring the navy to protect British traders, but at this point the Maori Wars drew all
available resources to New Zealand. The Australian Division had become an
independent naval station in 1859, but only in 1866 did Commodore Maguire
move the station headquarters back to Sydney.[2] Renewed naval contact with the
islands, and their mission stations, began again just as stories were beginning to
circulate about a slave trade in Pacific islanders.

Humanitarians had already invoked the specter of slavery to underline the
illegitimate nature of trade in the south Pacific. Their investigation of Benjamin
Boyd's labor practices had not found evidence of illegal activity, but missionaries, naval officers, and Governor Grey had combined forces to call for protective intervention on behalf of islanders. Their consular proposals and other
recommendations would languish for lack of support at the Treasury and the
Admiralty, but the story of "slavery" carried on. During debate on the 1872
Pacific Islanders Protection Bill, Bishop Selwyn (now in the House of Lords)
would recall how he had witnessed the beginning of the south Pacific slave trade

during the inquiry into Boyd's activities.[3] Having shaped interpretations of that incident to suit their own purposes, humanitarians would invoke their own representations of it in support of measures of benevolence over twenty years later.

"Labor trading," or "blackbirding," as the recruitment of Pacific islanders for plantation work was called, began as such in the late 1860s. Although islanders had been working for white men for decades, they had generally done so aboard sandalwood or pearlshell trade vessels, or at island shore stations in the bêche-de-mer trade. Now, for the first time, large numbers of them traveled abroad to work on the sugar and copra plantations of Queensland and Fiji. Before the labor trade ended in the early twentieth century, over 100,000 islanders, most of them young men from the New Hebrides and Solomon Islands, had taken at least one labor contract; most shipped for Queensland, but about 27,000 went to Fiji.[4] Plantation owners did not recruit islanders themselves, preferring to hire ships' captains experienced in island navigation. These recruiters varied widely in character and behavior during their distant negotiations, and there is no question that some of them resorted to kidnaping to fill their quotas.

However, Pacific historians have shown us how questionable humanitarian representations of the labor trade could be.[5] Many islanders learned to distinguish legitimate recruiters from criminals and appreciated the travel and prestigious European goods that serving a labor contract would bring them. Other islanders did not welcome recruiters and proved all too capable of defending themselves against undesirable contact. Much more than a simple formula of tit-for-tat retaliation, recruiting violence had various motives ranging from suspicion of strangers to the fluctuating nature of the labor market itself.[6] At times when demand for labor was high, recruiters moved into new areas that sometimes proved hostile.

During the late 1860s, stories of kidnaping began spreading through the Melanesian Mission and via visiting naval officers to Australian colonial governments, the Anti-Slavery and Aborigines Protection Societies in London, and ultimately to the British government. Public outrage, fanned by humanitarian publications and the agitation of sympathetic members of Parliament, produced the Pacific Islanders Protection Act in 1872.[7] In what seemed like a natural extension of Britain's antislavery campaign, the Royal Navy would attempt to enforce this legislation amid a complicated and ambiguous situation in the islands.[8] Ironically, it would not be British law that brought about the trade's demise: Fijian plantation owners began hiring indentured Indian laborers in the

1870s, and Queensland inaugurated a "White Australia" policy at the turn of the twentieth century.

If the labor trade was not a straightforward story of kidnaping, how did humanitarian images of it predominate? British missionaries played a large role, but it was to a much broader constituency of humanitarians that they turned in order to translate their representations into an antislavery crusade. This chapter will analyze the way that images of victimized islanders, already shaped by decades of benevolent interpretation, were able to influence British perceptions of the labor trade. Although humanitarian influence in government circles had declined since the 1840s, politicians still recognized the influence of benevolent organizations on public opinion, and humanitarians concerned about the labor trade were well aware of the importance of publicity in rousing the political power of Britain's antislavery tradition.

Shared antislavery rhetoric consolidated the efforts of missionaries and their supporters, who were already pressuring the British government when Bishop John Patteson was murdered by Nukapu islanders in 1871. After that, humanitarians in Parliament could point to a sensational example of retaliatory violence in support of their cause, translating their view of island conditions into the Pacific Islanders Protection Act. As usual, naval humanitarianism played a conspicuous role in linking mission and other humanitarian perspectives to political action. In the islands, naval captains gathered evidence of kidnaping for publication in Britain. At home, sympathetic members of Parliament, among them John Erskine, now an admiral and a member of the APS, helped introduce protective legislation. This sustained humanitarian influence established a rhetoric of protectiveness that allowed paternalistic interpretations of the labor trade to drown out other voices, including islanders' own.

British abolitionism was undergoing a revival in the 1860s. The journals of missionary David Livingstone were inspiring a new era of antislavery operations in Africa and, more important for our purposes, there was a brief slave trade in Pacific islanders by Peruvian guano miners. During the early 1860s, East Polynesian and Micronesian islanders were often worked to death extracting phosphate deposits from the seabird-haunted islets off the west coast of Peru, and kidnaping reached such extensive proportions in some areas that it left whole islands depopulated. H. E. Maude, whose *Slavers in Paradise* described the Peruvian guano operations, noted that it was humanitarian pressure—both British and French—that brought about the rapid suppression of this brutal practice.[9] Thus humanitarians in Britain had their attention fixed on the Pacific islands and were already predisposed to find evidence of a new slave trade when labor recruiting for Queensland and Fiji began.

There were enough cases of kidnaping and brutal treatment in the early years of the labor trade to provide missionaries with dramatic stories of "slavery," and in 1867 they began petitioning the colonial governments to investigate. As the missionaries saw it, labor recruiting could be nothing other than the victimization of helpless islanders: a reflection of assumptions made since the 1820s about islanders' response to European contact. It was, "in short, a revival of the slave trade," recalled one missionary.[10] The mission societies wrote to their headquarters in Britain and to the Foreign Office, urging government support for "a ship of war to come . . . to hunt down the rascals,"[11] and they began devoting considerable time to monitoring the labor recruiters that they blamed for their continued lack of progress in Melanesia. Robert Codrington, head of the Anglican Melanesian Mission's training center on Norfolk Island, lamented that "it is very trying certainly to have to encounter all the hindrances of a slave trade just when we thought we had got things into train for carrying out our own scheme."[12] Far from being a hindrance, humanitarian interpretations of the labor trade gave new moral support to missionaries and their crusade against white misbehavior and brought unprecedented publicity to the activities of the Melanesian Mission.

It was difficult for the Australian Station to muster sufficient resources for more than a single annual island cruise; even in the late 1860s this vast station's complement consisted only of the commodore's flagship, usually a steam corvette of about eighteen guns, four sixth-rate frigates (one of which was assigned to New Zealand), and a sloop. These vessels were dedicated to maneuverability and endurance, rather than firepower, and though most had steam capacity, it was rarely used, owing to scarcity of fuel. Telegraphic communications did not reach Australia until 1872, and these conditions of service meant that naval patrols in the south Pacific continued the traditional maritime struggle against time, distance, and winds. The station's responsibilities seemed to stretch further every year, past the New Hebrides and Banks Islands to the Solomon group and even, as in Captain John Moresby's 1871 cruise, to New Guinea. On an issue as traditional as slavery patrolling, however, it obtained some assistance from its neighboring station.

The Pacific Station, which had borne the brunt of investigation and suppression of the Peruvian slave trade, was already investigating complaints about French labor recruiting in the French territories of the Society Islands, New Caledonia, and the Loyalty Islands. Commodore Richard Powell of HMS *Topaze*, whose commander in chief was the former African Squadron antislaver Joseph

Denman, issued a strongly worded report on French "slavery" that was circulated among government departments in the autumn of 1867.[13] Many of his allegations proved unfounded or involved the recruitment of islanders already living in French territory: an issue the British government was reluctant to pursue. Government officials were skeptical about Powell's representations of French labor practices and regarded his humanitarian assumptions as exaggerated. Sir Frederick Rogers of the Admiralty, considering one of Powell's indignant reports at the Admiralty, noted that there was a vast difference between "rumours or conjectures" and Powell's own observations of healthy, well-run plantations and willing island migrants.[14] Invited to comment, the Colonial Office made a shrewd diagnosis of Powell's humanitarian bias, noting that his "slavery" allegations "seem to be made in foregone conclusions, on a theory advanced to any employ't of natives from certainty of abuse. 'The system of kidnapping Natives' is taken for granted, & easy inferences made against having any intercourse with them. We have urged precaution ag'st abuse & that is all we can do."[15] Once it became clear that kidnaping was not only a French problem, the British government would have difficulty maintaining this detached attitude.

The first naval reports on British recruiting for Queensland and Fiji seemed to contain more hard evidence than Powell's and pointed to the involvement of British subjects. Captain William Blake of HMS *Falcon* claimed that British recruiting abuses had led to the capture of a British trade vessel and the murder of its crew by islanders in the New Hebrides.[16] The murder of Britons prompted the Admiralty to express its concern to other government departments and to instruct Commodore Rowley Lambert, commander in chief of the Australia Station, to conduct a thorough investigation.[17] Meanwhile, the commodore had received a protest about the labor trade from the Reverend James McNair, missionary at Eromanga, who claimed this "slave traffic" was conducted "by a parcel of ruffians . . . old sandalwooders, who have acquired a smattering of some of the New Hebrides languages, and who have at the same time distinguished themselves for their treachery, foul murders, and gross immorality."[18] Statements like this linked the humanitarian reaction to the labor trade with its earlier objections to sandalwood trading practice, a connection made easier by the fact that sandalwooders, whose crop was now seriously depleted in Melanesia, often found a new source of income in labor recruiting. Missionaries like McNair simply transposed rhetoric about victimization in the sandalwood trade to a new, more sensational setting.

The difference between initial claims about the labor trade and subsequent investigation was striking. Commodore Lambert recalled that, during the period

covered by James McNair's account, another missionary in the New Hebrides
had written to the acting British consul at Fiji to state that he had no complaint
to make about labor recruiting.[19] In 1867, Captain Charles Hope of HMS *Brisk*,
visiting Fiji, had reported favorably on the conditions of employment of
islanders there, including the ones he met on the acting British consul's own plantation.[20] Lambert's predecessor, Commodore Sir William Wiseman, had been
concerned about the kidnaping of islanders by bêche-de-mer and pearlshell
traders on the Queensland coast,[21] but Captain Henry Bingham's report of his
visit in HMS *Virago* found laborers well treated and apparently content with the
terms of their contracts. Bingham concluded that, "taking an impartial view,"
he did not think any of them had come to Queensland unwillingly.[22] Commodore Lambert's own investigations in October 1868, when he "made particular
inquiries on this subject from the missionaries, who are the only persons from
whom information can be obtained," concluded "that labourers are transported
from island to island, but not in an improper manner."[23] Considering all the
evidence, Lambert declared that bona fide contracts were perfectly possible
between recruiters and islanders, and although there had been kidnaping incidents, recruiting in general could not be described as slavery.[24]

     This was also the view of the Queensland government, which was growing
sensitive to the unfavorable publicity generated by its search for labor. Knowing that kidnaping and other abuses were real enough, although less prevalent
than missionaries and their supporters believed, Queensland produced the 1868
Polynesian Labourers Act in an attempt to regulate recruiting practice, documentation, and conditions of transport and employment.[25] British legislation
already provided some regulation for conditions of employment and/or passage aboard British-registered vessels, but humanitarians in Queensland had
agitated for more rigorous provisions where south Pacific islanders were concerned. In Fiji, outside British jurisdiction, acting consul John Bates Thurston
could only attempt to control the situation through moral suasion. The shocking
case in 1868 of the *Young Australian,* whose captain had quelled a disturbance
among his recruits by firing indiscriminately into the hold, convinced Thurston
that more than moral authority was needed.[26] Thurston helped capture and send
the *Young Australian'*s captain for trial in Sydney, where a conviction for murder was overturned on appeal; the judges decided that islander testimony was
unacceptable. Amid this uncertainty, Thurston's successor March drew up a set
of recruiting regulations, which he feared were unenforceable.[27] After March,
Jones tried (unsuccessfully) to revive the issue of magisterial authority for
the Fiji consulate. His initiatives were overshadowed by the formation of the

Cakobau government in 1871 and by ongoing jurisdictional problems, but it is worth noting that the British government considered establishing a Fijian consular court based on the ones at Cape Coast Castle and Sierra Leone in West Africa.[28]

Queensland's claim that the labor situation was settling down, at least as far as its own plantations were concerned, seemed vindicated by the 1869 report of a royal commission set up by the Governor-General of New South Wales. After consulting witnesses ranging from missionaries to recruiters and planters, the commission concluded that "the existence of a migratory disposition on the part of the islanders of the Loyalty and New Hebrides Groups is borne out by the evidence of nearly all the witnesses who are familiar with them." After hearing contradictory reports about conditions of employment for islanders, the commission reported only that "there is great conflict of opinion" on the question.[29] When the commission's report reached London, the Admiralty decided that labor recruiting did not require the extension of naval patrols—a welcome respite for the parsimonious Admiralty Board—and hoped that recruiting abuses would soon die out.[30]

Humanitarians were disappointed by Britain's reaction to Queensland's legislation and the New South Wales commission report; it seemed that all three governments believed that the regulated importation of labor was possible, even desirable, and that kidnaping was a temporary phenomenon. After 1868, missionaries and their supporters began to change their tactics: instead of reporting catalogs of recruiting atrocities, they emphasized the childlike helplessness of islanders. Even though evidence showed that many islanders sought the recruiting ships, humanitarians could claim that they were accepting contracts they could not possibly understand. They pointed out that few recruiters spoke even one Melanesian language well, in an area where single islands might feature dozens, and argued that islanders were always exploited even when they appeared to recruit willingly. Only a total ban on the labor trade would protect them. In April 1869 the LMS wrote to the Colonial Office, declaring that labor recruiters victimized islanders by taking "advantage of their weakness and ignorance," thus making them "unwilling and helpless slaves."[31]

These "helpless slaves" soon found a champion in Commander George Palmer, who exploited his position as a naval officer in order to influence public opinion on the labor trade. Commodore Lambert, inundated by missionary complaints, ordered Palmer to take HMS *Rosario* on an extended island cruise in 1869.[32] Palmer's report, which he expanded and published in 1871, would do for the labor trade what Captain Erskine's book had done for sandalwooders. The commander's vivid descriptions of outrages against islanders, sprinkled with patriotic appeals for British intervention, gave humanitarian representations a higher profile than they had enjoyed before. Unlike official correspondence on the labor trade, Palmer's observations would be unequivocal, emotive, and widely accessible.

There was no question that some recruiters behaved with criminal irresponsibility, and Palmer acquired damning evidence about one of the worst of them. Ross Lewin, who had been tried (and acquitted) at Brisbane in January 1869 for raping an island woman, was recruiting islanders for his plantation on Tanna in the New Hebrides when Palmer called there at the end of March. The missionaries gave Palmer hair-raising accounts of Lewin's deceptive and violent recruiting methods, which including pulling men out of their canoes when they came to trade.[33] "I have ample proofs that a complete Slave Trade is being carried on," Palmer assured Governor Belmore of Queensland: "It ought to be distinctly understood that these natives (with very few exceptions) do not understand anything about engagements; they are just like children."[34]

During the cruise, Palmer boarded Lewin's recruiting vessel *Daphne* to find her "fitted up like an African slaver, *minus* the irons,"[35] and bound for Fiji with only a license for Queensland. Palmer sent the *Daphne* with a prize crew to Sydney, where, to his dismay, the Supreme Court of New South Wales could not find sufficient evidence to obtain a conviction under the British antislavery acts. Although the *Daphne* did not have a license to recruit for Fiji, shipboard conditions were hardly grueling: a hundred recruits wandered the decks under the supervision of nine unarmed men. The *Daphne* was guilty of violating aspects of colonial and merchant marine legislation and might have been successfully prosecuted on that basis, but the crown law officers of New South Wales had been unable to persuade the zealous Palmer to take this course.[36] The commander's obsession with "slaving" led to disaster; after the captain of the *Daphne* was acquitted, the ship's owners sued Palmer for false imprisonment and damages. It now seemed to many observers that Britain was failing to demonstrate the legal and political will necessary to combat the old evil of slavery in this new form. South Pacific traveler and naturalist Julius Brenchley lamented, "Where now is the Anti-Slavery Society? Where is the really benevolent Society of Friends? Where is the slightest flash of that frenzy of indignation not long since exhibited in the case of the Jamaica black?"[37] Missionary John Inglis at Aneityum reflected, "Had the philanthropic Wilberforce or Dr. Andrew Thomson been alive to-day," they would have denounced the labor trade "as strongly as they denounced the slavery and the slave-trade of their own times."[38]

Palmer eventually obtained immunity from the New South Wales government; he and his humanitarian friends then tried to make the most of what appeared to be a serious setback. The British *Anti-Slavery Reporter* told its extensive readership about the case and its outcome, hoping that, by publicizing Palmer's activities, "the force of public opinion is producing its effect, in bringing to an end the infamous traffic in South-Sea Islanders."[39] Palmer went directly to the British government, through the sponsorship of his naval brother-in-law, Captain Henry King, to obtain the support of Scottish M.P. Arthur Kinnaird. Kinnaird's connection with the APS and other humanitarian organizations inclined him to help, and he was able to convince the Colonial Office to refund Palmer's legal costs.

Clearly there was a special problem with Fiji, whose position outside British territory made legislative or judicial controls impossible. After visiting Thurston during his 1869 cruise, Palmer reported that the acting consul was forced to rely on personal influence, "having no means at his disposal to carry out English law, having neither magisterial power, nor force to back it."[40] Even the favorable New South Wales commission report had taken pains to separate the Queensland and Fijian situations, stating that the latter "demands a much more active supervision on the part of your Majesty's Government than it has yet received."[41] The Admiralty was reluctant to spare additional resources for the Australia Station and told the Colonial Office that any additional visits to Fiji would have to be made by the ship presently designated for New Zealand service.[42] However, Palmer's report and the publicity given to the *Daphne* and other cases were enough to prompt alterations to the standing orders for the Australia Station. Instructions to Commodores Wiseman and Lambert had made no mention of the labor trade,[43] but in 1870 the Admiralty's order to Commodore F. H. Stirling stated that "the operations for obtaining immigrants from the South Sea Islands have recently assumed a Slave Trade character, and their Lordships desire that you will act to the best of your judgment and in accordance with law in endeavouring to check the traffic."[44] This was a sea change in the Admiralty's attitude, the first clear sign that humanitarian representations were influencing official decision making.

A reminder of the serious legal problems still remaining confronted Captain Montgomerie after he took charge of a schooner, the *Challenge,* seized for suspected slaving at Fiji in June 1871. Montgomerie sent the vessel to Sydney in order to seek the New South Wales government's assistance with a Vice-Admiralty court trial, but Belmore did not want a repetition of the Palmer imbroglio and refused to have anything to do with the case. It was up to Montgomerie to prosecute on his own responsibility. As a naval officer he would be entitled to try to claim the *Challenge* as a prize if the vessel was proved to have been breaking existing antislavery legislation. However, it was Consul March who had seized the *Challenge,* and since he had no legal authority to do so, the chances of a successful prosecution were virtually nil. The Admiralty, equally reluctant to precipitate another *Daphne* crisis, supported Belmore. The British crown law officers added only that captains and consuls should be granted immunity to pursue cases of this kind in future. By this time, a proposed antikid-naping bill was under discussion, and the *Challenge* case was closed.[45]

Stirling had despatched Commander Henry Challis in the *Rosario* to conduct another labor trade investigation in the meantime. Challis' report was more ambiguous than Palmer's. At Fiji, the commander admired March's regulations about labor recruiting and was pleased to discover, after inspecting two newly arrived ships, that the islanders claimed to be willing recruits. He believed that, "in the absence of any law in Fiji, Mr. March's arrangements appear to me to be excellent."[46] Like Palmer, Challis noted stories about the misbehavior of individual recruiters such as the American "Bully" Hayes;[47] unlike him, he concluded that the activities of a handful of scoundrels were prejudicing observers against an otherwise acceptable recruiting system. At the Gilbert Islands in Micronesia, the chief of Aamana assured Challis that men from his territories recruited for Fiji, but "it was quite voluntary," and he "had no complaints to make against the masters of the vessels employed in their conveyance." This testimony and Challis' scrutiny of Gilbertese laborers he met at Fiji made him certain that they had not been kidnaped. More telling was his visit to Tanna, where, in the absence of missionary Neilson, Tannese leaders and local white residents declared "that a large number of natives voluntarily leave this Island in English vessels for employment in the Fiji Islands and Queensland, and are continually returning well satisfied with their treatment."[48]

This story was very different from the one Palmer had told in 1869. Bearing Challis' inquiry in mind and smarting from the indignities of the ongoing *Daphne* case, Commodore Stirling received a letter from Consul March, declaring that the 1,700 islanders registered with his office since the beginning of the year "understood the terms of their agreements."[49] All of this prompted the commodore to report, at the beginning of the fateful year 1871, "that the practice of kid-naping natives has somewhat abated, and is confined to such unscrupulous persons as the man Hayes and a few others."[50] Public outrage was gathering momentum in London, however, and Bishop Patteson's murder was about to create all the "frenzy of indignation" humanitarians could have wished for.

Bishop Selwyn of New Zealand had ordained his friend and colleague, John Patteson, the first Bishop of Melanesia in 1861. Following Selwyn's lead, the new bishop traveled extensively among the islands to recruit young men for mission training, taking full advantage of islanders' interest in travel and work abroad. There was an obvious element of competition between the Melanesian Mission and labor recruiters, aggravated by the fact that some unscrupulous recruiters pretended to be missionaries or claimed Patteson had sent them, a practice that could make island travel dangerous for the real missionaries who followed.[51] Even so, Patteson never condemned labor recruiting outright, knowing very well that many islanders willingly chose to emigrate. He believed instead in regulation by imperial statute and naval patrols.[52] While he visited Nukapu Island in the Santa Cruz group in October 1871, islanders attacked his party, killing him and fatally wounding his chaplain. Here was an apparent vindication of the humanitarian connection between recruiting, kidnaping, and retaliatory violence.

Just before Patteson's murder, *Rosario* left Sydney for an island cruise under Commander Albert Markham. Markham's first stop was the Melanesian Mission headquarters on Norfolk Island, where "the first intelligence I received was the news of the murder of Bishop Patteson and the Rev. Mr. Atkins."[53] Patteson's fate would haunt the rest of his voyage. The sensational news of the bishop's "martyrdom" naturally became the focus of his discussions with missionaries in the islands, and Markham's report—expanded and published as a book in 1873—presented well-established humanitarian images of malicious recruiters and backward islanders. Amid Patteson's grieving colleagues at Norfolk Island, Markham decided that "the attack on the bishop and party was made entirely in retaliation of wrongs and murders suffered by them at the hands of white people, whom I imagine to be those concerned in the nefarious practice of kidnapping natives for labour."[54] The commander later recalled that, "with these stories fresh in my memory, I felt that I had a most onerous and important duty to perform. . . . determined to do all in my power to shield and protect the Islanders."[55]

In this frame of mind, Markham visited the New Hebrides, Santa Cruz, and Solomon islands and Fiji on an extended four months' cruise. Everywhere he went he saw evidence of labor trade villainy. Met with hostility by Nguna islanders, he assumed that the recent visit of "Mr. Ross Lewin of notorious celebrity" had provoked them.[56] So dedicated was he to the retaliation explanation that he applied it even when islanders gave him a warm welcome. Investigating the case of the *Marian Rennie* at "Anuta" (probably Amota in the Banks Islands), where the islanders were supposed to have massacred everyone aboard except for the Fijian crew, Markham admitted that the Fijians were more likely to blame than the friendly, unarmed people he met at Anuta. He added, however, that the islanders must have been provoked to anger "in retaliation for some grevious wrong imposed on them."[57] Although he found only two improperly licensed recruiting vessels during his entire cruise, neither of which was carrying passengers under illegal conditions, Markham's final report declared "that the nefarious system of kidnapping is practised to a most inconceivable extent, and that it actually amounts to downright slavery, and in many cases, where blood is shed in a most wanton manner, to murder."[58]

The sensational circumstances of Patteson's death gave the labor trade and the Melanesian Mission wide publicity. Taking advantage of public outrage to press the case for imperial intervention in the islands, humanitarian organizations pointed out the retrospective significance of Commander Palmer's opinions, which had appeared in book form earlier in 1871. *Kidnapping in the South Seas* began with accusations familiar since the 1840s: it blamed sandalwood "scoundrels" for giving islanders "their first impressions of *civilisation,* which consisted chiefly in lying and treachery, interspersed with repeated acts of arson and murder."[59] Palmer knew that labor recruiters were often men with trading experience in the islands; since sandalwooders had all been rogues (as far as he was concerned), labor recruiters were too. If the British government did nothing to intervene, Palmer warned, "with our vaunted hatred of slavery, and all the evils that follow in its train, we shall become a laughing-stock to the rest of the civilized world."[60] Once designated "slavery," the labor trade inherited the political importance of Britain's African antislavery campaign and its images of international moral guardianship.

At a memorial for Patteson attended by two thousand people, the Bishop of Melbourne made a lengthy speech deploring the "lawless and cruel" labor trade, holding *Kidnapping in the South Seas* in his hand.[61] After hearing long extracts from the book, his audience approved the bishop's resolution asking for "Imperial intervention" to supress the recruiting of "ignorant and comparatively defenceless savages."[62] In London, the *Anti-Slavery Reporter* hoped Palmer's book "will prove especially valuable in opening the eyes of the public" and forcing the government to act.[63] Palmer's media campaign continued into 1872. After the government of Queensland began requiring recruiting ships to carry approved agents, the captain wrote an open letter to the APS accusing Queensland officials of appointing unscrupulous men as agents. The letter, which was carried by the *Morning Post* and the *Brisbane Courier,* outraged the governor of Queensland, who told the Colonial Secretary in London that, "when deliberately written for publication by a gentleman holding the high position of a Captain of the Royal Navy," allegations such as Palmer's required either retraction or substantiation by the British government.[64] The Colonial Office seems to have resolved the situation behind the scenes. Meanwhile, the Admiralty realized that greater resources would be necessary for the Australia Station to cope with labor patrolling; Commodore Stirling had made it clear that without new sailing schooners and expanded station limits, the Royal Navy could not be expected even to monitor the situation effectively.[65] In February 1872 the station boundaries were extended to include the Solomon Islands to the west and parts of Micronesia to the north; the Admiralty also authorized Stirling to build five one-hundred-ton sailing schooners to supplement his squadron.[66]

The change in attitude following Patteson's murder was not lost on plantation owners in Fiji. "Guileless persons love to represent the South Sea Islander as a grown-up child; but he is one who would prove a deal of trouble to his parents!" wrote William Wawn, a labor recruiter. Wawn, like others, claimed that plantation labor helped to civilize islanders by taking them away from indigenous barbarities, and he condemned missionaries and their supporters for turning real people into sentimentalized fantasies.[67] R. Beckwith Leefe, a retired Indian Army officer now running a Fiji plantation, lamented the way the consul's licensing system hindered access to labor while "Man of War after Man of War arrives and each and all refuse to enter into or satisfy the claims of British Subjects."[68] Men like these were in favor of a regulated labor trade but resented being branded "slavers" by those Wawn called "Narrow-minded Enthusiasts of the Southern Pacific."

Antislavery groups in Britain were now clamoring for imperial legislation, led by two seasoned humanitarians who were definitely "Enthusiasts": Admiral John Erskine and Bishop George Selwyn. Erskine, in consultation with the APS, helped arrange presentation of the Pacific Islanders Protection Bill in March 1872. Erskine's speeches revealed the extent of the paternalism under debate. Worried that the bill would regulate rather than abolish the labor trade, the admiral declared that it was "but a very small instalment of justice towards those who were absolutely at our mercy," because "it was a farce to talk of obtaining the free consent of these Polynesians."[69] Outright abolition was more than Parliament could endorse; there was simply too much evidence of islanders' willing recruitment. However, Bishop Selwyn's presence in the House of Lords helped rally support for a firmly regulatory bill. Selwyn pointed out that he had observed the beginnings of the south Pacific slave trade during the 1840s.[70] From the Commons, Erskine worked hard to ensure that an amendment guaranteeing the Royal Navy's right of seizure and protection from prosecution was included in the bill, which received royal assent on 27 June 1872. Although the development of new naval instructions took some time to work out,[71] the legislation was a public triumph for humanitarianism. John Kay, supervisor of Presbyterian missions, wrote from Scotland that he rejoiced "to know that the anti-slavery spirit, sustained by Christianity, is still as strong, and active, and vigorous as ever."[72]

Behind the scenes, there were doubts about enforcement. The Foreign Office reminded the Admiralty that "in the state of things now existing on and in the neighbourhood of Fiji it seems to us obvious that very much must be left to the discretion of the naval officers who are employed, and that no set of instructions can be drawn which will meet every case."[73] Enforcement was a familiar problem for officers on duty in the south Pacific, but there was a more fundamental difficulty in this case. Was the labor trade actually a widespread system of kidnaping or not? Commodore Stirling was concerned that the obsession with kidnaping, reflected in the wording of the Pacific Islanders Protection Act, was too restrictive.[74] His belief that the real situation was complex and changeable was confirmed when Captain John Moresby returned from his 1872 island cruise in HMS *Basilisk:* the results of Moresby's careful and extensive investigation—stretching from Fiji to the Ellice Islands in Micronesia—were decidedly ambivalent. In almost every place where he could obtain information, either through interpreters or with the help of local missionaries, he found little evidence of unwilling recruitment. Meeting the missionary vessel *Southern Cross* during his cruise, he was surprised to hear the missionaries admit that "they had not fallen in with any kidnapping or labour vessels, nor even heard of any searching amongst the Solomon Group this year." Realizing that this admission hardly squared with their usual story, the missionaries had added that "the new Act of Parliament, and the presence of men-of-war had frightened the labour vessels away."[75] Even Moresby had not known about the new legislation before he sailed, and naval vessels had been making annual cruises of the New Hebrides and Solomons for several years. The missionaries were grasping at straws. Moresby concluded that "all the evidence goes to prove that [kidnaping] has almost, if not entirely ceased . . . the cause being that force has been found not to pay so well as persuasion."[76] The cyclical nature of labor trade activity, as recruiters moved into new areas or were forced to change their tactics by increasingly sophisticated islanders, made it difficult to predict outbreaks of violence. It also made it difficult for the Royal Navy to maintain that the islands

were swarming with "slavers." Was it the "slavers" or humanitarian constructions of them that always seemed just out of reach?

The caution of captains like Moresby was out of step with public opinion
and with the more zealous members of the naval service. Commander Markham
published an expanded version of his 1871 report in 1873, in imitation of Palmer,
and echoed his predecessor's belief that "the enormities perpetrated by those
employed in the sandal wood trade, have of late years, if possible, been exceeded
by men engaged in the Labour Traffic."[77] It was to make "this state of things
known," wrote Markham, that he hoped to direct "a portion of public attention
to a question which very closely affects the honour of our country."[78] To
observers like Markham, believing that large numbers of kidnapers were victim-
izing islanders, the navy's failure to make a larger number of captures (or even
sightings) was due entirely to insufficient resources or political will. In reality,
humanitarian assumptions were taking on a life of their own, shaping images
of British moral guardianship in a way that rarely took notice of complex and
shifting realities in the islands. Even the pragmatic Moresby later found himself
swept up by humanitarian rhetoric; writing his memoirs in 1913, he recalled that
the purpose of his 1872 cruise had been "to check the kidnapping of natives, then
so common." Musing in old age on the heavy responsibilities of those who
patrolled Britain's expanding imperial frontier, he observed: "Truly the dark
places of the earth are full of cruelty, and the cost of an Empire's expansion,
with its tribute of blood and tears, is concealed except from those who keep watch
and ware upon its outposts."[79]

Convinced that the labor trade was really slavery, seeing their role in regulating it as a benevolent and Christian one, humanitarians in the 1860s and 1870s
reinforced perceptions of labor recruiting as illicit and brutal. Despite contradictory evidence, perceptions of the labor trade as "slavery" prevailed. Images
of victimized islanders and villainous white men, already well established, were
easily transferred to this new setting, and, thanks to an extensive public relations
campaign, humanitarians gained ground in their quest for imperial legislation.
After the murder of Bishop Patteson in 1871, they exploited political influence
and public support to launch the Pacific Islanders Protection Act: an official
endorsement of imperial benevolence.

8

Gunboat Diplomacy?

ALTHOUGH it could maintain a united front against misbehaving white men, humanitarian ambivalence about islander offenses made the issue of naval coercion problematic. Naval bombardments were rare and controversial before the 1870s, reflecting both their inadequacy as deterrents and their questionable morality in the minds of naval officers themselves. Only later do we begin to observe the demographic and social changes that prompted a redefinition of national honor and a new emphasis on demonstrations of vigor. By this time, formalized imperial rule was already under way through protective legislation and the cession of Fiji. Historians have made too many connections between the use of force and British expansion in the Pacific islands; this chapter will reveal more evidence of self-doubt than martial assertiveness among "gunboat" officers. Lives were at stake in each captain's decision about the use of force, and in this emotive context humanitarianism faced some of its greatest challenges.

We know how difficult it was for naval officers to bring either white men or islanders to trial; attempts to enforce fines too were often unsuccessful. These problems only underscore the wider dilemma of naval "policing." Some historians fall back on a generalized concept of "gunboat diplomacy," acknowledging the navy's position in international law and assuming that the use of force was "a language that was universal."[1] Descriptions of gunboat warriors assume that warship captains had few qualms about the use of force in principal; surely one could not be a professional naval officer otherwise? These assumptions are not borne out in the south Pacific. Between the start of regular island patrols in 1829 and the cession of Fiji in 1874, only eight ship's captains turned their guns on islanders.[2] At least forty-nine men commanded vessels in south Pacific waters during that time,[3] visiting a large number of islands on at least one cruise a year: "gunboat diplomacy" did not characterize the Royal Navy's presence in the south Pacific. Tension between different aspects of naval duty produced debate, not certainty. Assumptions about the effectiveness of naval force are equally questionable. The glimpses we have of islanders' own reactions indicate that two separate issues were at stake. Islanders were quite capable of realizing that the British outgunned them, and once they identified the destructive effects of musket, shot, and shell, they usually responded with fear. However, the recognition of power does not mean that its display was "salutary." The lessons supposed to be taught by the use of force were rarely understood in the same terms; how could they be? To reassure themselves about taking action they usually found distasteful, captains assumed that bombardments automatically conveyed Western notions of private property or criminal justice. We cannot accept this assumption at face value. Islanders might acknowledge a warship's destructive potential, but they did not necessarily consider themselves either educated or defeated by it.

In 1834, Governor Bourke of New South Wales despatched Captain Lambert of the *Alligator* to rescue crew members of the whaler *Harriet* from the Cape Egmont Maori of New Zealand. Bourke instructed Lambert to use force only as a last resort, but the captain retrieved the last of the captives only after two bombardments and a skirmish that killed and wounded a number of Maori. Called to account by the Select Committee on Aborigines in 1836, Lambert described his regret at having to use force but believed that it would deter further attacks on British subjects. The Maori certainly respected British power; they built a new war canoe bearing prow decorations derived from *Alligator*'s figurehead "to keep in memory a grief and the duty of revenge."[4] But had the Maori learned the lesson Lambert intended to teach? Maori chief Te Kahui's reminiscences about 1834 are dominated by the devastation of intertribal war; he did not mention *Alligator*'s activities.[5] Moreover, Maori who migrated from Cape Egmont to Port Nicholson after the *Alligator* incident seized the British brig *Rodney* to move to the Chatham Islands, where, in 1835, they captured a French vessel and killed the crew.[6]

Fourteen years later, the commander in chief of the Pacific Station instructed Captain Worth of the *Calypso* to provide vigorous support for Consul Pritchard, and the two men traveled to Fiji to investigate the complaints of British traders. Privately disgusted by Pritchard's opportunism and vindictiveness,[7] Worth decided that the murder of a British man after a dispute over provisioning seemed the most clear-cut of these complaints. When the Fijians refused to turn over those responsible for the murder, Worth tried to avoid inflicting casualties by warning them that he was about to attack their village.[8] Marines burned the deserted town after the Fijians fled and returned to the ship with only one man wounded; eight or nine Fijians had been killed and at least thirty wounded.[9] Pritchard had convinced Worth that, "if he punished one offence, it would be noised throughout the whole land, and be productive of as good an effect as if he punished a dozen."[10] However, when Captain Erskine arrived the following year, he condemned the action as "paltry and ineffectual," arguing that benevolent restraint was more effective than force. A Fijian chief warned by Erskine against attacking missionaries had "laughed at the power of a ship to punish him, as a retreat in the mountains would always secure his safety, and leave only empty houses at the mercy of the strangers."[11]

Almost ten years passed before the next punitive expedition: an attack on Woodlark Island made at the insistence of relatives of the murdered crew of the *Gazelle*. Their lobbying had prompted the Foreign Office to order naval reprisals, and the Admiralty's instructions to Loring left the captain in no doubt that he was to "take such measures as may be possible for ascertaining & punishing the murderers."[12] For the first time, instructions direct from London gave no option except the use of force. Loring made the long journey to Woodlark, where his marines burned houses and canoes without taking life, indeed, without seeing any islanders. Emphasizing that he took these steps only because he was ordered to, Loring did not believe that the incident had warranted punitive action. He confided to the First Lord of the Admiralty that the *Gazelle* lobbyists' real desire had been "that the Man of War should go to the Island & commit indiscriminate Massacre," and from this perspective, the captain perceived his limited raid as "judicious & just."[13] In fact, Loring regarded the whole Woodlark Island issue, drawn out over two years by now, as nothing more than a New South Wales political gimmick "to carry out party views and personal ill-will."[14]

Loring visited Tanna in the New Hebrides group on the same cruise, at the request of Governor William Denison of New South Wales, to investigate the murder of two sandalwood traders at Black Beach. Convinced that the Tannese had been deliberately provoked, the captain did not "think it right or advisable to fire, or to land, and commit indiscriminate slaughter and destruction on the Natives,"[15] and he left them with a warning. The *Iris* was barely under way, however, when the Tannese murdered the entire crew of another vessel at the very place where Loring had pursued his investigations. Returning in 1858, Loring detained the man he considered responsible and fired several shells at the Tan-

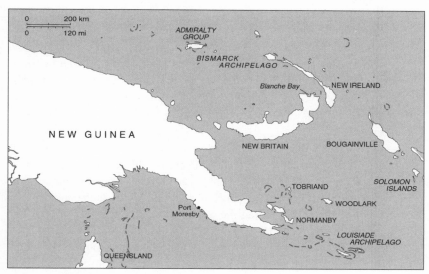

Map 7. Eastern New Guinea

nese gathered on the beach before sending men to destroy the nearby villages. Later, after the Tannese ambushed and killed two of his crewmen, Loring conducted a second raid, with a larger number of Tannese casualties. He reported the hope that his operations had been "salutary and sufficient,"[16] but Presbyterian missionary John Paton, who arrived at Tanna just after Loring's expedition, was unable to establish a mission station at Black Beach, where "no foreigners dare land unless well protected."[17]

At about the same time, HMS *Cordelia* was at Samoa, where Captain Charles Vernon was trying to arrest a man suspected of murdering the British trader William Fox. Fox was killed on Savai'i, and Williams accompanied Vernon there on 18 September to ask the ailing chief Malietoa for help. Williams noted that not all of Savai'i acknowledged the chief's authority, but he still asked Malietoa to produce the suspect, who was hiding with his family at a village in Palauli Bay. Malietoa died shortly afterward, and after further attempts to flush out the suspect, Vernon and Williams decided to fine the new Malietoa, who had been understandably preoccupied by his father's death and his own installation ceremonies. When the suspect's family still refused to surrender him, captain and consul decided to destroy their village by landing party; there were no casualties. They also burned a neighboring village, "more for intimidation than from a desire to hurt them."[18] They collected their fine from Malietoa, who was later able to have the suspect captured. Vernon convened a naval court to pronounce the sentence of death, and the man was hanged. "Thus my Lord, we have sought to satisfy Justice, and protect the lives of British subjects, while in accordance with our instructions, we have dealt as leniently as possible with the Natives," wrote Consul Williams.[19] However, the Samoans were so repelled by British methods of execution that they refused to attend the hanging. The carefully staged trial and its awful aftermath seemed more for Vernon and Williams' benefit than theirs.

In 1867 Captain William Blake of HMS *Falcon* investigated allegations of murder aboard the British trade vessel *Curlew*. He met one of the surviving crewmen at Tanna, and the man told him that the ship had been seized first by its own chief mate, who killed the ship's master. Hinchinbrook and Mare Island crewmen then took control of the vessel, killing the chief mate and a white cabin boy. The Hinchinbrook men forced the others to take them home, after which the Mare islanders and Blake's informant escaped. When Blake called at the Havannah Harbour mission station on Éfaté, the missionaries told him that the Hinchinbrook people had also murdered the crew of the *Kate* after it wrecked near their island. Blake sailed for Hinchinbrook, intending to determine the truth of these stories "and if there were any grievances they could bring forward in justification," a moderate enough approach.[20] Arriving on 1 August he found the remains of the *Curlew* and anchored nearby. Armed men appeared on the beach with their headman, and when the interpreter and a Hinchinbrook "chief " whom Blake had picked up at Fiji headed for shore in a boat, the warriors shouted that "they did not care for a man of war, at the same time gesticulating and yelling at the ship." The headman, who was carrying a ceremonial reed, solemnly struck the head off it with his hatchet, "which according to native custom is a signification of a declaration of war," Blake decided. The captain tried to communicate again the next morning, with the same results, and a landing party destroyed villages and canoes where relics of the *Curlew* were found. "The fact of this punishment having fallen upon those justly deserving it, will I trust have a salutary effect," Blake reported.[21]

In 1865 Commodore Sir William Wiseman took HMS *Curaçoa* to Tanna in response to requests for assistance from the New Hebrides Mission. John Paton had never felt secure at his Port Resolution station and wanted more vigorous measures taken to protect his safety. Even though there was no specific crime to avenge, Wiseman agreed to bombard the Tannese villages near Paton's station, using Paton's assistance as interpreter and guide, with the mission vessel *Dayspring* anchored nearby during the bombardment.[22] Paton then suggested that Wiseman's landing party could meet at "the dancing ground" on a hilltop above Port Resolution before setting fire to the villages. This spot, well known to the local Tannese and possibly of supernatural significance for them, left the exhausted marines and sailors open to attack, and in the resulting ambush one sailor and one Tannese man were killed.[23] The British force pulled back to the ship, and Wiseman contented himself with the damage done to fifteen villages by his bombardment and reports that the Tannese "were resolved to injure no more white people." This was not true; the people at Black Beach on the other side of Tanna killed a British sailor only a few days after Wiseman's bombardment of Port Resolution.[24] Perhaps word of the commodore's activities had not reached Black Beach before the murder was committed; perhaps other Tannese linked Wiseman's "lesson" only to the Port Resolution area. But the collaboration between Wiseman and Paton had been clear, and the consequences for the New Hebrides Mission were serious. The Tannese rebuffed John Geddie's attempt to reestablish the Port Resolution station, confronting him with the fact that earlier missionaries had "told them that it was wrong to fight, and advised them to give up their wars, and then brought a man-of-war to kill them and destroy their property."[25]

This was a shrewd diagnosis of the mission's contradictory position, but the Tannese interpretation of British actions was itself open to change. Historian Ron Adams has followed the stories of various naval bombardments at Tanna, beginning with an episode from 1774 when Cook threw one of his marines in irons for shooting a Tannese man. The Tannese told this story for generations, and by the time missionary George Turner recorded it in the 1840s, they had fitted it into their own cosmology. A big-man near Port Resolution had died just before the Cook incident, and the Tannese might have been wondering what magical forces had caused the death. When Cook's marine shot a Tannese man for no apparent reason, the islanders gave it a meaning of their own: Cook and his crew must have identified the man responsible for killing the big-man and then taken revenge for him. Thus an episode interpreted as a tragedy by scientist George Forster, who viewed it as a murder for which the marine should have been flogged, could also be seen as a triumph of supernatural justice by the observing Tannese.[26] We can see a similar process at work on the story of Wiseman's 1865 bombardment. Captain Markham, visiting in 1871, reported that the Port Resolution people regarded the reprisals "as a profound mystery, in which chiefs, naval officers, missionaries, shot and shell are mixed up in a sort of nautico-diplomatic confusion."[27] By 1875, Lieutenant Frank Henderson of HMS *Sappho* noticed that shells from *Curaçoa* were owned by men who considered them "as a great trophy," not as salutary symbols of British justice, but as evidence of when "Tanna men fight big ship."[28] Stories like to tie up loose ends, and these shells had been left on the beach too long; they had traded their intended meanings for Tannese ones.

An outbreak of measles in 1861 had led to the murder of Presbyterian missionary George Gordon and his wife on Eromanga. Wiseman left Tanna to search for the Gordons' murderers but quickly decided to go beyond inquiry. The murdered missionary's brother James, also stationed at Eromanga, complained that two local big-men were threatening to kill him and had seized land formerly promised to the mission station. Wiseman noted that "no direct act of Violence had been committed," but regarded the big-men's refusal to meet him as a confession of guilt and gave them an hour to remove women and children from the village before he began shelling. After his landing party destroyed the village, Wiseman expressed hopes that his actions would "prevent a recurrance of such serious outrages on the lives and property of British subjects."[29] After the *Curaçoa* departed, the apparently chastised islanders invited James Gordon to remain at Dillon's Bay, leading Wiseman to conclude that his bombardment there "appears to have had a most salutary influence throughout the Island."[30] A few years later, however, James joined his brother in martyrdom: killed by Eromangans from the interior. Did the inland people believe, perhaps, that Wiseman's bombardment was only aimed at the coastal islanders? We only know that the commodore's "salutary" message could be interpreted more ways than one.

In 1868 the people of Roviana Lagoon on New Georgia in the Solomon Islands captured the British schooner *Marion Rennie* and killed the crew. Captain Montgomerie took HMS *Blanche* to investigate, and after finding items from the schooner in several huts, he sent a landing party to burn the village. Worried that the islanders might not understand the lesson of his visit, Montgomerie accepted the help of a British trader called Ferguson, who suggested a fine of three tons of tortoiseshell to be ready for delivery by the end of the year. No Royal Navy ship was available to collect the fine, however, and the son of the *Marion Rennie*'s master wrote to Lambert to suggest that delay was undermining the navy's ability to teach "the Natives a lesson which they will not easily forget."[31] By 1873 the Roviana people had killed Ferguson too and were so hostile to Europeans that George Brown of the LMS was forced to begin his mission at Duke of York Island instead.

The best-publicized punitive action however, was *Rosario*'s bombardment of the Melanesian island of Nukapu in 1871. Commander Markham had been

Montgomerie's first lieutenant in *Blanche* before taking command of *Rosario*, and thus he had firsthand experience of punitive action. As his ship was departing on her island cruise, the Nukapu people killed Bishop Patteson and his chaplain. At their headquarters on Norfolk Island, the missionaries reminded Markham of Patteson's objection to punitive measures, and he promised to investigate peacefully. When the islanders shot arrows at his boat's crew, Markham decided that he needed "to teach them that the British Flag was not to be assailed with impunity" and sent marines, under cover of bombardment, to destroy the nearest village.[32] There was little contact with Nukapu for thirty-five years afterward, but when the Melanesian Mission finally established a station there, "it was the death of Patteson that the older inhabitants had become accustomed to regard as the great tragedy in their history, whereas they laughed as they recalled their bombardment."[33]

It is worth noting that the mere appearance of a naval vessel could have a profound significance for islanders if the circumstances were right. The Royal Navy's critics were fond of claiming that British lenience was counterproductive. Not wanting to accuse naval officers of cowardice, labor recruiter William Wawn blamed "Exeter Hall influence" and government interference for hampering the coercive power of the navy, with the result that "commanders of British warships have done more harm than good for the interests they have been supposed to protect."[34] Even missionaries could take this attitude, as Paton did when he claimed that the lenience of Commodore Wiseman's predecessor, Seymour, had only encouraged the Tannese to redouble their efforts to force him from his station. This was not what Paton had said at the time, however. It was an outbreak of measles in 1861 that seemed to confirm Paton's malign influence as far as the Tannese were concerned, and the missionary's description of their plotting states that they both expected and defied naval punishment, confident that their sorcerer would call up a hurricane to sink any hostile vessel and allow them to kill its crew.[35] This hardly suggests that *Iris'* bombardment in 1858 had been a "salutary" deterrent. When Seymour arrived at Port Resolution a few months after the measles outbreak, he quickly obtained a promise of good behavior from the Port Resolution people. According to Paton, the fact that Seymour had arrived at all and was not destroyed by the promised hurricane "confirmed Jehovah's supremacy over the Tannese deities and strengthened Paton's power in the vicinity of the harbour."[36] A humane captain, appearing at a significant time and acting in a meaningful way, could influence islanders more than a vengeful one whose punishment might not even be connected with the crime.

Islanders' varied responses to punitive action demonstrate that they were not necessarily cowed by British technological superiority or enlightened about British notions of justice. They responded with the full range and unpredictability of human emotion in the context of their own cultural background. Nor does the evidence show us swaggering naval warriors; instead, we see individuals of varying temperament struggling with a combination of humanitarianism, professional caution, and national pride. The rarity of naval punitive actions and evidence of their questionable effectiveness must challenge traditional assumptions about "gunboat diplomacy" in the Pacific islands. The relationship of naval force to the expansion of British trade or missionary activity in the south Pacific was ambiguous; bombardments had not protected the trader Ferguson or the missionary Gordon for long. Some naval officers condemned traders; some missionaries endorsed bombardments. Rather than a neat apportioning of attitudes, conflicting beliefs about the use of force reflected tensions in the wider debate about imperial "law and order."

We need to examine the legality of punitive action as early-nineteenth-century naval captains understood it. Customary rather than legislative, based on traditional theories of the law of war, the nineteenth-century "law of nations" regarded naval commanders as representatives of their nation's sovereignty, enabling them to take reprisals "when a specific wrong has been committed" by seizing or destroying property in compensation or directing violence against the individual or group responsible for the wrong. Such measures were "*prima facie* acts of war," although theorists realized that they were often the means of redressing grievances, rather than actual declarations of war.[37] Some naval captains tried to seek security in this legal framework; Loring was so uncertain about the legality of his punitive proceedings at Woodlark that he fired an opening volley "as a sort of declaration of war," casting himself as a representative of the British crown commencing hostilities.[38] Before the creation of the Western Pacific High Commission in 1877, this arbitrary option, dependent on the resources and discretion of individual naval captains, was the only legal way of dealing with islander offenses within British jurisprudence.[39] We have seen that the Foreign Office twice instructed naval captains to regard the Pacific islands as sovereign states; this definition was reinforced by the opinion of the law officers of New South Wales when they declared that islanders "must be treated as a separate nation and according to the Law of Nations."[40]

Naval captains were not at liberty to punish out of proportion to the crime, and concern about how to define appropriate reprisals testifies both to the legal uncertainty of the situation and the Royal Navy's protective attitude toward islanders. During the 1840s, debate about naval antislavery operations in West Africa drew attention to the question of whether a "civilised" state could punish an "uncivilised" one for "crimes against humanity."[41] Erskine worried about the implications for Pacific islanders, whose cannibalism, for example, might fall within this category and who could be judged "so low in the scale of humanity, as to place them quite beyond the pale of legal or moral obligations on the part of civilized countries."[42]

Controversial legal issues divided the supporters of indigenous sovereignty from those who regarded Pacific islanders as savages beyond the pale of natural law. Through the doctrine of sovereignty, humanitarians acknowledged the legitimacy of island codes of behavior, even if they regarded those codes as inferior to their own. Captain Lambert's friend Baron von Hügel, observing the way the New South Wales Executive Council sought to justify punitive action outside its jurisdiction in the *Harriet* investigation, remarked that Britain could not interfere in New Zealand unless it took possession: "For so long as [the Maori] have their own laws, strangers must submit to them."[43] Some nineteenth-century historians agreed, observing that "it was a national custom—indeed, a *law*—of the New Zealanders to appropriate all salvage from wrecks" such as the *Harriet,* and found fault instead "at home among the good *Christians* of Britain" who ignored the validity of indigenous self-determination.[44] In Britain, the APS declared that British subjects could not expect the protection of British law outside British territory,[45] while the *Daily Southern Cross,* commenting on Markham's bombardment at Nukapu, declared that it was inappropriate to exhibit "a vindictive display of power over misguided and ignorant savages, who probably to this day believe that they were perfectly justified by their own rude principles of equity."[46]

This stance was sharpened by the conviction that misbehaving Europeans were provoking violence in the islands. When the story of *Rosario*'s bombardment reached Britain, the *Telegraph* was outraged, claiming that islanders had been mistreated by labor recruiters and were merely retaliating for the brutalities they had endured: "Is it come to this that the British Navy has degenerated into butchering savages because they may have committed crimes after having been goaded to madness by the treachery and cruelty of white civilization?"[47] For humanitarians, the Royal Navy represented Britain's civilizing mission, and for its officers to use force against islanders was "too like the principles of their own wild code, that the only lesson taught them will be that 'might is right' —a lesson in which they will prove apt learners."[48] Instead, the "salutary" nature of naval visits should lie in moral elevation, as when Captain Erskine argued that "a system of forbearance and conciliation towards them should be the rule to be observed on our part, both as that best calculated to impress their minds with the dignity of our power, which had hitherto been often compromised by paltry and ineffectual attacks, and also with some notions of law and justice, which ought to govern their intercourse with foreigners."[49] From such a viewpoint, as Bishop Selwyn put it, punitive action was "called 'summary justice' but is, in fact, the violation of all justice."[50] The retaliation theory had a direct influence on this kind of interpretation. If humanitarians believed that islanders only committed crimes in response to previous white atrocities, how could they square punitive actions with their own consciences? Captain Chapman had been investigating labor recruiting at Fiji when Commodore Stirling asked him to identify the kidnapers of a white man, John Collins, at Malaita in the Solomon Islands. Chapman duly arrested three islanders (who could not be tried in any case) but resisted Collins' suggestions of punitive vengeance. Convinced that restraint would "have a better effect on the minds of the natives on board, in showing them both the power and clemency of Englishmen," Chapman justified his decision by deciding that "this murder was probably in revenge for some previous outrage by white men."[51] At home, the APS boasted about the effect of humanitarianism on naval behavior. Referring to an unspecified episode, the society's report for 1846 noted that a naval punitive raid was called off

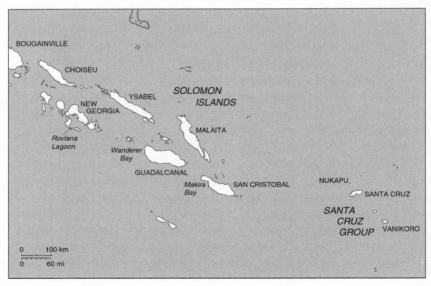

Map 8. Solomon/Santa Cruz Islands

when the commander recalled that "we shall have Mrs. Fry and the Philanthropists upon us on our return."[52]

Critics of humanitarianism argued that British justice existed for the protection of British interests and that natural law required the Royal Navy to take punitive action against those who committed crimes against humanity. Tackling the *Southern Cross* on the legality of *Rosario's* activities, the *New Zealand Herald* claimed that "it was obligatory on Capt. Markham to vindicate natural law" by punishing islanders.[53] It deplored the retaliation theory of "the ultra-humanitarians," believing that "the natives must be treated as accountable beings, and as such they should be punished in the only way their limited intelligence and local customs enable them to understand."[54] Those who wished for more and bigger punitive actions often compared the failings of the Royal Navy with the supposed vigor and effectiveness of French or American naval activities. It is worth pausing a moment to consider this accusation, because it was yet another example of wishful thinking. The evidence suggests that French and American punitive raids were no more "effective" than British ones.

The captain of the French trade vessel *L'Aimable Josephine* had often exchanged cargoes of bêche-de-mer for the transportation of warriors in one or other of Fiji's many internecine conflicts. In 1834, he and his crew were killed after their Vewan passengers lost a battle and decided to capture the French ship in order to use its weaponry against another group of enemies.[55] Word of the attack eventually reached the French commander Dumont d'Urville, who arrived to take vengeance on Vewa four years later. Unfortunately for him, his Fijian pilot prolonged the ship's passage through the islands so that the Vewans could be warned in time. D'Urville was forced to burn empty villages. Later, Wilkes of the U.S. Exploring Expedition heard the Vewan chief Verani boasting "that the French had only burned a few of his mud huts, which he could shortly build again; that it would give a very few days of labour to his slaves; and that he would cut off the next vessel that came, if he had an opportunity. He thinks that it was a very cheap purchase to get so much property for so little damage."[56] Tānoa and Cakobau of Bau, too, were gloating over their role in thwarting the French: "The Ambau people also spoke vauntingly of having given the French permission to destroy Viwa, as it was nothing, and satisfied the Papalangis; but they did not intend that any property or lives should be lost, for they had sent to inform the Viwa people that the attack was to be made, and even helped them to remove all their valuables."[57] This account sounds like Wilkes' observation about the chief Opotuno of Samoa, who eluded capture by living "in the mountains of Savai'i, where it was impossible to find him,"[58] or Tui Bua's boast, after

Calypso's raid in 1848, that a warship could not hurt him, "as he could always retire to the mountains, leaving his empty village in their possession."[59] Wilkes himself had burned Opotuno's village in an attempt to intimidate him, but the chief had laughed to see the common people punished on his behalf.[60]

The problem was not that the French or the Americans had an answer that Britain did not; there is no evidence that islanders found bombardment any more "salutary" with French or American colors flying. The problem was British confusion about the existence of international law in the Pacific islands and whether there was any justice in enforcing it. In some situations, British captains wanted to make it clear that they acted as the accredited representatives of their country, and the decks of their ships were part of Britain itself. The naval court held by Vernon and Williams at Samoa in 1858 was completely illegal: Williams did not have even a civil magistrate's powers, and naval courts were designed to try cases involving British subjects and British maritime law, not to condemn and execute foreigners. Even so, Williams assured Commodore Loring that *Cordelia*'s activities at Samoa "were only taken that the ends of Justice might be obtained."[61] Perhaps he or Vernon had read the journals of George Vancouver and knew how the captain had avenged the murder of members of his supply ship *Daedalus* by holding a trial in the Sandwich Islands as though he were a judge on the King's Bench. This was Vancouver's way of showing that he meant to do justice, but no matter how carefully he organized the ritual of a courtroom trial, others inevitably viewed the spectacle through different eyes; even his own officers "saw the shams and the absurdities."[62] Although chiefs from Waikiki volunteered to execute Vancouver's prisoners, they did not necessarily follow his reasoning. Nor were all islanders the same. In Samoa, where different sensibilities prevailed, Captain Vernon could not even get an audience for his drumhead execution.

While humanitarians debated the implications of sovereignty, the traders' champion, the *Sydney Morning Herald,* swept all legal qualms aside:

> In serious matters of this kind the public are not to be cajoled by questions of legal casuistry. They do not accurately know, neither do they much care, where one jurisdiction begins or where it ends, but they know that by the Constitution a power exists somewhere to call those to account who murder and mutilate British subjects, and when occasion arises they desire to see that power put in force.[63]

Here is a vivid example of the contradictory impulses that made the issue of naval punitive action so charged. A desire for vengeance and the exhibition of power scorns the niceties of law but then, pulling back from what seems like an endorsement of anarchy, searches for justification "by the Constitution."

Naval officers themselves found the legal ambiguities of their situation so worrying that descriptions of their activities as "policing" or the expansion of "British authority" are inappropriate. Whose laws did naval officers police, and on what authority? Behind the debate about humanitarianism lay contradictory definitions of British national identity. The *Southern Cross* guessed that other newspapers supported Markham's punitive raids not because they were convinced of their usefulness, but out of an "abject fear of being accused of sentimentalism."[64] Given the barbed criticism of writers like Lord Pembroke, such fears seemed justified. The earl, who championed the maligned labor recruiters, wrote in the spirit of those who complain today about "political correctness," confessing when he heard about the humanitarian excesses of the Royal Navy, "I have had ideas on native policy that I dare not utter in the latitude of Exeter Hall, and the era of the nineteenth century."[65] Humanitarians themselves were at a disadvantage when they could offer no simple, cure-all proposal to stand against the supposed deterrence of force. Amid the media sensation of Commodore Wiseman's mission-supported raids on Tanna and Eromanga, the Rev. J. Graham declared in the *Sydney Morning Herald* that "there must be something better than the military power to civilize the South Sea islanders." The *Herald's* editor, however, decided that the "loud and awful form" of Wiseman's actions was preferable to the "sickly humanity" of his detractors.[66]

Some never wavered in their humanitarian dedication. A. W. Murray, looking back over his establishment of mission stations in New Guinea, was convinced that he had never been attacked because he was never armed. In his view, "what we are to others, they are to us."[67] John Erskine, who had done so much to establish a tradition of benevolence on the Australian Division, had called for *Rosario's* reports to be published for Parliament, telling the secretary of the APS that "there are many officers who can't or won't see that they are sent among these islanders as 'messengers of peace' but who take the first opportunity that offers of trying to impose on the natives an exhibition of their power."[68] However, other officers had experienced challenges to their principles that Erskine never faced. A bitter Captain Loring, frustrated by the apparent mockery of his restraint at Tanna in 1857, confessed privately to the First Lord of the Admiralty that "these Savages do not understand the meaning of forebearance & the really humane object is to prevent future Murders."[69] The tangible loss of two crewmen also made Loring fear accusations of cowardice. His report to the Admiralty noted that, "but for the loss of Mr. Tupper and Wm Kennedy, I should have considered the day's work of destruction of property sufficient, But it now became advisable to show that this loss had nothing to do with our retiring, and on the following day we relanded and committed further destruction."[70] Loring's guesses about what the Tannese might think tell us less about them than about his own state of mind. He did not want to lose face, and he linked the use of force with the maintenance of personal and professional prestige.

There was a serious division of opinion in the missionary community too, especially after the *Curaçoa* episode. Bishop Patteson and the Melanesian Mission moved quickly to dissociate themselves from Paton and the other Presbyterian missionaries who had "urged the commodore to redress their wrongs."[71] It is true that the Presbyterians were more often in favor of naval reprisals than members of the other societies, but they were also the pioneering resident missionaries in the New Hebrides, Banks Islands, and other western island groups. The LMS in the Loyalty Islands and the peripatetic Melanesian Mission never faced the same dangers. However, it was not only fear that prompted men like John Paton and James Gordon to encourage naval retaliation. Both refused to leave their stations when invited to do so by their naval visitors; both seemed to be men who enjoyed courting danger. In the New Hebrides Mission's petition to Wiseman, Paton listed the roll of missionary martyrs in Eromanga, beginning with John Williams, and seemed to be savoring the mission's reputation for stubborn courage. "The natives count up how many white men they have killed without ever being punished," he wrote, "and say that it is all lies about a man of war coming to punish them."[72] Paton and his colleagues now requested "such steps as will most effectually prevent a repetition of similar scenes, and act so as to prove himself a terror to evil doers, and a praise to them that do well."[73] Here was the familiar invocation of naval knights-errant; the problem was that they were being asked to do battle against islanders for the benefit of white men. Humanitarians in New South Wales and Britain were outraged, writing a flood of newspaper articles that prompted Paton to complain that he was "probably the best-abused man in all Australia, and the very name of the New Hebrides Mission stinking in the nostrils of the People."[74] The published journal of one of *Curaçoa*'s lieutenants criticized Paton and Gordon for "the unctuous language of cant" and "exaggerated accounts of sundry attempts on their lives."[75] The APS devoted an article to Wiseman's activities, quoted extensively from an Australian newspaper hostile to the commodore's actions, and concluded that British subjects who chose for whatever reason to live and work in "barbarous countries" must do so at their own risk.[76]

Another Presbyterian missionary to find himself notorious was Peter Milne of Nguna. In March 1871 several Australian newspapers published the allegations of John Irving, chief officer of the schooner *Jason*, who claimed that while he was recruiting Nguna islanders in January, Milne had come down to the beach with one of his Samoan teachers "and by signs desired the natives to fire upon us, which they accordingly did."[77] The New Hebrides Mission was horrified by the wide and uncritical publicity given to Irving's accusations and to rumors of a naval investigation. Milne denied any connection with the story, suggesting that two of his Samoan teachers may have been responsible, and the synod forwarded a report on the incident to Commodore Stirling.[78] Stirling decided that Milne had not instigated the attack on the *Jason*, but the missionary was soon in trouble again: this time for recommending the punishment of the Nguna islanders themselves for killing the crew of another labor vessel, the *Fanny*. The *North Briton* published an extract from Commander Markham's report, which had noted that Milne expressed pleasure on hearing that *Rosario* might visit again the next day and "that if a few shot and shell . . . were thrown in it would have a salutary effect upon the natives as they seem to have a very poor idea of the power of a man-of-war."[79] Milne said later that he didn't specify "shot and shell," admitting that he had encouraged Markham "more than I ought to." He also expressed satisfaction that the Royal Navy had established a reputation as "a terror to evildoers, and the praise of them that do well," nearly a direct quotation from Paton.[80] Whatever Milne's intentions had been, they backfired; the two Nguna men he took as crew for his first island tour in 1870 warned other islanders (behind his back) "that before a missionary came to Nguna they had houses but that now they were all burned."[81] Whether the missionaries liked it or not, their role as informants was obvious to island observers.

Robert Codrington, who succeeded Patteson as head of the Melanesian Mission, condemned the way the Royal Navy made "the killing of a white man a crime to be heavily punished, without any knowledge of the reason of his death," especially when the Royal Navy's primary mission, as he saw it, was the defense of islanders against white men. He deplored actions like Commander Markham's not only because they ran contrary to the late Bishop Patteson's wishes, but also because they left "the impression that these little men of war go about to protect the traders and not the natives."[82] However, just as missionary activity in Melanesia was changing with the expansion of the Presbyterian society, so the Royal Navy's self-image was adapting to new circumstances. By the 1860s the navy was changing out of all recognition. The backlog of older officers was clearing, and men could obtain commands and promotions faster, at a younger age.[83] There were more ships for them, too: the extra vessels attached to the Australia Station during the Maori Wars were retained, and four small gunboats were added to patrol the labor trade in the early 1870s.

The new influx of commanders often had a different attitude. Captain Fremantle's comments about a "high and chivalrous feeling" were made in 1856 as he compared the Nelsonian officers of his own generation to what seemed like a new breed of cynical opportunists. Younger generations always seem to disappoint their elders, but this was a time when the influence of humanitarianism was declining in British society at large. Earlier captains could find prestige in the exhibition of virtue, but for later officers, reputation seemed to depend increasingly on the demonstration of power. Captain Blake, for example, decided that the armed warriors coming down to the beach at Havannah Harbour had been "emboldened by the appearance of our turning away" as the *Falcon* maneuvered around the harbor. After his punitive raid, he was satisfied that the islanders were in no doubt about the Royal Navy's "slaying power."[84] He believed that islanders despised restraint and exploited perceived weakness; the truth is that he despised those things himself. According to the missionaries, Commodore Wiseman had "thought that his honour was at stake" at Tanna, and John Geddie remarked that this new preoccupation with prestige "sweeps away at one stroke the character which we have been endeavouring for years to establish, as ambassadors of the Prince of Peace."[85] Likewise, Markham's bombardment of Nukapu baffled Bishop Selwyn, who joined Bishop Codrington of the Melanesian Mission in wondering "why he did not go away, when he saw friendly communication impossible."[86] Markham's explanation indicates his own worries: "What would every one have said & what would the natives have said? That I was afraid to attempt landing and that a Man of War had been beaten off by these savages."[87] The show of force was both an assertion of power and a reinforcement of personal courage: two powerful reasons for defending punitive expeditions even when there was little evidence of their effectiveness. Doubts were swept aside by a new confidence in "power whose action is found to be speedy, certain, and irresistible"[88] and that, even if it failed to teach islanders the desired lesson, would deal with worries about what everyone would have said at home.

Varying definitions of power and prestige were struggling for the control of British national symbols, too. In an 1854 article, the *Illustrated Sydney News* declared that "wherever the British flag cruizes it should carry with it protection and redress for those who may be wronged by British subjects."[89] Others, however, believed it represented British pride rather than British benevolence, as in Markham's remark that "the British Flag was not to be assailed with impunity"[90] and the *New Zealand Herald*'s comment that Markham could not "have gone quietly away after his boats and the British flag had been fired on."[91] The *Morning Post* agreed that "the measures which were taken by Commander Markham for upholding the British flag" seemed justified.[92] On the contrary, said the *Telegraph,* "the British flag lies draggled in the blood of the poor natives."[93] Since historians have so often described naval patrols as "showing the flag," it is worth emphasizing that this phrase implies a unity of purpose that the evidence does not sustain. As with so many other aspects of British naval activity in the south Pacific, detailed study reveals how the navy's perceptions of its duty came from a changeable and contradictory cultural background. When England's mission was to set an example of justice and civilization, force was counterproductive; when that mission became the pursuit of prestige and honor, force seemed the best way to accomplish it. What never changed was the sense of personal responsibility naval captains assumed over each situation they were faced with. Some of the younger knights-errant were beginning to question the older code of Christian chivalry, replacing it with a more vigorous one of their own. But there was one thing they all agreed on, and that was the exclusiveness of their maritime Round Table. No other men should usurp the paternal influence that seemed theirs by right—especially white men of dubious "respectability"—and Commodore James Goodenough would be willing to annex Fiji to prove it.

→→ *9* ←←

The Triumph of Tradition

B Y the time Britain accepted the sovereignty of Fiji in 1874, thirty-four years
had passed since the Treaty of Waitangi in New Zealand. Other cession
offers had been made and refused, while France colonized Tahiti, New Caledonia, and the Loyalty Islands with hardly a murmur from London. Colonial
officials in New Zealand, and later Australia, joined various mission and humanitarian organizations in appealing for protectorates in the islands, but the British
government usually resisted opportunities for territorial expansion. The 1874
Fijian deed of cession might therefore seem a new departure for British policy
in the islands, although economic theories of empire suggest that developments
in Fiji were the result of decades of British capital investment there.[1] A Pacific-
centered scholarship has scrutinized the roles played on the spot by Commodore
Goodenough and Cakobau's advisor John Bates Thurston. David W. McIntyre
explored Goodenough's journals in a 1962 article, revealing much about Goodenough's own perception of his duty in Fiji but also, to some extent, adopting
Goodenough's hostile view of Thurston.[2] Two years later, Deryck Scarr countered with an article based on Thurston's correspondence and, in turn, tended
to adopt Thurston's dislike of Goodenough.[3] John Bach's more recent treatment
of the cession seeks to swing the pendulum back in Goodenough's favor by praising the commodore's "preference for an orderly society conducted on British
principles over that of a remote war-torn and savage island."[4] Historians Peter
France and J. D. Legge have taken yet another approach, emphasizing the conflict
between different British groups in and about Fiji and the powerful role British
perceptions played in the creation of colonial Fiji's political and economic
identity.[5]

Against an extensive historiographical background, then, this final chapter seeks to do two things. First, it will locate Britain's decision to rule Fiji within the general framework of humanitarian representations of the Pacific islands, an argument very different from existing political or economic analyses. Second, it will move beyond the issue of side-taking in considering the relationship of Goodenough and Thurston. It is not a question of promoting one or other of these men as more influential, enlightened, or racist than the other. Instead, I will examine the way imperial benevolence constructed the roles of these two protagonists. Scarr's work argues persuasively that Thurston, and not Goodenough, was more concerned with what Fijians themselves might want. But this does not make Goodenough a racist cipher. Instead, it invites a closer scrutiny of the commodore's humanitarian self-image and its relationship to the Royal Navy's creation of British authority in the islands. We already know that humanitarian representations of island conditions were made without much reference either to British political policy or to islanders' own perspectives. The story of victimized islanders and villainous white men was self-validating, permitting naval knights-errant to ride to the rescue with a preconceived sense of authority. As John Galbraith put it in his 1963 article on humanitarianism and empire: "The preoccupation of Exeter Hall was not with understanding; it was engaged in a crusade against evil, and understanding would have blurred the issues."[6]

Seen in the context of imperial benevolence, the events of 1874 in Fiji become only one more scene in a familiar drama. Goodenough was preceded by a generation of British naval officers who believed that Fijians were being manipulated by unscrupulous white men. Most of his immediate predecessors had been concerned mainly with the planters, whose growing numbers and assertiveness were aggravating racial tension in Fiji from the late 1860s. Goodenough preferred to concentrate on the white men associated with the Cakobau government, especially John Bates Thurston, who seemed to be usurping the navy's preeminence in deciding what was best for the islanders.

After Rewa defeated Bau in August 1853, Cakobau's claim to the title "Tui Viti" appeared doomed. Hoping that his British friends could save him and under pressure from George Tupou of Tonga[7] Cakobau invited James Calvert to Bau and began studying the Bible. His conversion to Christianity in 1854 guaranteed the continuing loyalty of the Royal Navy and earned him vital Tongan military support, but declining health made his own survival uncertain. The death of Qaraniqio, chief of Rewa, in January 1855 helped Bau and its Tongan allies defeat Rewa at Kaba in April, but Cakobau's victory owed little to his own efforts or leadership. Qaraniqio died without naming a successor, and the Tongans were able to force a battle while Rewa was divided by an internal power struggle.[8] Many conflicting interests were being drawn into the Fijian situation. Even as he offered Ovalau to Britain through Captain Denham in 1855, Tui Levuka was writing to the French governor of Tahiti requesting French protection and offering to convert to Catholicism. This tactic proved a remarkably successful way of sharpening the Methodist misson's interest in the British cession proposal, but it is likely that Tui Levuka hoped only to enhance his own authority; he once boasted to Calvert that "my right hand is a Wesleyan, my left is a Catholic, but my whole body is Feejeean."[9]

As Cakobau's situation grew more precarious, Fiji's European community began to assert itself. The residents of Levuka had been hoping for British colonial rule since 1852 and the New South Wales proclamation against "enslaved" women. They seemed to believe that their interests would be better protected in a formal colony; meanwhile, the Royal Navy continued to ignore their petitions for retaliation against Fijians for robbery and murder, and in September 1853 they decided to take matters into their own hands. Overreacting to the rumored plunder of one of their trading vessels at Malaki, an island under Bauan influence, they combined forces with Tui Levuka to launch a revenge attack. The American commercial agent J. B. Williams, who had recently moved to Levuka, blamed British naval negligence for "taking no cognizance of past depredations and therefore encouraging Fijians to further violence."[10]

Williams took advantage of an American warship's visit in order to press claims of his own against Cakobau. The agent's house and store had been damaged by fire during a Fourth of July celebration in 1849, and Williams had tried unsuccessfully to persuade other American captains to exact compensation for his rapidly inflating losses. He now brought a claim of $43,000 before Commander Boutwell of the USS *John Adams,* arguing that "Tui Viti" was responsible for the behavior of all Fijians. Boutwell agreed and threatened the chief with imprisonment in America until he put his mark to an agreement to pay within two years.[11] Boutwell's superior officer, the humanitarian Captain Thomas Bailey of the USS *St. Mary's,* objected at once to this summary proceeding and wrote privately to Calvert to assure the Fijian missionaries that he would do his best to have the debt canceled.[12] Boutwell was summoned to an inquiry in Washington, but unfortunately for Cakobau, American politicians were not prepared to devote additional resources to investigation, and the "American Debt" was allowed to stand. Eighteen years later the captain of the USS *Tuscarora* renegotiated the payment schedule, but Cakobau was simply unable to pay. It was from this position that he received representatives of the Polynesian Land

Company in 1868, became interested in their offer to pay his debt in exchange for land, and was softened by their champagne. Commodore Lambert was horrified to see how much land and authority Cakobau signed away and was disgusted by the role of missionary William Moore, who had translated for Cakobau while pursuing trade and land speculations of his own.[13] John Bates Thurston, the acting British consul, helped persuade Cakobau to repudiate the charter and though the Company made payment toward the American debt, it obtained only a relatively small grant of land at Suva harbor in return.[14]

There were other threats to Cakobau's political and financial position in the meantime. The Tongan influence in Fiji was worrying. King George's brother Ma'afu was proving an ambitious and capable governor in the eastern Lau islands and had begun to intervene in the civil conflicts on Vanua Levu. King George lingered in Fiji himself after the battle of Kaba, touring Ma'afu's area of influence with a large and hungry entourage and leaving food shortages and rumors of Tongan imperialism in his wake. Fiji's missionaries were not idle; recognizing these developments as a threat to Cakobau's kingship, they moved rapidly to settle differences between the Tongans, Tui Levuka, Cakobau, and Ovalau's white population. Able to operate from Bau itself since Cakobau's conversion, Calvert—who was acting more and more like a consul—asked his superiors in London to bring the 1855 cession offer directly to the attention of the Foreign Office while Captain Fremantle went through Admiralty channels. "Rubbish will be cleared away," said Calvert, "and I hope a proper foundation laid for the English taking possession of Ovalau & indeed of all Feejee."[15] Calvert and Fremantle were in complete agreement about the "rubbish," and both saw their mission as the protection of Fijians from white exploitation. Fremantle was easily impressed by expressions of idealized affection and respect for Britain, declaring after a visit to Ovalau's Christianized villages that "they almost imagine they have no real friend but the English." He called on his government to offer protection to these beleaguered islanders who "all seem to look wistfully for sympathy and protection" from Britain.[16] It is worth comparing Fremantle's language to that of earlier naval visitors. Where captains Worth and Erskine had admired a robust Cakobau at the height of his power, Fremantle now spoke of "helpless Chiefs" looking "wistfully" for rescue. Fremantle believed that Cakobau's authority had to be strengthened quickly if the Tongans and the American debt were not to overwhelm him.

After Commander Boutwell's departure, Cakobau decided to renew his cession offer, and when William Pritchard arrived as Fiji's first British consul in 1858, the chief found a ready ally. Pritchard took the new offer to London in person later that year, making large claims for Cakobau's legal competence as Tui Viti by referring to the way he had been recognized as such by a succession of British naval officers.[17] It is important to understand how much of a moral quandary this new offer presented to government officials of both political parties in Britain. Lord Carnarvon, parliamentary secretary of the Colonial Office during the brief Tory government of 1858–1859, wrote that "it is painful to refuse [these] unfortunate islanders who are terrified by the licence of French sailors and the annexation ideas of the U.S. Government."[18] Prime Minister Palmerston's Whig administration found the issue no less difficult, choosing the safe option of sending a commission to Fiji to report.

Meanwhile, Pritchard had returned to Fiji and persuaded Cakobau and other leading chiefs to endow him with magisterial powers as head of a consular court to hear the complaints of British subjects. Something similar was already under consideration by the British government, but the Foreign Office was horrified by Pritchard's unauthorized initiatives. Fiji's missionaries too were treating the consul with increasing disdain. This relationship followed the usual pattern of mission-consular relationships and recalled Pritchard's father's difficulties in Samoa. Son William had become a trading consul despite the Foreign Office's instructions, and in this case, Fiji's missionaries were competitors rather than detractors. Although the LMS in Samoa conducted their own trade in tropical products, its scale was nothing like James Calvert's or John Binner's activities in Fiji. Political rivalry between mission station and consulate was also more pointed in Fiji, where the possibilities of centralized government and British rule had raised the stakes. Pritchard later claimed that the missionaries supported the 1858 cession proposal because "they were already the greatest power in Fiji" and hoped to retain this preeminence. By securing magisterial powers after his return from London, Pritchard seemed deliberately to be threatening that status; in his memoirs, the consul declared that in 1858 he had "secured the controlling power in the group in my own hands."[19] This clash of British wills discounted the importance of the indigenous polity, of course, but my main point here is that consuls could never win such battles for the moral high ground.

The extent of missionary influence over Fiji's naval visitors prompted the British government to issue strict instructions to the men appointed to the investigating commission. Retired colonel W. J. Smythe and naturalist Berthold Seemann were cautioned against allowing their admiration for missionaries "to affect your judgment upon the questions of policy. . . . The hope of the conversion of a people to Christianity, however specious, must not be made a reason for increasing the British dominions."[20] These instructions reflected the government's shock and disappointment at the outbreak of the Maori Wars in New Zealand, a series of conflicts that would shake humanitarian hopes that properly managed colonization would not alienate the indigenous population.[21] "In other words," I. C. Campbell has noted, "ideological considerations (whether nationalistic or humanitarian) were not to predominate in consideration of the issue."[22]

However, the instructions were not necessarily proof against the influence of Governor Denison of New South Wales; when he met Smythe in Sydney, the governor spoke of his fear that Pritchard intended to invite floods of white settlers to Fiji.[23] With warnings about the consul's sinister plans ringing in his ears, Smythe sailed for Fiji via Auckland, where settlers and the Maori were in open warfare. Smythe's opposition to Pritchard and the cession proposal was undoubtedly influenced by these factors and by the missionaries who provided him with "ready and efficient assistance" during his inquiries. Smythe was already prepared to worry about Fiji's two hundred white residents, most of them British, who "do nothing to civilize or improve the natives; on the contrary, they have in many instances fallen to a lower level." These were familiar references to white savagery, which Smythe now linked to Pritchard through the consul's trading activities. Recommending Pritchard's removal, Smythe added that the consul's background (meaning his birth outside Britain and his Samoan wife) made him unsuitable for his post and that only a native government "aided by the counsels of respectable Europeans" would allow Fiji to survive increased contact with the outside world.[24]

Smythe's description of Pritchard was thrown into sharp relief by the very different observations of Berthold Seemann, who befriended Pritchard during the inquiry, stayed in touch with him, and later helped to edit his memoirs. He published his own favorable response to the cession proposal, noting that it had the support of "all naval men who knew anything about the subject."[25] Although Seemann admitted that Cakobau's claim to the Tui Viti title was tenuous, he realized that the more orderly members of Fiji's European population (including Pritchard) were trying to create a Kingdom of Fiji in hopes that the islands would achieve "a state of peace and order when many were tired of the occasional anarchical atmosphere which suited the less respectable Europeans."[26] By this time, in order to underscore their opposition to Pritchard, Fiji's missionaries had become more favorable to the Tongans. Seemann agreed with the consul that British rule would be the best way of containing both Tongan and Methodist ambitions. Calvert was already presenting himself as an alternative consul; in 1862, when Captain Jenkins of HMS *Miranda* brought official word of Britain's rejection of the cession, Calvert reported, "Our aim will be at once to get a Native Government—with a Tongan element in it."[27] In such a government, the traditional relationship between Methodist missionaries and Tongans might increase mission influence over Fijians and precipitate Pritchard's downfall. For Captain Jenkins had come not only to announce the refusal of cession, but also to inquire into the consul's conduct. Jenkins found himself being led gently but firmly in the direction that his chief interpreter, Calvert, wished him to go. Calvert reported to his superiors that he "took good care that Capn J's light was increased daily" until the captain ceased to trust Pritchard and "so now looks to me."[28]

Pritchard was responsible for many of own his troubles: the consulate and all its files had burned down in a mysterious fire just before Jenkins arrived, and the consul's vanity and business activities had made him many enemies. Confident that the consul was doomed, Calvert left Fiji for England, where he met with old friends (including Admiral Erskine) in hopes of influencing the choice of Pritchard's replacement. But the Foreign Office had commissioned a retired army captain, Henry M. Jones, as the new consul. Jones, who arrived at his post in 1864, was not a natural politician, and his despatches were "reminiscent more of the parade ground than of the chambers of diplomacy."[29] However, he met the most important qualification of his office: he was not a trader. He also encouraged several leading chiefs, including Cakobau and Ma'afu, to form a nominal confederation in 1865, but like its New Zealand counterpart in the 1830s, traditional rivalries undermined the confederation's political unity, and it was a dead letter by the time Jones left Fiji in 1867.

The new acting consul was Jones' friend John Bates Thurston, another advocate of indigenous political reform and a new target for mission resentment. Thurston had been a labor vessel crewman and a cotton planter during his early days in Fiji; worse, he was a Roman Catholic. These things alone would be enough to set Calvert and the others against him, but then came the murder of Thomas Baker by the interior people of Viti Levu in 1867. The missionaries admitted that Baker had been reckless, and Thurston tried to show his good faith by accompanying a Bauan expedition to capture the murder suspects. Unfortunately, the Bauan forces failed to retrieve the suspects and were driven from the area. Calvert made pointed references to Thurston's Catholicism in his reports of the expedition, as if that alone explained its failure, and began campaigning to bring about Thurston's replacement.[30]

Visiting naval officers supported Thurston, to the point of providing a landing force to help Cakobau's forces quell an uprising on Viti Levu. There had been problems for years on the upper Rewa River; the interior of Viti Levu was populated by groups who owed no loyalty to the coastal people, or to Bau. With Commodore Lambert's help, Thurston decided to make an example of the town of Deuka. Because *Challenger* drew too much water to reach it directly, Lieutenant Charles Brownrigg and Thurston took three of the ships' boats upriver. The sailors and marines quickly became exhausted after dragging the boats and their heavy carronades into position in heavy rain, and they ran out of ammunition while the Fijians simply kept retreating into the bush. After burning the town in frustration, Browrigg found his party under ambush and abandoned the expedition with four wounded on his side and an unknown number of Fijian casualties.[31] The Admiralty reacted sharply to a case that appeared certain to attract controversy. Minutes on Lambert's report called it "a very questionable proceeding," suggesting that it would only aggravate Fijian hostility toward white settlers in the area. It certainly seems as though the Deuka people misunderstood the lesson Thurston and Brownrigg meant to teach. The town's warriors had assembled to confront the boats, but when Brownrigg fired what was meant to be a warning shot, "the result of this humanity was not as desired or expected."[32] Interpreting the shot as an opening of hostilities, the Fijians withdrew into cover and began returning fire. Brownrigg admitted that the burning of Deuka had "little effect"; the Fijians made a spirited attack on his boats every time they grounded in the shallow Rewa.[33]

This collaborative though ineffectual expedition reflected important aspects of the traditional naval viewpoint: support for Cakobau's leadership, control of misbehaving white men, and hopes for Fijian self-government. However, the growing complexity of the situation in Fiji was pulling the humanitarian position apart. Calvert, corresponding with Erskine in an attempt to have Thurston removed, also persuaded the admiral to criticize the Admiralty for endorsing *Challenger*'s "burning and killing for no purpose."[34] The Admiralty had its own reservations, as we know, but Erskine and his colleagues in the APS were upset by what seemed like naval injustice, just as they would be after the *Rosario* bombardments in 1871. Their hostility to Thurston also ensured that he was replaced rather than promoted; not content with criticizing the *Challenger* episode, Erskine had also persuaded his friend Childers, First Lord of the Admiralty, to confront the Foreign Office with Thurston's "extraordinary doings." Childers noted that Thurston was "probably a trader," thus defining him as irresponsible. He added that when Cakobau insulted Thurston during an argument, Thurston had responded by getting Captain Lyons to summon the chief aboard HMS *Charybdis* and lecture him until he apologized.[35] Childers threatened the Foreign

Secretary with questions in Parliament unless Thurston was replaced with a more suitable consul, and E. B. March duly arrived in Fiji in 1869. Humanitarians had once again deposed a "trading" consul whose conflict with missionaries made him seem hostile to the humanitarian crusade and had replaced him with a man they found more respectable.

We know how reluctant Britain was to recognize indigenous authority in the Pacific islands, despite its protestations about sovereignty; the situation was no different when Cakobau proclaimed himself Tui Viti in June 1871. Unlike previous attempts to rule from Bau, Cakobau was now able to obtain a degree of support from Ma'afu and the white planters. King Cakobau and his white resident advisors organized a district government system that was acceptable to most other Fijian chiefs and created a legislative assembly for which any man resident in Fiji could stand: a genuine attempt at mixed government.[36] However, Consul March objected loudly to what he regarded as the deliberate infringement of his prerogatives, and his despatches were full of allegations about legal and financial scandals. When Thurston reentered public life as Cakobau's chief secretary and minister for foreign relations, March's outbursts grew more personalized and his demands for magisterial jurisdiction more forceful. March's sympathy for opponents of the Cakobau government went to extremes; he refused to condemn or even warn the Levuka residents who formed a branch of the Ku Klux Klan.

Naval visitors to Fiji supported the new government; the Foreign Office had suggested that it be treated as a de facto authority until the issue of formal recognition was resolved.[37] Support for Cakobau was a long-established tradition in any case, and the Pacific Islanders Protection Act of 1872 gave added urgency to the need for united action against the labor trade. There was also the presence of retired Royal Navy lieutenant George Austin Woods: once "Magnificent George" to his messmates and now premier of Fiji. Woods had left a marine surveying job in New Zealand in 1871 after hearing about German designs on Fiji; these turned out to be baseless, and there was no work for a survey officer. Cakobau, always fond of naval officers, took a liking to Woods and adopted him as a member of the Bauan ruling family. Most of Fiji's white settlers, though complaining that Cakobau was too lenient with Woods, tolerated him as a relatively neutral premier when the Cakobau government was formed.[38]

After the departure of Captain Douglas and HMS *Cossack* in September 1872, Thurston wrote to the Fijian government agent in New South Wales, praising Douglas' help with the "disaffected class" at Levuka and hoping "that the internal power of the Kingdom may be now looked upon as thoroughly consolidated."[39] Although Douglas privately believed that Cakobau was only "by courtesy styled a King," he wished to endorse the government's authority and expressed his support by providing Cakobau with full royal honors, including a twenty-one-gun salute.[40] The following year, Captain Chapman of HMS *Dido* intervened at Thurston's request to stop what appeared to be an incipient race war in the Ba district. This area had been rapidly settled in recent years and lay between the territories of coastal and interior chiefs. It was a situation ripe for misunderstanding: the settlers were planning to arm themselves and take reprisals for various Fijian provocations. Chapman heard the settlers' stories of theft, arson, and assault but warned them against taking the law into their own hands and required them to sign a pledge of good behavior. To demonstrate his support for the Fiji government, he arrested one of the settler "hawks," De Courcey Ireland, and imprisoned him aboard *Dido*.[41] He also agreed to deport Thomas White, president of the British Subjects Mutual Protection Society at Levuka and, according to Thurston, the man responsible for organizing the Ku Klux Klan.[42] So far, the navy was acting out its traditional opposition to white settlers; Chapman lectured the Ba planters about "the error they were committing, being aliens in the Country in taking up arms against the lawfully constituted authorities."[43] The contradictions of this position were not lost on the settlers. Planter A. B. Brewster noted that Britain refused to recognize the Cakobau government but appeared to authorize its representatives to arrest Ireland for opposing what it now described as the lawful authorities. If they were lawful, why were they unrecognized?[44]

The legal crisis regarding the status of British subjects under the Cakobau government was the last straw for Consul March. "I shall be compelled in sheer despair to quit Fiji," he had told London in 1871, and after prolonged struggles with white residents (including Thurston) who were determined to claim Fijian nationality, he resigned his post in 1873. When Commodore Stirling arrived in HMS *Clio* later that year, he was scandalized to find the consul archives under the care of an unscrupulous man named Michell. Stirling and Thurston agreed to appoint *Clio*'s paymaster Alfred Nettleton as acting consul.[45] So concentrated was the navy's presence in Fiji by this time that, when Captain Simpson arrived in *Blanche* later in August, there were five warships in the group. Although Simpson forbade the sale of consular ammunition to government forces and warned Thurston against taking any action against settlers that might lead to bloodshed,[46] there was still no noticeable rift in the relationship between navy and government and no doubt, in the settlers' minds, that the Royal Navy was as set against them as ever. Planter E. J. Turpin observed bitterly that Captain Simpson was "being feted and *tea'd* till he does as he is required by the *'Matanitu.'* "[47]

Controlling the labor trade was a strong motive for the navy's ongoing cooperation with Thurston and its unprecedented intervention at the British consulate. Stirling's rationale for appointing Nettleton acting consul was based on his own interpretation of the "British interests" he was required to protect. He reported, "I have taken upon myself the responsibility of these unusual steps, believing that they were absolutely required for the welfare of British Interests in Fiji, and the regulation of the 'Labor Traffic.' "[48] Stirling was making a humanitarian judgment about which interests were to be considered legitimate, and he believed that the members of Cakobau's government should have that status. This was not the only interpretation of the current circumstances, however. As the situation in Fiji grew more complex, so did the humanitarian response to it. In 1872, during the same session of Parliament that passed the Pacific Islanders Protection Act, Sir William McArthur proposed British rule for Fiji. McArthur, who was related to the Methodist superintendent of south Pacific missions and had been well briefed in advance by Calvert and March, told the House of "a state of society as horrible as any existing upon the face of the earth" in Fiji, where the incompetence of Cakobau's advisors was allowing unscrupulous labor recruiters to flourish.[49] McArthur's colonization proposal was anathema to the government, but his allegations of slave dealing in Fiji moved Admiral Erskine to second the motion and other APS members of the Commons to support it. As in 1858, the government's response to the situation showed some turmoil of conscience. Edward Knatchbull-Hugessen, parliamentary undersecretary to the Colonial Office, was privately in favor of McArthur's motion and lamented the financial and political restraints that had (apparently) brought British imperial expansion to an end.[50] Prime Minister William E. Gladstone had rejected McArthur's proposal, but Knatchbull-Hugessen rebutted the motion in Parliament so ambivalently that the *Times* observed: "Officially bound to curse he ended up by nearly blessing it altogether."[51]

In Fiji, the Cakobau government organ, the *Fiji Gazette,* denounced McArthur's motion as "mock philanthropy,"[52] underlining the most important point at issue. Whose philanthropy was real? There were now two positions claiming humanitarian high ground: Thurston and his naval supporters working together to control interracial violence and labor abuses within the framework of the Cakobau government, on the one hand, and the more old-fashioned alliance of missionaries, the APS, and naval patrons like Erskine, who favored direct British intervention, on the other. Gladstone's response to McArthur's motion contained the essence of the whole problem, when he declared that the government refused to annex any territory "without the well-understood and expressed wish of the people to be annexed . . . authenticated by the best means the case would afford."[53] Which position represented the "authentic" wishes of Fijians? Which British voices would define what was "well understood" by them? Thus a man like Thurston could have two characters: "an honest man among rogues," as Captain Palmer had called him, and the manipulative self-seeker Commodore Goodenough would believe him to be: both designations made by men who considered themselves humanitarians with islanders' interests at heart.

Acting consul Michell, the man replaced by Commodore Stirling's paymaster, had written several resentful reports about Thurston for the APS. Michell agreed with Erskine that unscrupulous white advisors were encouraging Cakobau to embark on wars of conquest and enslavement throughout Fiji. He accused the British navy of allowing vessels to carry enslaved laborers "under the guns of a British man-of-war" and of preoccupying itself with adventures in the interior (like Captain Chapman's) when it should have been enforcing the Pacific Islanders Protection Act. "It is the duty of the Imperial Parliament to ascertain why our naval power has been used to bolster up Thakombau's tottering government," he wrote, claiming the white population was pursuing its own sinister agenda behind the navy's back.[54] Even as the APS was publishing Michell's accusations, a government commission consisting of Commodore James Goodenough and the new consul, E. L. Layard, was considering another cession offer. Goodenough, who completely dominated the inquiry, was an old-school naval officer, closer to Erskine than to Stirling, whose reaction to Fiji would have momentous consequences.

Prime Minister Gladstone was as eager as his predecessor Palmerston had been to use a commission of inquiry as a delaying tactic and was delighted to find that Goodenough was a churchman after his own heart who exhorted his crews to teetotalism and greater piety.[55] Goodenough recalled of their meeting that "Mr. Gladstone even more than Lord Kimberley said that I must report what wd. be most conducive to law & order and the best interests of the people black and white."[56] This was very telling: defining issues of "law and order" was one of the most conspicuous parts of the Royal Navy's mission in the Pacific islands. It was also significant that Goodenough visited the Wesleyan Methodist mission headquarters to gather information before leaving for the south Pacific.

Goodenough clashed with Thurston from the beginning, because his interpretation of the navy's mission predisposed him to. Before reaching Fiji, he had visited New Zealand and received the attentions of various New Zealand officials angling for a New Zealand protectorate in Fiji. In an attempt to outdo any adverse Australian influences, Julius Vogel and other members of the New Zealand government flattered the commodore by making him a member of their executive council.[57] Goodenough met Sir George Grey, who said he had been agitating for British rule in Fiji for years. He also met the brother of a Fiji planter, who warned the commodore that British rule was "only promoted by mean poor whites" in Fiji and that "the present Govt should be supported." Goodenough was bewildered, regretting how "the difficulties seem to thicken" regarding Fiji;[58] and in an attempt to concentrate his mind, he began a reading program that included Governor Philip's account of New South Wales, William Ellis' *Polynesian Researches*, John Williams' *Missionary Enterprises*, Erskine, Julius Brenchley's humanitarian account of the labor trade, and the reports of the London Missionary Society. These were standard works from the older benevolent tradition; already Goodenough was looking to the past for guidance about his mission to Fiji.

The commodore's next stop was Samoa, where he behaved in a way at odds with claims that he was always out of sympathy with attempts at indigenous government.[59] By the time of Goodenough's visit in November, Samoans had listened to decades of advice from missionaries and naval officers about the need to centralize in order to deal with outsiders. The LMS missionaries, in particular, had been interfering to an unprecedented extent in the conferral of titles during a series of civil conflicts.[60] They and British Consul Williams were now backing the claims of Laupepa to the office of Malietoa; they had manipulated the visit of HMS *Brisk* in 1866 by giving Captain Hope a false impression of Laupepa's status and encouraging him to hold peacemaking negotiations in Laupepa's favor.[61] By 1868 two rival Malietoas had been appointed in an attempt to halt the conflict, but Laupepa responded by trying to seize power as "king" of his district on Upolu. His rival promptly did the same, precipitating a war that ended in stalemate in 1873.

Samoa's European population had been expanding to include planters and substantial commercial interests, and when the civil war ended in 1873, seven of Samoa's highest chiefs formed a government known as the Ta'imua, which they hoped would act to preserve the sovereignty of their country. The American advisor Albert B. Steinberger arrived later that year on a reconnaissance mission for the U.S. government, bearing recommendations about the creation of an American protectorate. The Ta'imua authorized Steinberger to consult his government about the cession of Samoa while they began creating a system of representation and administration, but the United States repudiated Steinberger and refused to recognize the Ta'imua.[62] The British government had also refused to recognize the government, despite the pleas of Consul Williams; but Good-enough plunged in with typical recklessness. He decided to salute the Ta'imua and their new flag, referring to the Royal Navy's encouragement of central gov-ernment in Samoa and justifying his decision with reference to "ill-disposed British subjects" whose ambitions needed curbing.[63] The commodore's actions would force Britain to recognize the Samoan government in 1875, at a time when it was still resisting such recognition for the more comprehensive and long-standing Tongan government under King George Tupou.

Although his wife's brother was a planter in Fiji, Goodenough had no guar-anteed sympathy for planters as a group, as Deryck Scarr has suggested, nor can he be dismissed as a mindless racist.[64] He fulminated against the planters of Samoa, declaring that their Melanesian laborers led "precisely the slave life of Brazil."[65] Some of the settlers excused their conduct by declaring that Melane-sians were racially inferior; Goodenough responded by comparing them to the Australian squatters who exterminated Aborigines found on "their" property. "I have as good a right to a personal opinion as you," the commodore told one planter brave enough to take him on, "and I have formed my opinion on the study of books on Polynesia."[66] This was one of the most telling remarks in his journal, revealing the extent to which he took direction from his humanitarian reading.[67] It also helps explain the most conspicuous aspect of his actions in Samoa and one of the most traditional naval pastimes of all: hostility to consuls deemed unworthy of their moral responsibilities. Dismissing John Williams as "a weakly, puny little wretch" unequal to the great protective task before him,[68] Goodenough sailed for Fiji, full of wrath against self-seeking and incompetent white men in the islands, determined to dominate any stage on which he found himself.

It was unfortunate that Thurston's first action after the commodore's arrival was to try to obtain information behind his back from Captain Simpson. Simp-son went at once to Goodenough with Thurston's letter, and a series of missed appointments did little to improve the atmosphere between the two men. Neither did the unexpected appearance of a new Fijian constitution in the New South Wales press. The commodore went a step beyond the criticisms of March, McArthur, and the APS by deciding that the government's exploitation of Fiji was operating on more than one level. Thurston was using Cakobau to wage war on his white opponents, Goodenough believed; and this made Fiji's recent constitutional changes seem sinister. Many of Thurston's dealings with the Royal Navy in 1872 and 1873 had involved attempts to maintain law and order at Levuka, where opponents of the government and organizations like the

British Subjects Mutual Protection Society were causing havoc. But Thurston had also prepared a new constitution that would increase the power of ministers and reduce white representation in the legislative assembly, changes that Captain Simpson had convinced him not to promulgate until after Goodenough and Layard had arrived. When the new constitution appeared in the New South Wales press, Goodenough interpreted it as an attempted coup d'état by Thurston. He decided that the new government had no right to exist without the consent of all those who had played a role in developing the previous constitution and had paid taxes to support it. Before meeting Thurston for the first time, Goodenough had already decided to distrust him. The commodore's fellow commissioner, the new British consul, E. L. Layard, arrived six weeks behind Goodenough, too late to provide a restraining second opinion even if one had been sought. Within days, Goodenough decided that Layard was a cipher; "I shall have to tell Layard what to do in everything," he confided to his journal.[69] What followed was a personalized and acrimonious clash between Goodenough and Thurston that dominated the entire debate about cession.

Goodenough was particularly concerned about Cakobau's military operations. He believed that Thurston was encouraging the chief to extend his authority beyond anything sanctioned by traditional Fijian politics. One recent campaign attracted his particular attention. In February of 1873, planter William Burnes, his family, and twenty-six of their laborers were murdered at Vunisamaloa in the volatile Ba district of Viti Levu. Other planters, unwilling to trust the government to defend their interests, appeared ready to take matters into their own hands and to declare war on the mixed-race government force if necessary. Preferring not to risk a battle with the settlers, the force withdrew to investigate the murder of a Fijian at the inland village of Nakorowaiwai, a place that frequently launched attacks on other parts of the district. When the troops occupied the village, neighboring Fijians seized an opportunity for revenge and massacred about one hundred fifty of the Nakorowaiwai people. Civil war seemed imminent, and the government began a series of vigorous military campaigns, capturing several of the men accused of the Burnes murders. The men were tried at Levuka and sentenced to penal servitude. Other Fijians accused of various crimes were captured at Nubutautau and tried at Koro after Goodenough's arrival: many of these were also sentenced to hard labor.[70] Already sensitized to the possibility of slavery in the Pacific islands because of his observations at Samoa, Goodenough leapt to conclusions at once. He told Thurston that the interior people had never recognized Cakobau's authority (which was true enough) and had been made to acknowledge it by force "while fighting for their independence." Although he recognized the need to maintain stability in the interior, he objected to the designation of Cakobau's opponents as "rebels." He objected even more to their sentencing and issued a notice in December to all British subjects in Fiji that "the hiring or engaging of these men is an Act of Slavery."[71]

Thurston was astounded when the commodore seemed unable to grasp the seriousness of recent conflicts between settlers and Fijians, and the sincerity of government attempts to mitigate it. He was also concerned about losing the valuable naval support he had enjoyed since the 1860s. Goodenough refused to acknowledge that his statements were a departure from the supportive ones of his predecessors and angrily defended his place in the naval tradition of support for Cakobau. He qualified this, however, by declaring that although Cakobau had the right "to coerce his native subjects" in order to maintain order, he could not indulge in what appeared to be slave dealing; nor could he employ force against Englishmen.[72] This view was a familiar one: British representatives called for islanders to form their own governments and then refused to recognize their authority over British subjects.

Goodenough's interpretation involved a typically paternalistic emphasis on European agency; his definition of Thurston as an unscrupulous manipulator required a passive, vulnerable Tui Viti. The commodore's journals are full of references to "old Cakobau," a wayward chief who had broken his word once about upholding the constitution and might do it again if led astray by the devious Thurston. This approach was similar to Captain Fremantle's endorsement of the 1855 cession with reference to "helpless chiefs." It also recalls Prime Minister Gladstone's approach to the Fiji question. During the 1872 annexation debate, he had told Parliament that the British government could only accept free and open cession "authenticated by the best means the case would afford."[73] This ambiguous requirement was reflected in Gladstone's private chat with Goodenough about determining the interests of "law and order." As always, the issue was defining what was "authentic," desirable, or respectable in British eyes and, by extension, deciding what was illegitimate. Combining images of a helpless Cakobau with his hostility to the government's recent military campaigns, Goodenough questioned the government's ability to make crown grants of land in the king's name, when the land was "more or less the property of the Chiefs and people" of other districts.[74] He took a dim view of Cakobau's threats against Ritova of Macuata, who was refusing to attend meetings, and defied the government by sending HMS *Renard* to provide moral support for Ritova.[75] When Thurston objected to this interference with Cakobau's management of internal affairs, Goodenough replied that the Royal Navy had "constantly intervened between him and a portion of the Fijian people, generally in his interests, and that, in fact, he owes the consolidation of his power to the intervention of English Officers."[76] So determined was Goodenough to make Thurston and the other ministers into the villains of the piece that he described them as taking it "upon themselves" to set Fijians against Englishmen, a description from which Cakobau and the wider context of Fijian politics had completely disappeared.[77]

Cakobau had certainly benefited from the prestige and support of naval attentions over the years, although his family had been in the ascendant before regular naval visits began. To say that the Royal Navy had helped invent and consolidate his kingship was one thing, to claim that this gave naval officers the right to overrule him was another. But Cakobau had chosen advisors, Thurston among them, whom Goodenough identified as dangerous. Believing that the navy knew what was best for Fiji, the commodore declared that, "in the interest of the good order and good government of these islands," his own views should prevail.[78] The definition of law, order, and justice was a precarious business; Goodenough and Thurston were on opposite sides of an old debate. Thurston's long letters to the commodore attempted to explain the government's legitimacy and the right of Fijians and Britons to create a mixed government for a mixed population. For Goodenough, a man more interested in order than in law and swayed by notions of heroic naval intervention, such technicalities were overruled by higher moral imperatives that only he was qualified to interpret.

The missionaries kept a relatively low profile during Goodenough's visit; his dealings were mainly with Thurston and the other ministers, and there was no need for interpreters. However, when it appeared that Cakobau and the other chiefs were deciding against cession in February 1874, the Fiji mission committee petitioned Consul Layard. Modestly assuring him that they were forbidden to interfere with politics in Fiji, they expressed concern that King Cakobau was making a mistaken decision "under the influence and persuasions of those . . . who have not at heart the best interests of the Natives, and the Whites residing here."[79] They pleaded with Layard to maintain a strong naval presence in Fiji, for everyone's protection in case the government collapsed completely. At least one observer was convinced that the missionaries, especially Calvert, had been working as hard as ever to thwart Thurston and bring about cession. Jenkins, who had been promoted to admiral by the time of Calvert's death in 1892, wrote to the Methodist mission society to send his condolences, recalling Calvert's influence on him during his visit to Fiji thirty years earlier. "When the Fiji Islands became an English colony," he wrote, "I thought of sending congratulations to Mr. and Mrs. Calvert."[80]

Just as Jenkins had supported Calvert's criticism of Pritchard and his suspicions about the consul's manipulation of Cakobau, so Goodenough accepted criticism of Thurston and the others he believed were leading Cakobau astray. The Foreign Office had warned the commissioners against any statements or behavior that might "compromise or prejudice the ultimate decision to be taken,"[81] but Goodenough did things his own way. It was clear to Thurston that the commodore had already decided on British rule, and he confronted Goodenough with Britain's contradictory approach to the former and present governments. He stated bluntly that as long as Britain refused to recognize and assist Cakobau's kingship, while also refusing to administer the government itself or permit other British subjects to do so, "so long will a majority of British subjects refrain from uniting with Fijians in the effort to establish a National authority before which both races shall stand upon an equal footing."[82] Thurston wanted Goodenough to understand that this lack of support was encouraging the more militant settlers to continue defying the government in hopes of forcing the creation of a colony where they could exercise more power than enjoyed at present.[83] The ironies of this were observed by the *Fiji Gazette*, which quoted from Erskine's published description of the potential of Fijians for self-improvement. Now that a mixed government under a Fijian king seemed possible, "instead of that sympathetic assistance from England—which was so freely tendered on parchment," Cakobau was being "met with ridicule, slanderous assertions, and malignant obstructions" by Erskine himself, among others.[84] As Thurston put it, the British government was pursuing a policy that "can only terminate in the total destruction of a Government it almost called into existence."[85]

The situation recalled the predicament of W. T. Pritchard when he found himself vilified for attempting to create a mixed court and supporting Cakobau's status as Tui Viti. Just as Fiji's missionaries and their naval supporters had resented Pritchard's "usurpation" of influence they preferred to exercise themselves, so Thurston's critics seemed bent on destroying him and the government that gave him prominence. From his Taveuni plantation, Thurston had once described himself and other planters as "a kind of hedge or boundary between Heathenism and Christianity, between Barbarism and Civilisation."[86] Such a liminal space was dangerous; observers like missionaries and naval officers preferred clear-cut distinctions between the respectable and the disreputable. The beachcombers of the early nineteenth century, too, had attempted to occupy the boundary between two worlds and had paid for it by being denied the name of Englishmen. Perhaps Thurston understood and accepted this, writing in 1872 to his friend Captain Hope: "I am Fijian now."[87]

What status Thurston had lost in Goodenough's eyes the settler community gained. At the beginning of 1874 Goodenough learned that De Courcey Ireland was suing Captain Chapman for wrongful arrest, and the Admiralty had rebuked the captain for what it regarded as an unjustified intervention in Fiji's internal affairs. The crown law officers in London added that "H.M.'s officers should be instructed not to interfere except for the protection of British interests."[88] The identification of legitimate "British interests" was once again at the center of naval activity in Fiji, and Goodenough was determined to monopolize that process. He agreed that Ireland should not have been arrested, nor should Chapman have believed Thurston's claims that settlers were indiscriminately shooting at Fijians on their property. Declaring that Chapman should have listened to the planters' complaints, Goodenough delivered the ultimate accolade: the government should have adopted "a more conciliatory method of dealing with a respectable body of Englishmen."[89] Like Captain Home's recognition of "the Town of Levuka" in 1852, Goodenough's identification of the settlers as "respectable" marked an important redistribution of approval. This was the same process of inclusion and exclusion that we saw during the fracas about mixed-race households in Levuka. Then, missionaries and Levuka's white residents vied for leverage as the true civilizers of Fijian women, each regarding the other as destructive intruders. Now, Goodenough and Layard used issues like the "enslavement" of the Nakorowaiwai prisoners to suggest that Fijians needed protection from an exploitative government. The commissioners' instructions had clearly stated that Britain preferred Fijians to be ruled "by a Government which is in any real or even qualified sense their own and indigenous," but they were prepared to intervene if it appeared that the government was incapable of suppressing slavery.[90] Goodenough's shrewd manipulation of this issue was not lost on the progovernment *Fiji Gazette*. In December 1873 it speculated that because the commodore knew the British government's reluctance to accept cession, he had seized "a splendid opportunity, to raise his outcry 'The Fijian Government are Slavers.'. . . What a text for Exeter Hall! How the Wingfields, McArthur's, &c, would howl! . . . And the desideratum of the annexationists would be at once arrived at."[91]

Cakobau did not appreciate the commodore's bullying, resented the relentless meetings about cession, and worried about the machinations of his more restless chiefs, especially Ma'afu. After a particularly tense meeting in March 1874, he and the other chiefs decided to refuse British rule. Disappointed, Goodenough and Layard were convinced that Thurston was behind the decision, and their suspicions seemed confirmed when Cakobau accepted the resignation of all of his white ministers except Thurston. Thurston, in fact, was not opposed to British rule; he merely wished Cakobau and the other chiefs to choose it for their own reasons. In a poignant meeting with the chiefs after they declared against cession, Thurston told them "all their faults and all my doubts. They promised to work and go without pay if I would keep to them. I promised I would do my best for them."[92]

Thurston kept his promise, but he could not overcome Goodenough's hostility and his tendency to treat Cakobau and the other chiefs like recalcitrant children. "They must either trust me or Mr. Thurston," Goodenough declared, proposing a new government with himself and Layard as advisors and warning Cakobau, "You will get into greater trouble if you do not now come to us to consult with us." Cakobau, furious, told the commodore, "This country does not belong to foreigners. It is true foreigners have taught us writing but no one has taught us Fijians chiefs whether to give up our country or not."[93] Goodenough and Layard countered that they were "preparing, although with great reluctance, to assume the temporary Protectorate of the islands." One wonders how reluctant the commodore could be, when he explained his decision by announcing that "the necessary interference of the Senior Naval Officer here, during the past year, has already amounted at times to a virtual protectorate."[94] Invoking what he believed were the special privileges of his service, Goodenough might have been recalling Lord George Paulet and his naval protectorate at the Sandwich Islands. This was too much for Thurston to bear, and he bowed to the inevitable, realizing that statements of this kind had effectively destroyed the government. He advised Cakobau that a renewed cession offer was now the only possible option. Suspicious of Goodenough's motives and worried by his support for the settlers, Thurston also suggested a conditional cession that offered only the government and not the land or people of Fiji.[95]

Goodenough's prejudices and ambitions were obvious to the British government, and ministers worried that the commodore's enthusiasm was dragging them into an unnecessary and unwelcome commitment. British officials were wary of the conditional nature of the cession—it sounded more like the vague "protectorate" requests of past decades—and Foreign Secretary Lord Carnarvon declared that Goodenough had "so strongly a predisposition" for British rule that the government should seek a second opinion from the Governor-General of New South Wales. Sir Hercules Robinson duly left Sydney in August 1874 to make inquiries and was authorized to accept the cession only if it was made unconditionally. New South Wales had taken an official interest in Fiji since Denison's day, and members of the Legislative Assembly had voted to encourage Britain to accept the cession of 1858.[96] Emigration from Australia to Fiji and the activities of the Polynesian Company had attracted the interest of the Victoria government as well, and in 1870 the Victorian Legislative Assembly considered ruling Fiji itself. This was followed by a resolution of the Australian intercolonial conference, urging Britain to reconsider cession. The Colonial Office rejected this option, but indicated its willingness to discuss New South Wales control over Fiji; Governor-General Belmore, embroiled in labor trade disputes and aware of the Cakobau government's struggle to maintain its authority, declined to pursue it. New South Wales' commercial community did not give up agitating for some sort of British rule in Fiji: one of their spokesmen was Henry Parkes, a leading merchant and Sir Hercules Robinson's Colonial Secretary. Parkes had long been in favor of a trans-Pacific mail route with a coaling station at Fiji, and when the Fijian government's problems increased in 1873, he persuaded Robinson to cable the Colonial Office and recommend British rule to prevent anarchy.[97] This recommendation complemented Goodenough's activities, showing that Robinson was not a disinterested third party when he arrived in Fiji. It was no surprise that Robinson endorsed the commissioners' recommendations and hoisted the British flag in October 1874. "You have laid the foundation of a new English nation as the vanguard of Polynesian civilization," a delighted Parkes assured him.[98]

The cession of Fiji was far more than the story of personal animosity between Thurston and Goodenough or of racist collusion between the white settlers and their puppet commodore. Goodenough arrived at Fiji with decades of naval intervention at his back and a paternalist attitude that inclined him to oppose non-missionary white men like Thurston. It was a background full of contradiction about issues like indigenous government and the definition of British interests. The struggle between Thurston and Goodenough was patterned by similar clashes in the past between naval officers and consuls or government agents. Ironically, it was Thurston who would reach greater heights in the future. When Sir Hercules Robinson formed a provisional government for Fiji, he made Thurston the Colonial Secretary. Sir Arthur Gordon, Fiji's first governor, was equally impressed by Thurston's expertise and dedication, and confirmed the appointment. Thurston later went on, in turn, to the governorship of Fiji, leadership of the Western Pacific High Commission, and a knighthood. Goodenough, for his part, visited Fiji for the last time when he took Gordon there in 1875. Already one of Queen Victoria's most reckless knights-errant, still searching for a role heroic enough to hold him, the commodore would go from Fiji to his death.

Epilogue

GOODENOUGH and Gordon arrived at Fiji in June 1875, and the commodore marveled at how anxious Gordon was to sleep ashore among the mosquitoes. "He must be a romantic sort of fellow," Goodenough mused, but "no great or permanent harm ever came of over earnestness."[1] This would be a fitting epitaph for the tragic encounter to come at Santa Cruz, when Goodenough put himself and his crew at needless risk to demonstrate his own earnestness.

The Santa Cruz people had driven HMS *Sandfly* away from Carlisle Bay with poisoned arrows in 1874, and the commodore wanted to see if he could "make friends with the unfortunates, who seem most friendly and anxious to receive, by coming out to us in canoes and looking as if they wished to please."[2] The islanders had seemed friendly enough at first; a little light trading began, and Goodenough's party visited the village nearest their landing place. Then a man beckoned them to follow him down the beach toward another village. Goodenough and a few others began to follow; but when they saw how far away the village was, the commodore decided it was imprudent to go any further on foot. He "tried to explain" why he was turning back; Lieutenant Perry recalled that he "made friendly signs of goodbye" and then ordered everyone into the boats.[3] The islanders became agitated, waving their weapons, and one man fired an arrow into Goodenough's side. Who can know how those "signs of goodbye" were read by people who believed in sorcery? A shower of arrows followed, hitting two other men as the boats pulled away. The marines returned fire, stopping the attack and wounding one man. "My only object in firing was to stop their arrows," Goodenough wrote in his journal, and once safely aboard he intended "to do nothing to them."[4]

Lieutenant Hosken recalled that the junior officers "burned to be avenged," and they badgered the commodore until he compromised by ordering marines to burn the village.[5] Lieutenant Perry later told the Admiralty that Goodenough had forbidden any further action against "these poor savages still misunderstanding all attempts at conciliation, and themselves probably misunderstood."[6] This was a shrewd diagnosis. Goodenough had risked his life for a gesture on the beach, a place where gestures had meanings beyond his control. The effects of Santa Cruz poison were equally uncontrollable: all three wounded men developed tetanus. Goodenough, knowing he could not survive, began making preparations. It is not every man who can stage his own death, and the commodore (consciously or otherwise) emulated that most famous of naval farewells: Lord Nelson's. Goodenough's spiritual reflections and admonitions, coupled with the tearful sentimentality of his audience, challenge our current notions of masculine professionalism. But it is easy to suggest that a man's faith is empty posturing and impossible to prove its sincerity. At the very least, Goodenough's exhortations to faith and forgiveness must have helped others to cope with the shock of his death, and that was no bad motivation for a ship's captain. He first summoned all the officers privately and invited them to "come now one and all and kiss me to show that you all wish me well." Even through the pathos of Victorian deathbed prose, it seems clear that Lieutenant Hosken at least was deeply moved, not only by the dying man, but because "he met with his wound whilst trying to benefit the natives who killed him."[7] Not all the officers gathered round felt that this had been a worthwhile pursuit. Lieutenant Henderson of the *Sappho* talked with some of them later and confided to his journal that they felt the commodore had been needlessly reckless. High-minded principles were "very good and very right, but you cannot expect savages to look at these things in the same light," he wrote, putting his finger on the problem of "salutary" exhibitions of European behavior, benevolent or otherwise.[8] The *Times* would agree on 26 August, declaring that Goodenough had fallen victim to "imprudence," just as Bishop Patteson "fell a victim to his noble enthusiasm."[9]

The boundary between foolhardiness and heroism is thin, and if Goodenough's gestures were open to question on the Santa Cruz beach, he knew how to drive them home aboard his own vessel. He had himself carried to the quarterdeck, reclining there where all the crew could see him. He spoke of God's love and the need for forgiveness; then the petty officers were allowed to shake his hand. Goodenough was sending a clear message about how he saw himself and how he wanted to be remembered. It was clearly received. "One of the most touching incidents of his decease," wrote the *Newcastle Chronicle,* "is the fact that, like NELSON, at Trafalgar, our Commodore gathered round him his officers and men, and, in his dying moments, bade them, one and all, a sad, affectionate farewell."[10] Other commentators went further. Remembering Goodenough's injunction against retaliation at Santa Cruz, the *Allawarra Mercury* saw the image of Christ on the cross saying, "Forgive them, for they know not what they do."[11] Goodenough was not a Great Man, but he knew how to act like one, and that was enough for his apotheosis.

At the beginning of this study, I considered naval pilgrimages to places touched by Cook; and we come back to the Great Navigator now, nearly a century after his death. Just before leaving Sydney for the last time, Goodenough had unveiled a monument to Cook at Randwick. In the press reports of the commodore's death, many recalled the tribute he had paid to Cook's "devotion to duty," which "was one which shows perseverance, constancy, courage, and generosity."[12] Time and Victorian hindsight was making both men into symbols of what Britain wished itself to be: that is what heroes are for. *The Saturday Review* observed, "We seem to be carried back a hundred years, and to mourn afresh the untimely fate of Captain Cook,"[13] and ran both men's biographies in its obituary for the commodore.

Ordinary seamen Edward Rayner and Frederick Smale, both aged eighteen, were also laid to rest in Sydney's North Shore Cemetery, but little was said about their two young lives, except that it had been their privilege to die with such a noble man. We do not know what stories their friends and families told in order to give their deaths meaning. The death of Goodenough, for its part, added shape to Britain's imperial destiny. We have seen much discussion of "duty" among officers as they contemplated their responsibilities in the Pacific islands. We know how different aspects of duty could conflict in life, but death was more forgiving. On 17 November 1881, the *Pall Mall Gazette* announced the unveiling of a bust of Goodenough in the Painted Hall at the naval college in Greenwich. It added that the commodore had "combined the ideal qualities, sometimes supposed to be contradictory, of true Christian, perfect gentleman, and thorough seaman: in life the representative of the best type of naval officer, and in death the emblem of conduct and duty." Here was the perfect, gentle knight; an epitome of Christianization and Civilization that no living man could ever achieve. As *Pearl's* chaplain explained after the commodore's funeral, "We should never have known what he was had he not died."[14] Who had he been to the Santa Cruz islanders? What had he *really* been like? It no longer mattered.

As for what he seemed to be, he died as he had lived: perversely quixotic, tilt-ing at windmills to the last.

The Pacific spoke to the hopes and fears of many Europeans. It inspired stories of a great southern land, rich beyond belief, which drew generations of sailors around the geographical barrier of the Americas. The financial speculation of the "South Sea Bubble" grew and burst, while equally speculative geographers encouraged islands to swoop like swallows across maps that could not hold them. The Age of Discovery ushered in a new Pacific: one more definitively mapped, but peopled by islanders whose beauties and cruelties captivated the European imagination. For Britons, the voyages of Captain Cook seemed to trace a path to empire. Traders sought oil, fur, and sandalwood among islands whose positions could now be fixed. Missionaries took ships to follow the voice of God and to make their own stories of peril and salvation. By the early nine-teenth century the south Pacific had an enormous impact on Britain, enhanced by the images published in exploration narratives and missionary journals, and eagerly consumed by an increasingly literate public. Sunday school children felt they knew the King of the Cannibal Islands and mourned the martyrdom of John Williams in darkest Melanesia. British colonies in Australia and New Zealand were demanding an oceanic destiny of their own. As Henri Baudin points out in *Paradise on Earth*, the "Age of Discovery" did not end with Cap-tain Cook and his contemporaries; instead, Europe continued to interpret the outside world through metaphor and fantasy that remained "infinitely variable, infinitely interpretable."[15] Commerce, Christianity, politics, and technology prompted various degrees of collaboration or resistance from islanders and from Britons themselves, as different definitions of Britain's mission in the Pacific competed with each other.

British benevolence in the Pacific islands was based on the assumption that islanders had the same potential for "civilization" as any other human beings. The duties of Britain's naval representatives were, therefore, much more than "policing." Officers believed they had moral obligations, as members of a Christian and civilized society, to help primitive peoples improve themselves. Island leaders, especially in Polynesia and Fiji, could be useful catalysts for "reforming" island societies, something naval captains were determined to do without violence or coercion. In other areas, especially Melanesia, they believed the activities of British traders to be a greater threat than island "savagery." Images of victimized islanders moved easily between stories about European beachcombers, sandalwooders, or labor recruiters, but finding the means to protect islanders through legal or political action remained elusive. Kingmaking fell short of treaties that recognized sovereignty; calls for the prosecution of British villainy were thwarted by the rules of evidence and due process. Above all, the definition of "British interests" was hampered both by the disparate nature of British activities in the islands and by uncertainties at home about imperial identity, prestige, and honor. Nothing illustrated this better than the problematic nature of "gunboat diplomacy" in the south Pacific. The annexation of Fiji in 1874 would usher in a new era of formal British involvement in which the Royal Navy would play a significant role. But the form of its self-assigned mission was shaped in the early decades of the century and would change in detail, rather than substance, over time.

The need for greater debate about humanitarianism's history is acute: relationships between benevolent intentions, armed force, and national prestige remain as precarious today as they were over a century ago. We read familiar calls in newspapers for humanitarian intervention abroad, often perceived as "the West's" moral obligation, followed later by accusations of impotence and emasculation when humanitarian efforts fail to secure their objectives. Moreover, one person's humanitarian intervention is another's neocolonialism. We still wrestle with the legacy of imperial benevolence and its contradictory imperatives. I have suggested that the conduct of any armed service rests on perceptions of duty derived from a changeable and often ambiguous cultural background. When England's mission was to set an example of justice and civilization in the south Pacific, force was counterproductive, but when the mission was defined as the pursuit of prestige and honor, force seemed the best way to accomplish it. There was no golden age of Victorian absolutes rejected—for good or for ill —by the twentieth century. Instead there was emotive debate, as there is now, about society's expectations of those who "show the flag" abroad.

Notes

INTRODUCTION

1. Quoted in David Lowenthal, *The Past Is a Foreign Country* (Cambridge: Cambridge University Press, 1985), xvi. The same point has been made by anthropologists, as in Paul Rabinow's call "to anthropologize the West" in "Representations Are Social Facts: Modernity and Post-Modernity in Anthropology," in James Clifford and George E. Marcus, *Writing Culture: The Poetics and Politics of Ethnography* (Berkeley: University of California Press, 1986), 241, and Nicholas Thomas' "colonial projects," which he sees as "culturally and strategically complex"; *Colonialism's Culture: Anthropology, Travel and Government* (Cambridge: Polity, 1994), 106.

2. Greg Dening, "A Poetic for Histories: Transformations That Present the Past," in Aletta Biersack, ed. *Clio in Oceania: Toward a Historical Anthropology* (Washington: Smithsonia, 1991), 355.

3. John Bach, *The Australia Station: A History of the Royal Navy in the South West Pacific, 1821–1913* (Kensington, N.S.W.: University of New South Wales Press, 1986), x, 69.

4. The Earl [of Pembroke] and the Doctor [G. H. Kingsley], *South Sea Bubbles*, second ed. (London: Bentley and Son, 1872), 286.

5. [F. E. Manning], *Old New Zealand* (London: Bentley, 1876), ix.

6. O. K. H. Spate, *Paradise Found and Lost* (London: Routledge, 1988), 224.

7. John M. Ward, *British Policy in the South Pacific, 1786–1893* (Sydney: Australasian, 1948), 165.

8. The debate about islander agency in Pacific Studies continues unabated; see Tom Brass, "The Return of 'Merrie Melanesia': A Comment on a Review of a Review," *Journal of Pacific History* 31:2 (1996), 215–223. Rather than an attempt to identify what islanders "really" experienced, my own treatment of the labor trade is an exploration of British interpretations of events.

9. K. R. Howe, "The Future of Pacific Islands History: A Personal View," in Brij Lal, ed.,

Pacific Islands History: Journeys and Transformations (Canberra: Journal of Pacific History, 1992), 225–242; K. R. Howe, Robert C. Kiste, and Brij V. Lal, eds., *Tides of History: The Pacific Islands in the Twentieth Century* (St. Leonards, N.S.W.: Allen and Unwin, 1994), xi–xiv; Peter Hempenstall, " 'My Place': Finding a Voice within Pacific Colonial Studies," in Lal, *Pacific Islands History,* 70–73; Nicholas Thomas, "Fear and Loathing in the Postcolonial Pacific," *Meanjin* 51:2 (1992), 265–276, and *Colonialism's Culture.*

1 MEASURES OF BENEVOLENCE

1. See Ronald L. Meek, *Social Science and the Ignoble Savage* (Cambridge and New York: Cambridge University Press, 1976), 131–176; P. J. Marshall and Glyndwr Williams, *The Great Map of Mankind: British Perceptions of the World in the Age of Enlightenment* (London: Dent, 1982), 258–298, and Glyndwr Williams, " 'Savages Noble and Ignoble': European Attitudes towards the Wider World before 1800," *Journal of Imperial and Commonwealth History* 6:3 (1978), 300–313.

2. Niel Gunson, *Messengers of Grace: Evangelical Missionaries in the South Seas, 1797–1860* (Melbourne and Oxford: Oxford University Press, 1978), 96, 195–214; I. C. Campbell, "Savages Noble and Ignoble: The Preconceptions of Early European Voyagers in Polynesia," *Pacific Studies* 4:1 (1980), 45–59; and K. R. Howe, "The Intellectual Discovery and Exploration of Polynesia," in Robin Fisher and Hugh Johnston, eds., *From Maps to Metaphors: The Pacific World of George Vancouver* (Vancouver: University of British Columbia Press, 1993), 245–262.

3. Marshall and Williams, *Great Map of Mankind,* 214. Materialistic means of classification would continue into the twentieth century; Meek, *Social Science and the Ignoble Savage,* 2.

4. René Gonnard, *La légende du bon sauvage* (Paris: Librairie de Medicis, 1946), 121.

5. William Ellis, *Polynesian Researches* (London: Fisher, Son and Jackson, 1829), vol. 1, 42–53.

6. Quoted in Marshall and Williams, *Great Map of Mankind,* 191–192.

7. James Prichard, *Researches into the Physical History of Man* (1813), edited with a valuable introduction by George W. Stocking (Chicago and London: University of Chicago Press, 1973); also see Prichard's *The Natural History of Man,* third ed. (London: Hippolyte Baillier, 1848).

8. George W. Stocking, *Victorian Anthropology* (New York and London: Macmillan, 1987), 49–52.

9. Robert Gordon Latham, *The Natural History of the Varieties of Man* (London: J. Van Voorst, 1850), 12.

10. "The Black Races of Polynesia," *Journal of Civilization* 23 (London, 1841), 357.

11. Quoted in Gunson, *Messengers of Grace,* 199.

12. Howe, "The Intellectual Discovery of Polynesia," 256–258.

13. Much work has been done on humanitarianism in the British domestic context reminding us that we must consider gender and class as well as racism and colonialism when studying this phenomenon. See Ian Bradley, *The Call to Seriousness: The Evangelical*

Impact on the Victorians (London: Cape, 1976); Peter Marsh, ed., *The Conscience of the Victorian State* (Hassocks: Harvester Press, 1979); Boyd Hilton, *The Age of Atonement: The Influence of Evangelicalism on Social and Economic Thought, 1795–1865* (Oxford: Clarendon, 1988); and David Turley, *The Culture of English Antislavery, 1780–1860* (New York and London: Routledge, 1991).

14. The literature on these developments is large and controversial; see Margaret Steven, *Trade, Tactics and Territory: Britain in the Pacific, 1780–1823* (Melbourne: Melbourne University Press, 1983); David Mackay, *In the Wake of Cook: Exploration, Science and Empire, 1780–1801* (London: Croom Helm, 1985); Spate, *Paradise Found and Lost;* Alan Frost, *Convicts and Empire: A Naval Question, 1776–1811* (Melbourne: Oxford University Press, 1980), and his *Botany Bay Mirages: Illusions of Australia's Convict Beginnings* (Melbourne: Melbourne University Press, 1994), 98–109.

15. See Alan Frost, "New South Wales as *Terra Nullius:* The British Denial of Aboriginal Land Rights," *Historical Studies* 19:77 (1981), 513–523, and Jane Samson, "British Voices and Indigenous Rights: Debating Aboriginal Legal Status in Nineteenth-Century Australia and Canada," *Cultures of the Commonwealth* 2 (1996–1997), 5–16.

16. [George Craik], *The New Zealanders* (London: C. Knight, 1830), 432.

17. Jane Samson, " 'Protective Supremacy': The Royal Navy, Pacific Islanders, and the Limits of Benevolence, 1829–1859" (Ph.D. thesis, University of London, 1994), 26–27, 43–45; Bach, *The Australia Station,* 17–18.

18. PRO, ADM 1/5531, "Special Instructions for the Captains and Commanders of the Squadron Employed on the East India Station," by Rear Admiral Capel for the guidance of captains dealing with Indian authorities, dated 26 March 1835.

19. PRO, ADM 13/2, Admiralty to Seymour, 31 January 1833.

20. Ibid.

21. See Augustus Earle, *Nine Months Residence in New Zealand in 1827* (Christchurch: Whitcombe, 1909; first publ. 1829); and Otto von Kotzebue, *A New Voyage round the World* (London: H. Colbum and R. Bentley, 1830). Missionaries countered with William Ellis, *A Vindication of the South Sea Missions* (London: F. Westley and A. H. Davis, 1831); William Orme, *Defence of the Missions in the South Sea and Sandwich Islands* (London: B. J. Holdsworth, 1827); and John Williams, *A Narrative of Missionary Enterprises in the South Sea Islands* (London: J. Snow and J. R. Leifchild, 1837).

22. PRO, ADM 1/197, Owen to Sandilands, 20 July 1830.

23. F. W. Beechey, *Narrative of a Voyage to the Pacific and Beering's Strait . . . in the Ship "Blossom"* (Philadelphia: Carey, 1832), vol. 1, 286.

24. Earle, *Nine Months Residence in New Zealand,* 136–139.

25. BUL, CMS, C/N/O93, Henry Williams Journals, 10 March 1834.

26. Ibid.

27. Edward Belcher, *Narrative of a Voyage Round the World* (London: H. Colbum, 1843), vol. 1, 266.

28. They issued strict directives about involvement in trade, much to John Williams' disgust; Gunson, *Messengers of Grace,* 115–121.

29. Ellis, *Polynesian Researches,* vol. 2, 78.

30. Ibid.

31. Quoted in Gunson, *Messengers of Grace,* 172–173.

32. SOAS, WMMS, FBN 12/541, Turner to General Secretaries, 23 May 1830.

33. His story was published for children in "A Contrast and Its Lessons," *The Church Missionary Juvenile Instructor* (London, 1862), 35–36.

34. Frederick Walpole, *Four Years in the Pacific in Her Majesty's Ship Collingwood from 1844 to 1848* (London: Richard Bentley, 1849), 372–373.

35. *Journal of Civilization*, 20 (1841), 317.

36. *The Gentleman's Magazine* 100 (1830), 242.

37. SOAS, WMMS, FBN 13/601, Thomas to General Secretaries 11 June 1840.

38. SOAS, WMMS, FBN 13/603, Rabone to Secretaries, 21 November 1840.

39. Ibid. Croker's actions are analyzed more fully below on pp. 66–68.

40. PRO, ADM 1/5548, Home to Cochrane, 15 October 1844.

41. At this time French naval visits were normally confined to a brief annual "tournée des missions" of the most prominent mission stations; Robert Aldrich, *The French Presence in the South Pacific* (Basingstoke: Macmillan, 1990), 81. This neglect would intensify; see Colin Newbury, "Aspects of French Policy in the Pacific, 1853–1906," *Pacific Historical Review* 27:1 (1958), 45–56.

42. PRO, FO 58/69, Erskine to Admiralty, 10 October 1849.

43. John Elphinstone Erskine, *Journal of a Cruise among the Islands of the Western Pacific* (London: Dawsons, 1967; orig. publ. 1853), 395.

44. Ibid., 140.

45. BCRO, FR, 216/F9, Fremantle to Stirling, 6 August 1855.

46. For studies of the relationship between masculinity, neo-chivalry, and empire see "Knights of Empire," in Mark Girouard, *The Return to Camelot: Chivalry and the English Gentleman* (London and New York: Yale University Press, 1981), 220–230; Philip Mason, *The English Gentleman: The Rise and Fall of an Ideal* (London: Andre Deutsch, 1982), 214–221; and Joseph Bristow, *Empire Boys: Adventures in a Man's World* (London: Harper Collins Academic, 1991).

47. PRO, ADM 1/217, Crozier to Hobson, 27 December 1836.

48. PRO, FO 58/59, Blake to Seymour, 30 March 1847.

49. Alice E. J. Fanshawe, *Admiral Sir Edward Gennys Fanshawe* (London: Spottiswoode and Co., 1904), 179.

50. SCL, Selwyn Papers, Box D, George to Dr. Selwyn, 15 April 1850.

51. John Inglis, *In the New Hebrides: Reminiscences of Missionary Life and Work* (London: T. Nelson and Sons, 1887), 308.

52. Many other Britons idolized him as well; see Bernard Smith, "Cook's Posthumous Reputation," in his *Imagining the Pacific: In the Wake of the Cook Voyages* (New Haven and London: Yale University Press, 1992), 225–240.

53. PRO, ADM 1/208, Laws to Admiralty, 11 March 1829.

54. Robert Fitzroy, *A Narrative of the Voyage of H.M.S. Beagle* (London: Folio Society, 1977, first publ. 1839), 289.

55. ML, CY Reel 2538, Journal of the *Sparrowhawk*, entry for 16 September 1839.

56. ML A2881–6, Rev. George Nobbs MSS, Moresby to Nobbs [May 1853].

57. Greg Dening discusses the process of Christian mapping with reference to Spanish and Portuguese explorations in the Marquesas islands; see *Islands and Beaches: Discourse on a Silent Land* (Melbourne: Melbourne University Press, 1980), 9–11.

58. ATL, QMS MSS 1850–51/P, Henry Gabriel Swainson, "Journal of a Cruise in H.M.S. Havannah, 1850" (unnumbered folios).

59. ML, CY MSS 369, Lieutenant Frank Henderson, journal written on HMS *Sappho*, 1875–1876.

60. ML, MS 6658, Lyth Letters, Mary Ann to Mrs. Lyth, 2 December 1837 aboard *Conway*; and ML B570, Hazelwood Journals, 20 August 1849.

61. SCL, Selwyn Papers, Box D, George to Dr. Selwyn, 6 December 1849.

62. BCRO, FR, 92/2, Stephen to Thomas Fremantle, 1 November 1856.

63. William Barrett Marshall, *A Personal Narrative of Two Visits to New Zealand in His Majesty's Ship Alligator* (London, J. Nisbet, 1835). For a fuller discussion of this episode, see Jane Samson, "The 1834 Cruise of HMS Alligator: The Bible and the Flag," *The Northern Mariner* 3:4 (1993), 37–47.

64. *Great Britain Parliamentary Papers* (hereafter *P.P.*), 1836, VII [538], "Report of the Select Committee on Aborigines (British Settlements)," 436–454. Marshall's career would end tragically when he died of fever during the idealistic, ill-fated Niger Expedition to West Africa in 1841. See William Allen and T. R. H. Thomson, *A Narrative of the Expedition Sent by Her Majesty's Government to the River Niger in 1841* (London: R. Bentley, 1848), vol. 2, 22–23.

65. *P.P.*, 1837, VII [425], "Report from the Select Committee on Aborigines (British Settlements)," 22.

66. SOAS, WMMS, FBN 13/603, Journal of Francis Wilson, 30 June 1840.

67. Walter Lawry, *Friendly and Feejee Islands: A Missionary Visit to Various Stations in the South Seas in the Year 1847* (London: J. Mason, 1850), 71.

68. ML, MS A836, Lyth Letters, Richard to Mrs. Lyth, 5 November 1853.

69. Erskine, *Journal of a Cruise*, 1.

70. Quoted in Jocelyn Linnekin, "Ignoble Savages and Other European Visions: The La Pérouse Affair in Samoan History," *Journal of Pacific History* 26:1 (1991), 8.

71. PRO, ADM 1/208, Laws to Admiralty, 11 March 1829.

72. R. D. Bethune, "Samoan Group, or Navigator's Islands," *Nautical Magazine* 11 (London, 1840), 755.

73. Erskine, *Journal of a Cruise*, 58.

74. PRO, ADM 1/217, Crozier to Hobson, 27 December, 1836.

75. RGS, JMSS, Henry Worth "Account of a Visit to Feejee."

76. APL, Grey Letters, E23, Erskine to Grey, 22 September 1849.

77. PRO, ADM 1/5617, Home to Admiralty, 20 December 1852.

78. *The Sandwich Island Gazette*, February, 1839, cited in "The New Hebrides," *Nautical Magazine* 9 (1839), 605–606.

79. ATL, QMS MSS VIG 2081, Philip D. Vigors, "Private Journal of a Four Months Cruise through Some of the 'South Sea Islands' and New Zealand in H.M.S. Havannah," 121.

80. Erskine, *Journal of a Cruise*, 393.

81. See "The First Missionaries to Britain," *The Journal of Civilization* 23 (London, 1841), 252–254; and "Ancient Britons," ibid. 24 (1842), 110–112.

82. Compare Erskine, *Journal of a Cruise*, 213, with its reference to Scott's *Rob Roy*, with Daniel Tyerman and George Bennett's references to Scott's *History of Scotland* in their *Voyages and Travels round the World* (London: London Missionary Society, 1841), vii.

83. PRO, ADM 1/5617, Home to Admiralty, 20 December 1852.

84. Boris Ford, *The Romantic Age in Britain* (Cambridge: Cambridge University Press, 1992), describes the Victorians' "complex set of attitudes to history—as the place of a past barbarity and yet also as the place whence we can derive such confidence as we have in a continuous future"; 28–29.

85. APS, *Extracts from the Papers and Proceedings of the Aborigines' Protection Society* 4 (London, 1839), 99. Published on the first page of each annual report, the object of the society was altered in 1842 to read as follows: "The object of this Society is, to record the history, and promote the advancement of Uncivilized Tribes."

86. See Saxe Bannister, *British Colonization and Coloured Tribes* (London: W. Ball, 1838); and William Howitt, *Colonization and Christianity: A Popular History of the Treatment of the Natives by the Europeans in All Their Colonies* (London: Longman, Orme, Brown, Green and Longman's, 1838).

87. PRO, CO 201/175, CO to Admiralty, 14 June 1826; and PRO, ADM 1/4246, CO to Admiralty, 5 January 1831, enclosing Darling to CO, 12 August 1830.

88. Marshall, *A Personal Narrative*, 107–111.

89. This episode is discussed in Peter Adams, *Fatal Necessity: British Intervention in New Zealand, 1830–1847* (Auckland and Oxford: Auckland University Press and Oxford University Press, 1977), 68–69, 164; and in Claudia Orange, *The Treaty of Waitangi* (Wellington: Allen and Unwin, 1987), 21–22.

90. Quoted in John Beecham, *Remarks upon the Latest Official Documents Relating to New Zealand* (London: James Nichols, 1838), 5.

91. *P.P.*, 1838, XXI [680], "Report from the Select Committee of the House of Lords, Appointed to Inquire into the Present State of the Islands of New Zealand and the Expediency of Regulating the Settlement of British Subjects Therein."

92. Quoted in Beecham, *The Latest Official Documents*, 12.

93. Patricia Burns, *Fatal Success: A History of the New Zealand Company* (Auckland: Heinemann Reed, 1989).

94. Adams, *Fatal Necessity*, 41.

95. Ibid., 59–64.

2   WHITE SAVAGES

1. Quoted in Marshall and Williams, *Great Map of Mankind*, 280.

2. James Cook, *The Journals of Captain James Cook:* vol. 3, *The Voyage of the Resolution and Discovery, 1776–1780*, ed. J. C. Beaglehole (Cambridge: Hakluyt, 1967), 174.

3. PRO, ADM 1/2371, "Owners of Vessels Engaged in the Southern Whale Fishery" to Admiralty, 23 July 1836. The Admiralty forwarded copies of this letter to the East Indies and Pacific stations. For background on the current controversy about the merchant service, leading up to the Merchant Shipping Acts of mid-century, see A. G. Course, *The Merchant Navy: A Social History* (London: F. Muller, 1963), 195–221.

4. Howe, *Where the Waves Fall*, 103.

5. Caroline Ralston, *Grass Huts and Warehouses: Pacific Beach Communities of the Nineteenth Century* (Canberra: Australian National University Press, 1977), 24.

6. PRO, ADM 1/34, Baker to Admiralty, 22 November 1830.

7. PRO, ADM 1/204, Owen to Admiralty, 5 August 1831, enclosing Owen to Desausmarez, 9 July 1831.
8. Marshall, *A Personal Narrative*, 162.
9. *P.P.*, 1837, "Select Committee on Aborigines," 14.
10. Ibid.
11. Ibid., 23–24.
12. Gunson, *Messengers of Grace*, 38.
13. Ibid., 133–136.
14. Michael Lewis, *The Navy in Transition, 1814–1864: A Social History* (London: Hodder and Stoughton, 1965), 21–39.
15. Erskine, *Journal of a Cruise*, 197, 195, 272, 309.
16. PRO, ADM 1/5548, Home to Admiralty, 15 October 1844.
17. PRO, FO 58/69, Erskine to Admiralty, 10 October 1849.
18. Howe, *Where the Waves Fall*, 295.
19. Erskine, *Journal of a Cruise*, 18.
20. NLA, MS 2180, Diary of John Geddie, 24 August 1849.
21. Ibid., 19 May 1851.
22. Ellis, *A Vindication of the South Sea Missions*, 47.
23. Wheeler, *Extracts*, part 3, 235.
24. Ron Crocombe and Marjorie Crocombe, eds., *The Works of Ta'unga* (Canberra: Australian National University Press, 1968), 108.
25. Williams, *A Narrative of Missionary Enterprises*, 582.
26. SCL, Selwyn Papers, 6/25 (c), George to Dr. Selwyn, Epiphany, 1848.
27. APL, Grey Letters I/2 (3), John Inglis to Grey, 21 March 1859.
28. Benjamin Morrell, *A Narrative of Four Voyages* (New York: J. and J. Harper, 1832), 372.
29. Ibid., 380.
30. ML, Uncat MSS Set 307, item 42, Towns to Paddon, [April] 1858.
31. Erskine, *Journal of a Cruise*, 379.
32. Ibid.
33. Inglis, *In the New Hebrides*, 53.
34. PRO, FO 58/84B, Fremantle to Admiralty, 12 December 1855.
35. *The Australian Dictionary of Biography*, vol. 4, (Melbourne: Melbourne University Press, 1972), 141.
36. Turley, *The Culture of English Antislavery*, 232.
37. J. Gallagher, "Fowell Buxton and the New African Policy," *Cambridge Historical Journal* 10 (1950), 36–58; Howard Temperley, *White Dreams, Black Africa: The Antislavery Expedition to the River Niger, 1841–1842* (New Haven and London: Yale University Press, 1991), 1–19.
38. Philip Curtin, *Image of Africa: British Ideas and Action, 1780–1850* (Madison: University of Wisconsin Press, 1964), 429–430; Brian Stanley, " 'Commerce and Christianity': Providence Theory, the Missionary Movement, and the Imperialism of Free Trade, 1842–1860," *The Historical Journal* 26:1 (1983), 71–94; Andrew Porter, " 'Commerce and Christianity': The Rise and Fall of a Nineteenth-Century Missionary Slogan," *The Historical Journal* 28:3 (1985), 597–621.
39. Fanshawe, *Admiral Fanshawe*, 180.

40. APL, Grey MSS, Geddie to Grey, 11 October, 15 October, and 2 November 1855.
41. *Quarterly Review* 106 (1859), 177.
42. [Craik], *The New Zealanders*, 81–99.
43. Ernest Dieffenbach, *New Zealand and Its Native Population* (London: Smith, Elder, 1841), 28.
44. Erskine, *Journal of a Cruise*, 197. See Dorothy Shineberg, "Guns and Men in Melanesia," *Journal of Pacific History* 6 (1971), 61–82; K. R. Howe, "Firearms and Indigenous Warfare: A Case Study," *Journal of Pacific History* 9 (1974), 21–38; and I. C. Campbell, "The Historiography of Charles Savage," *Journal of the Polynesian Society* 89:2 (1980), 143–166.
45. George Vason, *An Authentic Narrative of Four Years' Residence at Tongataboo*, edited by S. Piggott (London: Longman, Hurst, Rees, Orme and Longman's, 1810); and John Martin, *An Account of the Natives of the Tonga Islands . . . Arranged from Extensive Communications of Mr. William Mariner*, 2 vols. (London: J. Martin, 1817).
46. SOAS, WMMS, FBN 12/541, Thomas to General Secretaries, 5 August 1830.
47. William Waldegrave, "Extracts from a Private Journal Kept on Board H.M.S. Seringapatam, in the Pacific, 1830," *Journal of the Royal Geographical Society* 3 (1833), 190–193.
48. PRO, ADM 1/34, Waldegrave to Baker, 12 June 1830.
49. SOAS, WMMS, FBN 12/541, Thomas to General Secretaries, 5 August 1830.
50. PRO, ADM 1/5497, Josiah Tubou and George Tāufaʻāhau to Croker, 23 June 1840.
51. The following account is taken from an undated paper titled "Jimmy the Devil," found in a collection of papers belonging to the late-nineteenth-century anthropologist Adolph B. Brewster. The author of this account had met Jimmy, by then an old man, at Nukuʻalofa; CUL, G. K. Roth Papers, ADD 8780, Box 10.
52. W. T. Pritchard, *Polynesian Reminiscences* (London: Chapman and Hall, 1866), 293.
53. SOAS, WMMS, FBN 1/52, Orton to General Secretaries, 30 July 1830. The death of British soldiers at the hands of "savages" was often difficult to accept; for examples of the same type of explanation with regard to engagements with the Maori, see James Belich, *The New Zealand Wars and the Victorian Interpretation of Racial Conflict* (Auckland: Penguin, 1988), 315–318.
54. PRO, ADM 1/5497, Josiah Tupou and George Tāufaʻāhau to Croker, 22 June 1840.
55. Sione Lātūkefu, *Church and State in Tonga* (Canberra: Australian National University Press, 1974), 105.
56. Ralston, *Grass Huts and Warehouses*, 54–55.
57. Lawry, *Friendly and Feejee Islands*, 71.
58. PRO, FO 58/84B, Fremantle to Admiralty (confidential), 12 December 1855.
59. Levuka on Lakeba, rather than the village of the same name on Ovalau.
60. [David Cargill], *Diaries and Correspondence of David Cargill, 1832–1843*, ed. Albert Schutz (Canberra: Australian National University Press, 1977), 89.
61. PRO, FO 58/1, Bethune to Gipps, 4 October 1838.
62. Mary Wallis, *Life in Feejee: Or Five Years among the Cannibals* (Boston: W. Heath, 1851), 389, 402.
63. Erskine, *Journal of a Cruise*, 159.
64. C. S. Stewart, *Journal of a Residence in the Sandwich Islands* (London: H. Fisher, Son and Jackson, 1828), xxii.

65. Albert Hastings Markham, *The Cruise of the Rosario amongst the New Hebrides and Santa Cruz Islands* (London: S. Low, Marston, Low and Searle, 1873), 210–211.

66. Erskine, *Journal of a Cruise*, 344 and 159; Swainson, "Journal of a Cruise."

67. PRO, ADM 7/851, John MacGillivray, "Voyage of H.M.S. Herald under the Command of Capt. H. Mangles Denham RN, Being a Private Journal Kept by John MacGillivray, Naturalist," f. 88.

68. A detailed study of this episode can be found in Jane Samson, "Rescuing Fijian Women? The British Anti-slavery Proclamation of 1852," *Journal of Pacific History* 30:1 (1995), 22–38.

69. Thomas Williams, *The Islands and Their Inhabitants*, vol. 1 of *Fiji and the Fijians*, with James Calvert (London: Alexander Heylin, 1860), 168.

70. For a comparative discussion of this issue, see Roger Bastide, "Color, Racism and Christianity," *Daedalus* 96:2 (1967), 319–320.

71. Joseph Nettleton, *John Hunt: Pioneer, Missionary and Saint* (London: C. H. Kelly, 1906), 105.

72. James Calvert, *Mission History*, vol. 2 of *Fiji and the Fijians* (see n. 69), 299, 303–319.

73. Williams, *The Islands and Their Inhabitants*, 168.

74. AONSW 4/3215, Nimmo to Colonial Secretary, 1 October 1852.

75. Charles Wilkes, *Narrative of the United States Exploring Expedition* (Philadelphia: Lea and Blanchard, 1844), vol. 3, 72–73, 97, 309, 351.

76. SOAS, WMMS, FBN 6/289, Calvert to Secretaries, 29 September 1852 and enclosure.

77. AONSW 4/3215, Law Officers to Colonial Office, 15 August 1851, enclosing final draft of proclamation.

78. Ibid., Newcastle to FitzRoy, 10 January 1853.

79. Ibid., Home to Colonial Secretary, 19 December 1852.

80. Ibid., Nimmo to Colonial Secretary, 1 October 1852.

81. John Orlebar, *A Midshipman's Journal on Board H.M.S. Seringapatam during the Year 1830* (San Diego: Tofua, 1976), 51. This episode left a lasting impression; later in his career, Orlebar would found a mission to the Micmac Indians of New Brunswick in Canada.

82. Walpole, *Four Years in the Pacific*, 385.

83. BCRO, FR, 92/1, Stephen to Tom Fremantle, 6 November 1855.

84. BCRO, FR, 43/L, Stephen to Lady Fremantle, 4 January 1856.

85. NLA, MS 2180, Diary of John Geddie, 29 January 1852.

86. H. E. Maude, *Of Islands and Men: Studies in Pacific History* (Melbourne and New York: Oxford University Press, 1968), 134–177; and Ralston, *Grass Huts and Warehouses*.

3 PROTECTIVE SUPREMACY?

1. W. P. Morrell, *Britain in the Pacific Islands* (Oxford: Oxford University Press, 1960), 63.

2. For example, PRO, ADM 1/197, Owen to Sandilands, 20 July 1830.

3. PRO, ADM 1/204, Owen to Admiralty, 5 August 1831, enclosing Owen to Desausmarez, 9 July 1831.

4. PRO, ADM 1/5531 "Special Instructions for the Captains and Commanders of the Squadron Employed on the East India Station," by Rear Admiral Capel for the guidance of captains dealing with Indian authorities, dated 26 March 1835.

5. PRO, ADM 1/204, Owen to Admiralty, 5 August 1831, enclosing Owen to Desausmarez, 9 July 1831.

6. Tyerman and Bennett, *Voyages and Travels*, 127.

7. Gavan Daws, *Shoal of Time: A History of the Hawaiian Islands* (New York: Macmillan, 1968), 77.

8. PRO, FO 58/3, Croker to Byron, 14 September 1824.

9. Alexander Simpson, *The Sandwich Islands* (London: Smith, Elder and Co., 1843).

10. Daws, *Shoal of Time*, 117.

11. PRO, FO 534/16, Canning to Pomare, 3 March 1827.

12. Ibid., FO to Admiralty, 19 July 1839.

13. Ibid., FO to Admiralty, 4 October 1842.

14. John S. Galbraith, *Reluctant Empire: British Policy on the South African Frontier, 1834–1854* (Englewood Cliffs, N.J.: Prentice Hall, 1963), 78.

15. PRO, FO 534/1, Nicolas to FO, 15 March 1843.

16. PRO, ADM 50/229, Thomas to Nicolas, 12 June 1843.

17. PRO, FO 534/1, FO to Admiralty, 19 August 1843.

18. Quoted in Bach, *The Australia Station*, 29.

19. J. I. Brookes, *International Rivalry in the Pacific Islands, 1800–1875* (New York: Russell and Russell, 1941), 164.

20. John Moresby, *Two Admirals* (London: John Murray, 1909), 264, 308.

21. Ibid., 326–327.

22. ML, PMB 626, Lt. Francis Hayter, Logbook and Journal, Jan. 1871–1873, entry for 24 April 1873.

23. Ibid., entries for 10 and 11 June 1873.

24. Moresby, *Two Admirals*, 337.

25. ML FM4/1767, Goodenough MSS, Journals of Commodore Goodenough (hereafter "Goodenough Journals"), entries for 27 and 29 September 1873.

26. PRO, FO 58/63, George Tāufaʻāhau to Grey, 28 August 1847.

27. J. Rutherford, *Sir George Grey, K.C.B., 1812–1898* (London: Cassell, 1961), 53–54; and W. H. Oliver, ed., *The Dictionary of New Zealand Biography* (Wellington: Department of Internal Affairs, 1990), which also notes Grey's later attempts to "civilize" South African blacks as governor of the Cape colony; vol. 1, 160–164.

28. PRO, FO 58/63, Grey to CO, 14 March 1848.

29. Quoted in Angus Ross, *New Zealand Aspirations in the Pacific in the Nineteenth Century* (Oxford: Clarendon, 1964), 30.

30. PRO, FO 58/63, Josiah Tupou to Queen Victoria, 19 February 1844.

31. PRO, CO 209/59, Grey to CO, 14 March 1848.

32. Ibid., with minutes.

33. Ibid.

34. Ibid., CO to FO and Admiralty, 9 February 1849.

35. PRO, FO 58/66, Admiralty to FO, 12 March 1849.

36. Ibid.

37. John Connell, *New Caledonia or Kanaky? The Political History of a French Colony* (Canberra: Research School of Pacific Studies, 1987), 36; D. K. Fieldhouse, *The Colonial Empires: A Comparative Survey from the Eighteenth Century* (London: Weidenfeld and Nicolson, 1966), 204; and Colin Forster, "French Penal Policy and the Origins of the French Presence in New Caledonia," *Journal of Pacific History* 26:2 (1991), 135–150.

38. Fieldhouse, *The Colonial Empires*, 206; Connell, *New Caledonia or Kanaky?* 40; and Brookes, *International Rivalry in the Pacific Islands*, 241.

39. PRO, CO 209/504, Denison to CO, 5 October 1858.

40. SOAS, WMMS, FBN 6/289, Erskine to Calvert (undated), cited in Calvert to Secretaries, 18 October 1852.

41. ML, CY Reel 721, Deas Thompson Papers, Erskine to Thompson, 26 July 1851.

42. Ibid., Erskine to Thompson, 20 July 1852.

43. PRO, FO 58/84B, Fremantle to Admiralty (confidential), 12 December 1855.

44. Some speculated that news of the French annexation had been the final straw in Home's fatal illness; see Brookes, *International Rivalry in the Pacific Islands*, 202.

45. Ibid.

46. Ibid.

47. Merze Tate, *The United States and the Hawaiian Kingdom: A Political History* (New Haven: Yale University Press, 1965), 3–4.

48. NANZ, Micro Z/2670, RG 84, Mervine to Bailey, 27 February 1855.

49. NANZ, G16/1, Maxwell to Grey, 4 March 1848.

50. SCL, Selwyn Papers, Box D, George to Dr. Selwyn, 7 April 1848.

51. *Sydney Morning Herald*, 8 October 1856.

52. BCRO, FR 43/L, Fremantle to Lady Fremantle, 4 January 1856.

53. For a full discussion of St. Julian's character and involvement in the islands, see Marion Diamond, *Creative Meddler: The Life and Fantasies of Charles St. Julian* (Melbourne: Melbourne University Press, 1990), 52–84.

54. PRO, FO 58/82, CO to FO, 14 January 1855, enclosing FitzRoy to CO, 26 August 1854, and Charles St. Julian, "Suggestions as to the Policy of Her Majesty's Government with Reference to the Various Groups of Central, Western, and North-Western Polynesia."

55. Ibid., FO 58/82, FO to Treasury, 12 April 1855.

56. Ibid., Admiralty to FO, 24 September 1855, enclosing Fremantle's report.

57. PRO, ADM 1/5672, Fremantle to Admiralty (confidential), 12 December 1855.

58. Ibid. Again there are echoes of St. Julian; compare PRO, FO 58/84B, St. Julian to Denison, 28 September 1855, on the need for British intervention to halt the Samoan civil war.

59. PRO, FO 58/84B, Fremantle to Admiralty (confidential), 12 December 1855.

60. PRO, ADM 1/5672, Fremantle to Admiralty (confidential), 12 December 1855.

61. Ibid.

62. PRO, FO 58/82, FO memorandum, 5 January 1855.

63. W. Ross Johnston, *Sovereignty and Protection: A Study of British Jurisdictional Imperialism in the Later Nineteenth Century* (Durham, N.C.: Duke University Press, 1973), 13–22.

64. BLO, Clarendon Deposit, C/4, Aberdeen to Clarendon, 24 March 1853, and Graham to Clarendon, 17 April, 1853.

65. Ibid., C/127, Clarendon to Crampton, 23 December 1853, and C/224, despatch to Minister at Washington, 30 December 1854.

66. NMM, STK/52, Gladstone to Stokes, 30 August 1858, and Stokes to Gladstone, 6 September 1858.
67. R. P. Gilson, *Samoa, 1830 to 1900: The Politics of a Multi-Racial Community* (Melbourne: Oxford University Press, 1970), 228–229.
68. Gunson, *Messengers of Grace,* 150.
69. PRO, FO 58/38, Pritchard to FO, 8 September 1845. For background on Pritchard's career and character, see George Pritchard, *The Aggressions of the French at Tahiti and Other Islands of the Pacific,* ed. Paul de Deckker (Auckland and Oxford: Auckland University Press and Oxford University Press, 1983), 13–31.
70. PRO, FO 58/59, Blake to Seymour, 30 March 1847.
71. Ibid., "Case I."
72. PRO, FO 58/59, Blake to Seymour, 30 March 1847.
73. Ibid., "Extract from Lieutenant Turnour's Report," 26 February 1847, enclosed in "Case I."
74. PRO, FO 58/59, Blake to Seymour, 30 March 1847.
75. Ibid., Blake to Pritchard, 20 March 1847.
76. *Historical Records of Australia* (Sydney, 1924), series I, vol. 20, 664. For analysis of Blake's activities from the Ngatik islanders' perspective, see Lin Poyer, "The Ngatik Massacre," *Journal of Pacific History* 20 (1985), 4–22.
77. NANZ, G16/1, Maxwell to Grey, 4 March 1848.
78. Erskine, *Journal of a Cruise,* 75.
79. PRO, FO 58/72, Erskine to Admiralty, 14 January 1851.
80. Conway Shipley, *Sketches in the Pacific* (London: T. McStan, 1851), 25.
81. PRO, FO 58/72, Hornby to FO, enclosing Worth's report of proceedings, 20 October 1849. Minutes on the file indicate that the Foreign Office agreed but noted that Pritchard's instructions gave him "permission to exercise commerce."
82. PRO, ADM 1/5617, Home to Admiralty, 20 December 1852.
83. Ibid., Home to Pritchard, 9 September 1852.
84. Ibid., Home to the Chiefs of Samoa (undated).
85. PRO, FO 58/72, Pritchard to Erskine, 4 December 1850.
86. PRO, ADM 1/5672, Fremantle to Admiralty, 15 November 1855.
87. Ralston, *Grass Huts and Warehouses,* 83; and Gilson, *Samoa, 1830 to 1900,* 221.
88. PRO, FO 58/84B, Morshead to Bruce, 23 November 1855.
89. PRO, ADM 1/5672, Fremantle to Admiralty, 15 November 1855.
90. PRO, CO 201/486, Denison to CO, 3 October 1855.
91. NANZ, G16/1, Maxwell to Grey, 4 March 1848.
92. This foreshadowed the tense relationship between the Western Pacific High Commission and the Royal Navy later in the century. See Deryck Scarr, *Fragments of Empire: A History of the Western Pacific High Commission, 1877–1914* (Canberra: Australian National University Press, 1967); and Bach, *The Australia Station,* 130–153.

4 KINGMAKING

1. Examples include the short-lived Maori confederacy, based on the flag and Declaration of Independence of 1834–1835, and the (briefly) more successful attempt to create a

Samoan kingship in the 1860s (see below pp. 160–161). For a general analysis of indigenous polities and their response to European-style nation building, see Howe, *Where the Waves Fall*, 125–277.

2. PRO, ADM 1/34, Waldegrave to Baker, 12 June 1830.

3. William F. Wilson, ed., *With Lord Byron at the Sandwich Islands in 1825* (Honolulu: Petroglyph, 1922), 13.

4. Stewart, *Journal of a Residence*, 348–352.

5. H. G. Cummins, "Tongan Society at the Time of European Contact," in Noel Rutherford, ed., *Friendly Islands: A History of Tonga* (Melbourne and New York: Oxford University Press, 1977), 63–89; and Christine Ward Gailey, *Kinship to Kingship: Gender Hierarchy and State Formation in the Tongan Islands* (Austin: University of Texas Press, 1987), 170–193. The English translation of *tu'i* as "king" must be treated with caution, since Tongan titles were held through a combination of inherited rank and election.

6. PRO, ADM 1/218, Bethune to King George, 15 January 1838.

7. H. G. Cummins, "Holy War: Peter Dillon and the 1837 Massacres in Tonga," *Journal of Pacific History* 12 (1977), 25–39; and Lātūkefu, *Church and State in Tonga*, 100–117.

8. SOAS, WMMS, FBN 13/586, Thomas to General Secretaries, 15 January 1838.

9. Wilkes, *Narrative of the United States Exploring Expedition*, vol. 3, 7.

10. Ibid., 11.

11. Compare Wilkes' report with Thomas West, *Ten Years in South-Central Polynesia* (London: J. Nisbet, 1865), which says "instead of manfully acknowledging that the representations made by the Missionaries were true, he left the islands in anger"; see p. 283.

12. PRO, ADM 1/5497, Josiah Tupou and George Tāufa'āhau to Croker, 23 June 1840.

13. Ibid.

14. Ibid., Dunlop to Nias, 24 July 1840.

15. Ibid., Croker, "Terms of Peace Offered."

16. Ibid.

17. Ibid., Josiah Tupou and George Tāufa'āhau to Croker, 22 June 1840.

18. SOAS, WMMS, FBN 13/603, Rabone to General Secretaries, 21 November 1840.

19. PRO, ADM 1/5497, Dunlop to Nias, 24 July 1840.

20. Ibid.

21. Ward claimed that the captain was "induced by the Wesleyan missionaries"; *British Policy in the South Pacific*, 68. See also Morrell, *Britain in the Pacific Islands*, 52; and Bach, *The Australia Station*, 118.

22. PRO, ADM 1/5497, Josiah Tupou and George Tāufa'āhau to Croker, 22 June 1840.

23. SOAS, WMMS, FBN 13/603, Rabone to General Secretaries, 21 November 1840, and FBN 14/612, Rabone to General Secretaries, 18 April 1844.

24. SOAS, WMMS, FBN 13/602, Thomas to General Secretaries, 1 September 1840.

25. Ibid., Wilson to General Secretaries, [March] 1842, enclosing journal for 30 June 1840.

26. SOAS, WMMS, FBN 1/52, Orton to General Secretaries, 30 July 1840.

27. PRO, ADM 1/5497, Nias to Admiralty, 25 July 1840.

28. PRO, ADM 1/5530, Sulivan to Parker, 18 August 1842.

29. Ibid., Sulivan to Parker, 18 August 1842.

30. SOAS, WMMS, FBN 14/632, Amos to General Secretaries, 17 August 1852.

31. PRO, ADM 1/5548, Home to Cochrane, 15 October 1844.

32. PRO, FO 58/63, Grey to Maxwell, 23 December 1847.

33. Ibid.

34. PRO, FO 58/63, Maxwell to Grey, 9 March 1848.

35. NANZ, G33/1, Grey to George Tubou, 3 April 1849.

36. Howe, *Where the Waves Fall*, 190–191; I. C. Campbell, *A History of the Pacific Islands* (Christchurch: University of Canterbury Press, 1989), 81; and Lātūkefu, *Church and State in Tonga*, 118–132.

37. PRO, FO 59/69, Erskine to Admiralty, 10 October 1849.

38. Ibid.

39. Erskine, *Journal of a Cruise*, 125.

40. Hugh Laracy, "The Catholic Mission," in Rutherford, ed., *Friendly Islands*, 143.

41. PRO, FO 58/69, Erskine to Admiralty, 10 October 1849.

42. PRO, ADM 1/5617, Home to Admiralty, 20 December 1852.

43. SOAS, WMMS, FBN 14/632, Amos to General Secretaries, 17 August 1852.

44. Ibid.

45. PRO, ADM 1/5617, Home to Pupulu and Nivello, 11 August 1852.

46. Lātūkefu, *Church and State in Tonga*, 151–153; and Laracy, "The Catholic Mission," 143–144.

47. SOAS, WMMS, FBN 14/632, Thomas Adams to General Secretaries, [August] 1852.

48. Aldrich, *The French Presence in the South Pacific*, 52.

49. SOAS, WMMS, FBN 14/632, Turner to General Secretaries, 2 September 1852.

50. Ibid., Home to George Tupou, King of Tongatabu, 18 August 1852, enclosed in Adams to General Secretaries, [August] 1852.

51. Ibid.

52. PRO, ADM 1/5785, Seymour to Admiralty, 16 May 1862.

53. Howe, *Where the Waves Fall*, 192.

54. PRO, ADM 1/6380, Hoskins to Admiralty, 19 May 1876.

55. David Routledge, *Matanitū: The Struggle for Power in Early Fiji* (Suva: Institute of Pacific Studies, 1985), 54–55.

56. There was a ceremonial leader as well, known as the Rokotui Bau, who technically outranked the *vūnivalu*. Ibid., 43.

57. David Routledge, "The Failure of Cakobau, Chief of Bau, to Become King of Fiji," in G. W. Wood and P. S. O'Connor, eds., *W. P. Morrell: A Tribute* (Dunedin: University of Otago Press, 1973), 125–139.

58. PRO, FO 58/69, Erskine to Admiralty, 10 October 1849.

59. J. D. Legge, *Britain in Fiji, 1858–1880* (London: Macmillan, 1958), 12; and Routledge, *Matanitū*, 91.

60. Walter Lawry, *Missions in the Tonga and Feejee Islands* (New York: n.p., 1852), 116.

61. RGS, JMSS, Worth, "Account of a Visit."

62. Shipley, *Sketches in the Pacific*, 28.

63. SOAS, WMMS, FBN 6/281, Calvert to Secretaries, 10 October 1849.

64. PRO, FO 58/69, Erskine to Admiralty, 10 October 1849.

65. Ibid.

66. PRO, FO 58/26, Miller to Aberdeen, 4 October 1844, enclosing Rees (at Vewa) to Miller, July 1844, and Miller "to Seru and others," 4 October 1844.

67. Erskine, *Journal of a Cruise*, 179.

68. Ibid., 207.
69. PRO, FO 58/69, Erskine to Admiralty, 10 October 1849.
70. SOAS, WMMS, FBN 6/282, Erskine to Cakobau, 19 May 1850.
71. ATL, QMS MSS, Swainson, "Journal of a Cruise."
72. Howe, *Where the Waves Fall*, 267–268.
73. PRO, FO 58/69, Erskine to Admiralty, 10 October 1849.
74. Ibid.
75. Erskine, *Journal of a Cruise*, 227–228.
76. SOAS, WMMS, FBN 6/282, Erskine to Cakobau, 19 May 1850.
77. Routledge, *Matanitū*, 91.
78. PRO, ADM 1/5617, Home to Admiralty, 20 December 1852.
79. Ibid.
80. Quoted in Routledge, *Matanitū*, 83.
81. R. A. Derrick, *A History of Fiji* (Suva: Printing and Stationery Department, 1946), 112; SOAS, WMMS, FBN 6/292, Waterhouse to Secretaries, 11 June 1855; and PRO, ADM 7/852, MacGillivray, "Voyage of H.M.S. Herald," 69.
82. Andrew David, *The Voyage of HMS Herald to Australia and the South-west Pacific* (Melbourne: Miegunyah Press, 1995), 204.
83. Ibid., 61–62.
84. Ibid., 70.
85. Missionary William Wilson wrote that after the cession offer had been made "the French cannot interfere." SOAS, WMMS, FBN 12/292, Wilson to Secretaries, 9 July 1855.
86. FO 58/84B, extract from Denham's 1855 report attached to Fremantle to Admiralty (confidential), 15 November 1855.
87. Ibid.
88. BCRO, FR 154/1, Denham to Fremantle, 29 July 1855.
89. PRO, FO 58/84B, extract from Denham's 1855 report attached to Fremantle to Admiralty (confidential), 15 November 1855.
90. BCRO, FR, 154/1, Denham to Fremantle, 29 July 1855.
91. PRO, FO 58/84B, extract from Denham's journal attached to Fremantle to Admiralty (confidential), 12 December 1855.
92. David, *Voyage of HMS Herald*, 177.

5 THE SANDALWOOD CRUSADE

1. ATL, QMS MSS VIG 2081, Vigors, "Private Journal of a Cruise," 324.
2. K. R. Howe, *The Loyalty Islands: A History of Culture Contacts, 1840–1900* (Honolulu: University of Hawai'i Press, 1977).
3. Dorothy Shineberg, *They Came for Sandalwood: A Study of the Sandalwood Trade in the South-west Pacific, 1830–1865* (Melbourne: Melbourne University Press, 1967), 7–9, 16–28.
4. Ibid., 136–144.
5. Erskine made extensive use of Andrew Cheyne's published trading journal, *A Description of Islands in the Western Pacific* (London: J. D. Potter, 1852), in compiling his own

book for publication the following year. He also used Cheyne's navigational charts; see Erskine, *Journal of a Cruise,* 338, n. 3; 341, nn. 1 and 2; 346, n. 1; and 385, n. 2.

6. H. W. Tucker, *Memoir of the Life and Episcopate of George Augustus Selwyn, D.D.* (New York: Pott, Young, 1879), vol. 1, 265–266. No other account of this part of *Dido*'s voyage survives.

7. *Nautical Magazine* 10 (1844), 608.

8. Shineberg, *They Came for Sandalwood,* 62.

9. Erskine, *Journal of a Cruise,* 143–145.

10. Quoted in Shineberg, *They Came for Sandalwood,* 209–210.

11. Anonymous, *Isles of the Pacific* (Melbourne, n.p., 1861), 10.

12. *Hansard's Parliamentary Debates,* third series (hereafter *Hansard*), 1872 [1667].

13. Samuel Hinds, *The Latest Official Documents Relating to New Zealand* (London: J. W. Parker, 1838), 15.

14. Ibid., 3–4.

15. Inglis, *In the New Hebrides,* 303–304.

16. Howe, *Where the Waves Fall,* 304, and Gunson, *Messengers of Grace,* 323.

17. David Hilliard, "Bishop G. A. Selwyn and the Melanesian Mission," *New Zealand Journal of History* 4 (1970), 120–137.

18. Howe, *Where the Waves Fall,* 303–306.

19. Erskine, *Journal of a Cruise,* 3, n. 3.

20. PRO, FO 58/69, Erskine to Admiralty, 10 October 1849.

21. *Quarterly Review* 106 (1859), 176.

22. Dorothy Shineberg, ed., *The Trading Voyages of Andrew Cheyne, 1841–1844* (Wellington and Auckland: A. H. and A. W. Reed, 1971), 96–97 and 139–140.

23. Shineberg, *They Came for Sandalwood,* 83–85, 100–103.

24. ML, Uncat MSS Set 307, item 59, Towns to Lewis, 6 March 1850.

25. Cheyne, *A Description of Islands,* 68, 12.

26. Shineberg, *They Came for Sandalwood,* 207–208.

27. "Sandalwood Voyage," *Nautical Magazine* (May 1850), 299.

28. AONSW 4/3375, Towns to Colonial Secretary, 12 November 1857.

29. ML, Uncat MSS Set 307, item 40, Towns to Underwood, 20 November 1857.

30. Ibid., Towns to Henry, 19 November 1857; Towns to Edwards, [November] 1857; Towns to Mair, 26 November 1857; and Towns to Geddie and Inglis, 28 November 1857.

31. AONSW 4/3375, Loring to Denison, 15 December 1857.

32. Ibid.

33. NLA, MS 2180, Diary of John Geddie, 11 December 1857.

34. ML, Uncat MSS Set 307, item 42, Towns to Paddon, [April] 1858.

35. AONSW 4/3375, Loring to Denison, 15 December 1857.

36. AONSW 4/1665, Denison to Loring, 14 November 1857.

37. AONSW 4/3375, Governor's minute on Loring to Denison, 15 December 1857.

38. Shineberg, *They Came for Sandalwood,* 199–214.

39. For example, Michael Gilding, "The Massacre of the *Mystery:* A Case Study in Contact Relations," *Journal of Pacific History* 17 (1982), 66–85.

40. Erskine, *Journal of a Cruise,* 379.

41. ML, Uncat MSS Set 307, item 69, Towns to Brooks, 12 August 1851.

42. Quoted in Shineberg, *They Came for Sandalwood*, 201.
43. "The Murders at the Islands," *Sydney Morning Herald*, 29 January 1850.
44. PRO, ADM 1/5606, Erskine to Admiralty, 2 April 1850.
45. Ibid., Erskine to Oliver, 14 March 1850.
46. This chief was almost certainly the powerful district leader Bweon; Bronwen Douglas, "The Export Trade in Tropical Products in New Caledonia, 1841–1872," *Journal de la Société des Océanistes* 27: 31 (1971), 162.
47. NMM, BEL 53, Oliver to Erskine, 10 June 1850.
48. Douglas, "The Export Trade," 163.
49. ATL, QMS MSS VIG 2081, Vigors, "Journal of a Cruise," 256.
50. PRO, ADM 1/5617, Home to Admiralty, 20 December 1852.
51. AONSW 4/3182, Inspector General of Police to Colonial Secretary, 10 January 1852.
52. NLA, MS 2180, Diary of John Geddie, 5 January 1852.
53. Ron Adams, *In the Land of Strangers: A Century of European Contact with Tanna, 1774–1874* (Canberra: Australian National University Press, 1984), 39–40.
54. Ibid., 40.
55. Erskine, *Journal of a Cruise*, 393, and Shineberg, *They Came for Sandalwood*, 92, n. 42.
56. Shineberg, *They Came for Sandalwood*, 207.
57. Erskine, *Journal of a Cruise*, 381.
58. SCL, Selwyn Papers, C/1/c, Selwyn to Dr. Selwyn, 15 August 1850.
59. APS, *Colonial Intelligencer, or Aborigines' Friend* 3/4 (1848), 51.
60. PRO, ADM 1/5696, Loring to Admiralty, 15 February 1858.
61. PRO, FO 58/86, CO to FO, [November] 1857.
62. PRO, FO 58/82, FO to Treasury, 12 April 1855.
63. PRO, FO 58/86, MS comments (unsigned) after Admiralty to FO, 25 February 1858, enclosing Fremantle to Admiralty, 4 October 1856.
64. PRO, FO 58/89, Geddie and Inglis to Loring, 15 December 1857.
65. PRO, ADM 1/5696, Loring to Admiralty, 15 February 1858.
66. PRO, FO 58/91, "Memorial on the Subject of a Consulship for the New Hebrides."
67. Marion Diamond, *The Seahorse and the Wanderer: Ben Boyd in Australia* (Melbourne: Melbourne University Press, 1988), 2.
68. Ibid., 129.
69. NANZ, G16/1, Lawry to Grey, 22 December 1847.
70. Ibid.
71. Ibid., Grey to Maxwell, 23 December 1847.
72. Ibid.
73. Ibid., Maxwell to Grey, 4 March 1848. Maxwell worried about "the want of a good interpreter," which hampered his questioning, but he also insisted that these points were "distinctly stated."
74. Ibid., "Statement of Uatsum."
75. Ibid.
76. Ibid. These were ironic comments to come from a Royal Navy captain during the age of impressment.
77. Erskine, *Journal of a Cruise*, 342.
78. Inglis, *In the New Hebrides*, 198. This interpretation was durable; writing in 1958, C. E.

Fox (himself a missionary) declared in his study of the Melanesian Mission that aboard *Dido* Bishop Selwyn had seen "the shadow of the slave trade . . . already falling over the islands." *Lords of the Southern Isles* (London: A. R. Mowbray and Co., 1958), 5.

79. Shineberg, *They Came for Sandalwood*, 212.
80. PRO, ADM 1/5606, Erskine to Admiralty, 2 April 1850.
81. ML, Uncat MSS Set 307, item 55, Towns to Jones, 16 November 1844.
82. Ibid., item 61, Towns to Orton, 28 August 1852. Earlier that year, he had told the same vessel's previous commander, "I feel sure 9 cases in ten our side are the agressors [*sic*]." Ibid., Towns to Oliver, 4 March 1852.
83. Ibid., item 62, Towns to Cooney, 19 March 1853.
84. ML, MSS 88605, Towns to Erskine, 16 November 1858.
85. ML, Uncat MSS Set 307, item 69, Towns to Brooks, 12 August 1851.
86. Ibid., Towns to Pollard, 14 June 1852.
87. AONSW 4/3190, Home to Colonial Secretary, 29 January 1853.
88. Ibid., Attorney General to Colonial Secretary, 9 February 1853.
89. AONSW 4/3362, Bingham to Colonial Secretary, 21 June 1856.
90. AONSW 4/3440.1, CO to Admiralty, 20 June 1860.

6 *A HOUSE DIVIDED*

1. In addition to Ward's *British Policy in the South Pacific* and Morrell's *Britain in the Pacific Islands,* there is a detailed study titled "The Structure of British Authority before the Cession of Fiji" in Scarr, *Fragments of Empire,* 1–22, and a large literature on legal aspects of Britain's colonization of New Zealand. The best attempt to set Britain's legal relationship with the south Pacific into full historical context is still W. Ross Johnston's *Sovereignty and Protection.*
2. "An Act for the more effectual Punishment of Murders and Manslaughters committed in Places not within His Majesty's Dominions" (1817), 57 Geo. III, cap. 53.
3. "An Act to provide for the Administration of Justice in New South Wales and Van Diemen's Land, and for the more effectual Government thereof, and for other Purposes relating thereto" (1828), 9 Geo. IV, cap. 83.
4. PRO, ADM 1/218, Bethune to Maitland, 9 February 1838.
5. Ibid., and AONSW 4/2411.3, Bethune to Bourke, 9 February 1838.
6. PRO, ADM 1/34, Baker to Admiralty, 22 November 1830.
7. PRO, ADM 1/5617, Home to Admiralty, 20 December 1852.
8. PRO, ADM 1/204, Owen to Desausmarez, 9 July 1831.
9. AONSW 4/3799, Colonial Secretary to Lambert, 29 April 1834, and ADM 1/217, Capel to Admiralty, 28 May 1837.
10. PRO, ADM 1/218, Maitland to Admiralty, 18 May 1838.
11. Ralston, *Grass Huts and Warehouses,* 48–49.
12. Erskine, *Journal of a Cruise,* 308–309.
13. PRO, ADM 1/1749, Desausmarez to Admiralty, 10 December 1831.
14. PRO, ADM 1/5617, Home to Admiralty, 20 December 1852.
15. PRO, ADM 1/5672, Fremantle to Admiralty, 15 November 1855.

16. Ibid.

17. PRO, ADM 1/212, Blackwood to Bourke (undated).

18. PRO, ADM 1/3720, Jones to Admiralty, 4 March 1834.

19. Ibid.

20. PRO, ADM 1/212, "Statement of George Harris," 3 June 1833.

21. Ibid., Admiralty minute on Gore to Admiralty, 26 October 1833, enclosing Blackwood's report and depositions.

22. ML A1959, John Thomas Papers, Thomas to Secretaries, 3 June 1833.

23. For a comparative discussion of this issue, see Samson, "British Voices and Indigenous Rights."

24. APS, *Address of the Aborigines' Protection Society* [London, 1838].

25. Saxe Bannister, *Humane Policy, or, Justice to the Aborigines* (London: T. and G. Underwood, 1830); idem, *British Colonization and Coloured Tribes;* and Standish Motte, *Outline of a System of Legislation for Securing Protection to the Aboriginal Inhabitants of All Countries Colonized by Great Britain* (London: John Murray, 1840).

26. Motte, *Outline of a System,* 19—20.

27. "An Act to Authorise the Legislatures of Certain of Her Majesty's Colonies to Pass Laws for the Admission, in Certain Cases, of Unsworn Testimony in Civil and Criminal Proceedings, 1843," 6 & 7 Vict., cap. 22 (1843).

28. AONSW 4/662, Martin to Belmore, 2 July 1869, and 4/680, CO to Belmore, 2 October 1869. Also see O. W. Parnaby, *Britain and the Labor Trade in the Southwest Pacific* (Durham: Duke University Press, 1964), 20—21.

29. AONSW 4/2832, Attorney General to Colonial Secretary, 2 April 1849.

30. Erskine, *Journal of a Cruise,* 381—383 and Appendix B.

31. Lewis to Pollard, 20 September 1850, in Appendix B, ibid., 480. The statement, written at Pollard's request, was signed at Lifu and formed the basis of Pollard's deposition before the Water Police magistrate.

32. AONSW 4/5732, Crown Solicitor's Judgment Books, 26 June 1851.

33. Erskine, *Journal of a Cruise,* 308.

34. Ibid., 382.

35. AONSW 4/3182, Superintendent to Inspector General of Police, 10 January 1852.

36. Ibid., Inspector General of Police to Colonial Secretary, 10 January 1852.

37. Home's letter to the colonial secretary does not appear to have survived, but reference to it is made in PRO, ADM 1/5617, Home to Admiralty, 20 December 1852, and in the correspondence below.

38. AONSW 4/3182, Attorney General to Colonial Secretary, 11 January 1853.

39. AONSW 2/3114, Justice Dickinson notebooks, 12 August 1854.

40. J. Gordon Legge, *A Selection of Supreme Court Cases in New South Wales from 1825 to 1862* (Sydney: Charles Potter, 1896), vol. 2, 861.

41. ML, Uncat MSS Set 307, item 63, Towns to Fletcher, 16 December 1853.

42. Quoted in Shineberg, *They Came for Sandalwood,* 96.

43. ML, Uncat MSS Set 307, item 118, Towns to Home, 25 February 1853.

44. Ibid., Towns to Home, 28 February 1853.

45. Ibid., Towns to Colonial Secretary, 5 March 1853.

46. PRO, ADM 1/5606, Erskine to Admiralty, 9 April 1850.

47. PRO, FO 58/106, Solicitor General to Young, 13 December 1864.

48. PRO, FO 58/108, Pritchard to FO, 31 December 1860.

49. PRO, FO 58/96, Pritchard to FO, 1 January 1862; the first despatch describing the "Mercantile Court of Fiji" is at FO 58/94, Pritchard to FO, 1 August 1861.

50. PRO, FO 58/94, minutes on Pritchard to FO, 1 August 1861.

51. PRO, FO 58/1, Bethune to Gipps, 4 October 1838.

52. AONSW, 4/3440.1, Loring to Cowper, 31 May 1859.

53. PRO, FO 58/69, Erskine to Admiralty, 10 October 1849.

54. PRO, FO 58/59, "Case Six," enclosed in Blake to Seymour, 30 March 1847.

55. Ibid., Blake to Seymour, 30 March 1847.

56. PRO, FO 58/84B, Fremantle to Admiralty, 15 November 1855.

57. Ibid.

58. BCRO, FR 92/1, Stephen to Tom Fremantle, 6 November 1855.

59. PRO, ADM 1/210, McMurdo to Owen, 8 November 1832.

60. PRO, FO 58/69, Erskine to Admiralty, 10 October 1849.

61. PRO, FO 58/59, Blake to Seymour, 30 March 1847.

62. PRO, FO 58/1, Bethune to Gipps, 4 October 1838.

63. PRO, FO 58/69, Erskine to Admiralty, 10 October 1849.

64. Erskine, *Journal of a Cruise*, 96.

65. PRO, FO 58/1, Bethune to Colonial Secretary, 3 July 1838.

66. AONSW 4/2411.3, Crown Solicitor's Office to Colonial Secretary, 20 June 1838.

67. PRO, FO 58/63, Cochrane to Admiralty, 11 June 1846.

68. AONSW 4/3190, Home to Colonial Secretary, 29 January 1852.

69. Ibid.

70. Ibid., Home to Deas Thompson, 29 January 1853.

71. Ibid., Law Officers to Colonial Secretary, 9 February 1853. Forwarding their opinion to Captain Home, the governor expressed his "regret" at their response; ibid., Colonial Secretary to Home, 3 February 1853.

72. Ibid.

73. Curtin, *The Image of Africa*, 301. For a discussion of the British treaty system in South Africa, see Galbraith, *Reluctant Empire*, 133.

74. I. C. Campbell, "British Treaties with Polynesians in the Nineteenth Century," in William Renwick, ed., *Sovereignty and Indigenous Rights: The Treaty of Waitangi in International Contexts* (Wellington: Victoria University Press, 1991), 67–82.

75. Ibid., 80.

76. Curtin, *Image of Africa*, 476.

77. PRO, FO 58/62, Pritchard to FO, 12 August 1848.

78. SOAS, CWM, Samoa 1848, Box 21/5, Stallworthy to Directors, 3 July 1848, and Mills to Directors, 18 August 1848.

79. PRO, ADM 1/5785, Burnett to Admiralty, 11 December 1862.

80. PRO, ADM 1/6261 Stirling to Admiralty, 4 January 1873, and Goodenough to Admiralty, 14 November 1873.

81. PRO, FO 58/111, Thurston to FO, 31 December 1867.

82. SOAS, WMMS, FBN 5/235, Carey to Secretaries, 22 August 1867.

83. PRO, FO 58/111, minutes on Thurston to FO, 31 December 1867; FO 58/114, FO to Admiralty, 5 May 1868, and reply of 8 May 1868.
84. PRO, FO 58/124, FO to Jones, 14 September 1863.
85. Ibid., Jones to FO, 15 December 1864.
86. Ibid., Thornton to FO, 10 April 1869.
87. Ibid., minutes on Jones to FO, 24 November 1865.
88. Ibid., Jones to FO, 18 July 1867.
89. AONSW 4/3362, Fremantle to Colonial Secretary, 12 November 1856.
90. Ibid.
91. AONSW 4/3440.1, Loring to Admiralty, 11 March 1860.
92. Ibid.
93. Ibid., Admiralty to CO, 8 May 1860.
94. Ibid., CO to Admiralty, 20 June 1860.

7 ANTISLAVERY IMPERATIVES

1. An earlier version of this chapter was published as Jane Samson, "Imperial Benevolence: The Royal Navy and the South Pacific Labour Trade, 1867–1872," *The Great Circle* 18:1 (1997), 14–29.
2. Bach, *The Australia Station,* 78.
3. *Hansard,* 1872 [188], 211.
4. Kay Saunders, "The Workers' Paradox: Indentured Labour in the Queensland Sugar Industry to 1920," in her *Indentured Labour in the British Empire, 1834–1920* (London: Croom Helm, 1984), 220; and Jacqueline Leckie, "Workers in Colonial Fiji: 1870–1970," in Clive Moore et al. eds., *Labour in the South Pacific* (Townsville: James Cook University of Northern Queensland Press, 1990), 47.
5. Peter Corris, *Passage, Port and Plantation: A History of Solomon Islands Labour Migration, 1870–1914* (Melbourne: Melbourne University Press, 1973); Deryck Scarr, "Recruits and Recruiters: A Portrait of the Labour Trade," in J. W. Davidson and Deryck Scarr, eds., *Pacific Islands Portraits* (Wellington: A. H. and A. W. Reed, 1970), 95–126; Clive Moore, "Pacific Islanders in Nineteenth Century Queensland," in Moore et al., eds., *Labour in the South Pacific,* 124–127.
6. Adrian Graves, "The Nature and Origins of Pacific Islands Labour Migration to Queensland, 1863–1906," in Shula Marks and Peter Richardson, eds., *International Labour Migration: Historical Persectives* (Hounslow: Institute of Commonwealth Studies, 1984), 114.
7. "Act of the British Parliament, for the Prevention and Punishment of Criminal Outrages upon Natives of the Islands in the Pacific Ocean (Kidnapping) (1872)," 25 & 36 Vict., ca p. 19. The official short title of the act was "The Kidnapping Act, 1872," but "Pacific Islanders Protection Act" is the usual reference.
8. Earlier studies of the Royal Navy's role in this process include Scarr, *Fragments of Empire,* and Bach, *The Australia Station,* 57–68, 130–53.
9. H. E. Maude, *Slavers in Paradise: The Peruvian Slave Trade in Polynesia, 1862–1864*

(Stanford: Stanford University Press, 1981), 149. However, Maude barely mentions the role of the Royal Navy's Pacific Station, whose ships enforced the international anti-slavery agreements and often shared patrolling duties with the Australia Station; Bach, *The Australia Station*, 49–50.

10. Robert Steel, *The New Hebrides and Christian Missions* (London: J. Nisbet, 1880), 392.

11. PRO, FO 58/112, Logan to FO, 24 June 1867.

12. David Hilliard, *God's Gentlemen: A History of the Melanesian Mission, 1849–1942* (St. Lucia, Qld.: University of Queensland Press, 1978), 64; Howe, *Where the Waves Fall*, 305–307.

13. PRO, FO 58/112, Admiralty to FO, 1 October 1867.

14. PRO, CO 234/21, minute of 3 November on Admiralty to CO, 28 October 1868.

15. Ibid., minute of 5 November on Admiralty to CO, 28 October 1868.

16. PRO, FO 58/112, Admiralty to FO, 9 December 1867.

17. PRO, ADM 1/6054, Admiralty to Lambert, 9 December 1867.

18. PRO, ADM 1/6096, McNair to Lambert, 22 October 1868, enclosed in Lambert to Blackall, 28 January 1869.

19. PRO, ADM 1/6054, McCullagh to Jones, 11 October 1865, enclosed in Lambert to Admiralty, 5 October 1868.

20. PRO, ADM 1/6008, Lambert to Admiralty, 13 December 1867; and Deryck Scarr, *I, the Very Bayonet* (Canberra: Australian National University Press, 1973), 71.

21. PRO, ADM 1/6054, Wiseman to Admiralty, 14 April 1868.

22. Ibid., Bingham to Admiralty 28 March 1868, and enclosures.

23. Ibid., Lambert to Admiralty, 1 October 1868.

24. Ibid.

25. "An Act to regulate and control the introduction and treatment of Polynesian labourers" (1868), 31 Vict., cap. 47.

26. Scarr, *I, the Very Bayonet*, 96–97.

27. PRO, ADM 1/6192, Stirling to Admiralty, 30 January 1871; and Scarr, *Fragments of Empire*, 17.

28. PRO, FO 58/124, Treasury to FO, 25 January 1868 and attachments.

29. Report of the Royal Commission "to inquire into, and report on, certain cases of alleged kidnapping of natives of the Loyalty Islands in the years 1867–68 . . . and generally to inquire into, and report on, the state and probable results of Polynesian immigration," 27 September 1869; *P.P.* 1871, XIX [399], "Further Correspondence Respecting the Deportation of South Sea Islanders," 56, 58.

30. PRO, ADM 1/6126, minute by Childers on Blackall to CO, 7 October 1869.

31. LMS to Earl Granville, 6 April 1869, in *P.P.* 1868/69, XLIII [408], "Correspondence Relating to Importation of South Sea Islanders into Queensland," 37–38.

32. PRO, ADM 1/6096, Lambert to Admiralty, 11 February 1869.

33. Ibid., Palmer to Lambert, 5 April 1869, enclosed in Lambert to Admiralty, 1 July 1869.

34. Palmer to Belmore, 25 May 1869, in *P.P.* 1871, XIX [399], 18.

35. PRO, ADM 1/6096, Palmer to Lambert, 24 April 1869.

36. PRO, ADM 1/6197, Williams to Belmore, 6 September 1871.

37. Julius Brenchley, *Jottings during the Cruise of H.M.S. Curaçoa among the South Sea Islands in 1865* (London: Longmans, Green and Co., 1873), x.

38. Inglis, *In the New Hebrides*, 214–215.
39. The British and Foreign Anti-Slavery Society, *Anti-Slavery Reporter* 16:11 (1869), 264.
40. PRO, ADM 1/6096, Palmer to Lambert, 24 April 1869, enclosed in Lambert to Admiralty, 1 July 1869.
41. "Commission on Polynesian Immigration," in *P.P.* 1871, XIX [399], "Further Correspondence Respecting the Deportation of South Sea Islanders," 58.
42. PRO, ADM 1/6126, Admiralty to CO, 5 January 1870.
43. PRO, ADM 13/5, Admiralty to Wiseman, 19 May 1863, and Admiralty to Lambert, 3 June 1867.
44. PRO, ADM 13/6, Admiralty to Stirling, 7 April 1870.
45. PRO, ADM 1/6198, FO to Admiralty, 15 December 1871.
46. PRO, ADM 1/6192, Challis to Stirling, 10 October 1870.
47. Ibid.; and Alfred Basil Lubbock, *Bully Hayes: South Sea Pirate* (London: Martin Hopkinson, 1931).
48. PRO, ADM 1/6192, Challis to Stirling, 19 November 1870.
49. Ibid., March to Stirling, 14 October 1870.
50. PRO, ADM 1/6230, Stirling to Admiralty, 30 January 1871.
51. Hilliard, *God's Gentlemen*, 63.
52. Ibid., 64–65; extract from article by Patteson in the *Southern Cross*, enclosed in CO to Blackall, 18 February 1870, *P.P.* 1871 [468], 75–76; and David Hilliard, "John Coleridge Patteson: Missionary Bishop of Melanesia," in Davidson and Scarr, *Pacific Islands Portraits*, 177–200.
53. PRO, ADM 1/6230, Markham to Stirling, 1 November 1871.
54. Ibid.
55. Albert Hastings Markham, *The Cruise of the Rosario amongst the New Hebrides and Santa Cruz Islands* (London: S. Low, Marston, Low and Searle, 1873), 46.
56. PRO, ADM 1/6230, Markham to Stirling, 14 November 1871.
57. Ibid.
58. Ibid., Markham to Stirling, 10 February 1872.
59. George Palmer, *Kidnapping in the South Seas* (Edinburgh: Edmonston and Douglas, 1871), 183.
60. Ibid., 194.
61. *Melbourne Argus*, 4 December 1871.
62. Ibid.
63. *Anti-Slavery Reporter* 17:6 (1871), 176.
64. Normanby to CO, 21 March 1872, in *P.P.* 1873, L [244], "South Sea Islands," 110.
65. PRO, ADM 1/6230, Stirling to Admiralty, 22 April 1872.
66. The new boundaries ran from 95° E to 160° W longitude along the Antarctic Circle to the south, with the northern limits extended to 12° N between 130° and 160° E longitude; PRO, ADM 1/6230, Admiralty to Stirling, 14 February 1872.
67. William T. Wawn, *The South Sea Islanders and the Queensland Labour Trade* (London: Swan Sonnenschein, 1893), vi, 16.
68. PRO, FO 58/127, R. Beckwith Leefe to Belmore, 17 August 1869.
69. *Hansard* (1872), [209] 1154 and [210] 1666.
70. Ibid., [188] 211.

71. PRO, ADM 1/6230, "Instructions for the guidance of the Commanders of Her Majesty's Ships of War employed in the supression of the Kidnapping Trade, 1872," was not promulgated until 1873; Bach, *The Australia Station*, 56–57.

72. John Kay, *The Slave Trade in the New Hebrides* (Edinburgh: Edmonston and Douglas, 1872), 39.

73. PRO, ADM 1/6284, enclosed in Admiralty to Stirling, 2 April 1873.

74. PRO, ADM 1/6230, Stirling to Admiralty, 22 April 1872.

75. Ibid., Moresby to Stirling, 12 September 1872.

76. Ibid., Moresby to Stirling, 12 September 1872.

77. Markham, *The Cruise of the Rosario*, 46.

78. Ibid., vi–vii.

79. Moresby, *Two Admirals*, 266, 217.

8 GUNBOAT DIPLOMACY?

1. Bach, *The Australia Station*, 37. Also, "Matters of island government [were] . . . effectively coerced, where necessary, by British men-of-war," in Ward, *British Policy in the South Pacific*, 165; "many flag-showing and punitive expeditions [went] to protect Europeans," in G. A. Wood, "Pax Britannica: The Royal Navy around 1860," in Wood and O'Connor, eds., *W. P. Morrell: A Tribute*, 67; R. P. Gilson's *Samoa, 1830 to 1900*, which makes the Royal Navy a symbol of the British oppression of Samoans; and Claudia Knapman, *White Women in Fiji, 1835–1930: The Ruin of Empire?* (Sydney and London: Allen and Unwin, 1986), 159, which claims that "European punitive power . . . became a factor in restraining Fijians' freedom of action as early as the 1840s."

2. I have excluded two incidents where marines destroyed single dwellings or canoes as a warning and the assistance provided to King Cakobau and his ministers in 1868 by HMS *Challenger* (discussed in the next chapter). None of these episodes has features at odds with this argument.

3. This figure includes vessels from the East Indies and Pacific stations before 1859 and the Australia Station thereafter.

4. Elsdon Best, *The Maori Canoe* (Wellington: A. R. Shearer, 1976), 216.

5. S. Percy Smith, *Maori Wars of the Nineteenth Century* (Christchurch: Whitcombe and Tombs, 1910), 67–71, 108–109; Ian Church, *Heartland of Aotea: Maori and European in South Taranaki before the Taranaki Wars* (Hawera, N.Z.: Hawera Historical Society, 1992), 18–19.

6. Smith, *Maori Wars*, 127.

7. They had traveled to the village to trade, "and the chief had them killed for the sake of their goods"; Shipley, *Sketches in the Pacific*, 34. Shipley was Worth's first lieutenant during *Calypso*'s 1848 cruise, and since only a fragment of Worth's official report survives, his is the only complete naval account of this episode.

8. Ibid.

9. Ibid., 35.

10. Ibid., 34.

11. Erskine, *Journal of a Cruise*, 227.

12. PRO, ADM 2/1614, Admiralty to Loring, 13 October 1857, enclosing FO to ADM, 29 September 1857.

13. BM, Halifax MSS, Add MS 49551, Loring to Wood, 1 March 1858.

14. Ibid., Loring to Wood, 17 May 1858.

15. AONSW 4/3375, Loring to Denison, 15 December 1857.

16. PRO, ADM 1/5696, Loring to Admiralty, 6 September 1858.

17. George Patterson, *Missionary Life among the Cannibals* (Toronto: James Campbell, 1882), 433; Adams, *In the Land of Strangers*, 78.

18. PRO, FO 58/89, Williams to FO, 22 November 1858.

19. Ibid.

20. PRO, ADM 1/6008, Blake to Lambert, 4 August 1867.

21. Ibid.

22. PRO, ADM 1/5925, Wiseman to Admiralty, 1 October 1865.

23. Brenchley, *Jottings during the Cruise of H.M.S. 'Curaçoa,'* 202.

24. PRO, ADM 1/5969, Hope to Wiseman, 6 September 1866, enclosing Underwood to Hope, 17 August 1866.

25. Patterson, *Missionary Life among the Cannibals*, 488.

26. Adams, *In the Land of Strangers*, 30–32.

27. Palmer, *Kidnapping in the South Seas*, 33.

28. ML, CY MSS 269, Henderson, "Journal Written on HMS Sappho," 731–732.

29. PRO, ADM 1/5925, Wiseman to Admiralty, 16 October 1865.

30. Ibid., Wiseman to Admiralty, 20 November 1865.

31. ML FM4/1654, RNAS, Delany to Stirling, 3 April 1871.

32. *P.P.* 1872, XXXIX [543], Markham to Stirling, 12 February 1872, 11.

33. Hilliard, *God's Gentlemen*, 75.

34. Wawn, *The South Sea Islanders and the Queensland Labour Trade*, 98, 166.

35. Adams, *In the Land of Strangers*, 129.

36. Ibid., 132.

37. William Hall, *A Treatise on International Law* (Oxford, 1890), 66–67, 364–365.

38. PRO, ADM 1/5696, Loring to Admiralty, 6 September 1858.

39. Johnston, *Sovereignty and Protection*, 125.

40. AONSW 4/2411.3, Crown Solicitor's Office to Colonial Secretary, 20 June 1838.

41. Joseph Denman, *The African Squadron* (London: John Mortimer, [1850]), 63, citing the eighteenth-century theorist Vattel. Like captains Toup Nicholas and Paulet in the south Pacific, Denman suffered when the Foreign Office did a volte-face: he was sued after bombarding a slave factory at Gallinas in West Africa.

42. Erskine, *Journal of a Cruise*, 274.

43. Baron Charles von Hügel, *New Holland Journal*, ed. and trans. Dymphna Clark (Melbourne: Miegunyah Press, 1994), 426.

44. Richard A. A. Sherrin, *Early History of New Zealand from Earliest Times to 1840*, ed. Thomson W. Leys (Auckland: H. Brett, 1890), 458.

45. *Aborigines' Friend* 2 (1865), 290.

46. NMM, MRK/8, *Daily Southern Cross*, 5 February 1872.

47. Ibid., *Telegraph*, 18 [January] 1872.

48. Ibid., *Daily Southern Cross*, 5 February 1872.

49. Erskine, *Journal of a Cruise*, 4.
50. SCL, Selwyn MSS, Box D/1/C, Bishop Selwyn to his father, 15 April 1850.
51. PRO, ADM 1/6261, Chapman to Stirling, enclosed in Goodenough to Admiralty, 27 December 1873.
52. APS, *Annual Report* 1846 (London, 1846), 11.
53. NMM, MRK/8, *New Zealand Herald*, 28 February 1872.
54. Ibid.
55. Routledge, *Matanitū*, 59–60.
56. Wilkes, *Narrative of the U.S. Exploring Expedition*, vol. 3, 116.
57. Ibid.
58. Ibid., vol. 2, 97.
59. PRO, FO 58/69, Erskine to Admiralty, 10 October 1849.
60. Wilkes, *Narrative of the U.S. Exploring Expedition*, vol. 2, p 97–107.
61. PRO, FO 58/89, Williams to Loring, 22 November 1858.
62. Greg Dening, *History's Anthropology: The Death of William Gooch* (Lanham: University Press of America, 1988), 17.
63. *Sydney Morning Herald*, 22 July 1857.
64. NMM, MRK/8, *Southern Cross*, 27 February 1872.
65. Pembroke in [Manning], *Old New Zealand*, xii.
66. *Sydney Morning Herald*, 18 October 1865.
67. Murray, *Forty Years' Mission Work*, 499.
68. Rhodes House, British and Foreign Aborigines' Protection Society MSS, MSS Br Emp s 18/C133 (138) Erskine to Chesson, 27 February 1875.
69. BM, Halifax MSS, Add MS 49551, Loring to Woods, 17 May 1858.
70. PRO, ADM 1/5696, Loring to Admiralty, 6 September 1858.
71. *Sydney Morning Herald*, 24 October 1865.
72. ML, PMB 31, Synod Minutes of New Hebrides Presbyterian Mission, memorial to Commodore Wiseman, 1 August 1865.
73. Ibid.
74. James Paton, ed., *John G. Paton, D. D. Missionary to the New Hebrides: An Autobiography* (reprint ed.: London: Banner of Truth Trust, 1965), 298.
75. Herbert Meade, *A Ride through the Disturbed Districts of New Zealand, Together with Some Account of the South Sea Islands* (London: John Murray, 1870), 231.
76. *Aborigines' Friend* 2 (1865), 490.
77. ML, PMB 31, Minutes of New Hebrides Presbyterian Mission Synod, 3 July 1871, 93.
78. Ibid. See also PMB 197, Milne MSS, Peter Milne to his parents, 24 July 1871.
79. ML, PMB 197, Peter Milne MSS, Milne to brother, 24 December 1872.
80. Ibid.
81. Ibid., Milne to his parents, 20 October 1870.
82. ML, PMB 216, Papers of the Melanesian Mission, Voyages of the Southern Cross 1874–77, report of Robert Codrington, 7 May 1875.
83. Michael Lewis, *The Navy in Transition, 1814–1864: A Social History* (London: Hodder and Stoughton, 1965), 122.
84. NMM, BLK/1, journal entry, 23 July 1867.
85. Quoted in Patterson, *Missionary Life among the Cannibals*, 477, 482.

86. ML FM4/2411, Selwyn to Markham, 29 May 1872.
87. ML, MS 802, Mitchell Library, Markham to Tilly, 24 February 1872.
88. Ibid.
89. *Illustrated Sydney News*, 19 August 1854.
90. *P.P.* 1872, XXXIX [543], Markham to Stirling, 12 February 1872, 11.
91. NMM, MRK/8, *New Zealand Herald*, 27 February 1872.
92. Ibid., *The Morning Post*, 14 May 1872.
93. Ibid., *Telegraph*, 18 [January] 1872.

9 THE TRIUMPH OF TRADITION

1. D. K. Fieldhouse, *Economics and Empire, 1830–1914,* second ed. (London: Macmillan, 1984), 225–245; and Michael Havinden and David Meredith, *Colonialism and Development: Britain and Its Tropical Colonies, 1850–1960* (London and New York: Routledge, 1993), 48, 60–62.

2. W. David McIntyre, "New Light on Commodore Goodenough's Mission to Fiji 1873–74," *Historical Studies* 39 (1962), 270–288.

3. Deryck Scarr, "John Bates Thurston, Commodore J. G. Goodenough, and Rampant Anglo-Saxons in Fiji," *Historical Studies* 11:43 (1964), 361–382. David Routledge took both McIntyre and Scarr to task for neglecting wider historical contexts in "The Negotiations Leading to the Cession of Fiji, 1874," *Journal of Imperial and Commonwealth History* 2:3 (1974), 278–293.

4. Bach, *The Australia Station,* 125.

5. J. D. Legge, *Britain in Fiji, 1858–1880;* and Peter France, *The Charter of the Land: Custom and Colonization in Fiji* (Melbourne and London: Oxford University Press, 1969).

6. John S. Galbraith with George Bennett, "The Humanitarian Impulse to Imperialism," in Robin Winks, ed., *British Imperialism: Gold, God, Glory* (Berkeley: University of California Press, 1963), 71–76.

7. Whether this constituted Tongan imperialism is debated in I. C. Campbell, "The Alleged Imperialism of George Tupou I," *Journal of Pacific History* 25:2 (1990), 159–175; and Deryck Scarr, "Cakobau and Ma'afu: Contenders for Pre-eminence in Fiji," in Davidson and Scarr, *Pacific Islands Portraits,* 95–126.

8. Routledge, *Matanitū,* 86.

9. CUL, Add 8780, G. K. Roth Papers, "Notes" on early Fijian history.

10. AONSW 4/3224, Williams to Colonial Secretary, 18 April 1853. The date is incorrect; according to notes on the file, it was received in Sydney in December, and it clearly refers to the September episode.

11. David Routledge, "American Influence on the Politics of Fiji, 1849–1874," *Journal of Pacific Studies* 4 (1978), 73.

12. WMMS, FBN 6/300, Bailey to Calvert, 4 May 1857.

13. FO 58/113, Thurston to FO, 27 May 1868; and FO 58/114, CO to FO, 3 December 1868, with enclosures and abstract.

14. Routledge, *Matanitū,* 120.

15. SOAS, WMMS, FBN 6/292, Calvert to Secretaries, 24 July 1855, writing aboard *Herald.*

16. Ibid.

17. *P.P.* 1862, XXXVI [701], "Correspondence Relating to the Fiji Islands," Pritchard to FO, 8 February 1859.

18. W. David McIntyre, *The Imperial Frontier in the Tropics, 1865–75* (London, Melbourne, Toronto: Macmillan, 1967), 218.

19. Pritchard, *Polynesian Reminiscences*, 234.

20. *P.P.* 1862, "Correspondence Relating to the Fiji Islands," "Instructions to Colonel Smythe," 23 December 1859.

21. James Belich tackles this and other "myths of empire" in his *Making Peoples: A History of the New Zealanders from Polynesian Settlement to the End of the Nineteenth Century* (Auckland and London: Penguin, 1996). Legge has argued that fear of another race war in the south Pacific was the British government's main reason for rejecting the 1858 cession proposal; Legge, *Britain in Fiji*, 34.

22. Campbell, "British Treaties with Polynesians," 74.

23. *P.P.* 1862, "Correspondence Relating to the Fiji Islands," Denison to CO, 10 April 1860.

24. Ibid., Smythe to CO, 1 May 1861; and Routledge, *Matanitū*, 98.

25. Berthold Seemann, *Viti: An Account of a Government Mission to the Vitian or Fijian Islands, 1860–1861* (Folkestone and London: Dawson's, 1973; first publ. 1862), vii–viii.

26. Ibid., xv.

27. SOAS, WMMS, FBN 35/1559, Calvert to Rowe, 31 July 1862.

28. SOAS, WMMS, FBN 5/226, Calvert to Secretaries, 25 July 1862.

29. Routledge, *Matanitū*, 105.

30. Scarr, *I, the Very Bayonet*, 99–106.

31. PRO, ADM 1/6054, Lambert to Admiralty, 4 August 1868.

32. Ibid., Thurston to Lambert, 1 August 1868.

33. Ibid., Brownrigg to Lambert, 31 July 1868; and Henry Britton, *Fiji in 1870* (Melbourne: Samuel Mullen, 1870), 25.

34. SOAS, WMMS, FBN 5/236, Calvert to Boyce, 4 March 1869.

35. PRO, FO 58/116, Childers to FO, 18 February 1869.

36. Routledge, *Matanitū*, 126–139.

37. *P.P.* 1873, XLII [76], "Fiji Islands (Instructions to Naval Officers)," Admiralty to Stirling, 2 January 1872, with enclosure. I. C. Campbell has pointed out that the situation at this point was almost exactly like that in New Zealand in the late 1830s, and if Britain had accepted cession at this point, the two cases would have been even more alike; Campbell, "British Treaties with Polynesians," 76.

38. A. B. Brewster, *King of the Cannibal Islands* (London: Robert Hale, 1937), Journals of Commodore J. G. Goodenough (hereafter 150; and "Goodenough Journals"), 18 December 1873.

39. ML, MSS A6975–1, Central Archives of Fiji and the Western Pacific High Commission (hereafter CAF), Thurston to Sahl, 13 September 1872.

40. ML FM4/2143, CAF, Douglas to Thurston, 4 June 1872.

41. ML FM4/2144, CAF, Chapman to Thurston, 23 March 1873.

42. Ibid., Thurston to Chapman, 8 April 1873, and Chapman's reply of 9 April.

43. PRO, ADM 1/6261, Stirling to Admiralty, 18 April 1873.

44. Brewster, *King of the Cannibal Isles*, 70.

45. ML FM4/2144, CAF, Stirling to Thurston, 9 and 11 August 1873.
46. Ibid., Simpson to Thurston, 3 September 1873.
47. ML FM4/3042, CAF, Diary of E. J. Turpin, entry 4 September 1873.
48. PRO, ADM 1/6261, Stirling to Admiralty, 23 August 1873.
49. *Hansard,* vol. CCXII, 25 June 1872.
50. McIntyre, *Imperial Frontier in the Tropics,* 247.
51. Ibid., 250.
52. ML FM4/4018, CAF, *Fiji Gazette,* 12 October 1872.
53. Quoted in McIntyre, *Imperial Frontier in the Tropics,* 250.
54. APS, *Annual Report, 1874* (London, 1874), 6–12.
55. See McIntyre, *Imperial Frontier in the Tropics,* 321–322.
56. ML FM4/1767, "Goodenough Journals," 10 June 1873.
57. Ibid., 9 October 1873.
58. Ibid., 4 October 1873.
59. Scarr, "John Bates Thurston, Commodore J. G. Goodenough, and Rampant Anglo-Saxons in Fiji," 370–371. He puts the case even more strongly in his *Fiji: A Short History* (Sydney and London: Allen and Unwin, 1984), 68.
60. Howe, *Where the Waves Fall,* 248–249.
61. PRO, ADM 1/5969, Hope to Williams, 5 September 1866.
62. Howe, *Where the Waves Fall,* 250–251.
63. PRO, ADM 1/6261, Goodenough to Admiralty, 14 November 1873.
64. See Scarr, *Fiji: A Short History,* 67–68.
65. ML FM4/1767, Goodenough Journals, 24 October 1873.
66. Ibid., 12 November 1873.
67. Fiji's first governor, Arthur Gordon, recalled Goodenough's formidable shipboard library of four hundred volumes; quoted in McIntyre, *Imperial Frontier in the Tropics,* 322.
68. ML FM4/1767, Goodenough Journals, 8 November 1873.
69. Ibid., 22 November 1873 and 4 January 1874.
70. Routledge, *Matanitū,* 173–178.
71. ML FM4/2144, CAF, Goodenough to Thurston, 9 December 1873.
72. Ibid., Goodenough to Thurston, 2 December 1873.
73. McIntyre, *Imperial Frontier in the Tropics,* 250.
74. ML FM4/2144, CAF, Goodenough to Thurston, 5 December 1873.
75. PRO, ADM 1/6303, Goodenough to Admiralty, 3 July 1874; and ML FM4/2144, CAF, Layard to Thurston, 4 June 1874.
76. Ibid., Goodenough to Thurston, 14 January 1874.
77. ML FM4/1767, Goodenough Journals, 26 November 1873.
78. ML FM4/2144, CAF, Goodenough to Thurston, 14 January, 1874.
79. SOAS, WMMS, FBN 5/236, Committee to Layard, 12 March 1874.
80. SOAS, WMMS, FBN 35/1584, Jenkins to Nettleton, 16 April 1892.
81. PRO, ADM 1/6303, FO to Goodenough and Layard, 18 April 1874.
82. ML, MSS A6975–2, CAF, Thurston to Goodenough, 15 December 1873.
83. Ibid.
84. ML FM4/4018, CAF, *Fiji Gazette,* 11 October 1873.

85. ML, MSS A6975–2, CAF, Thurston to Layard, 16 January 1874.
86. Quoted in John Young, "Evanescent Ascendancy: The Planter Community in Fiji," in Davidson and Scarr, *Pacific Islands Portraits,* 147.
87. Quoted in Routledge, *Matanitū,* 185.
88. PRO, ADM 1/6086, Crown Law Officers to CO, 27 June 1873.
89. PRO, ADM 1/6303, Goodenough to Admiralty, 23 April 1874.
90. *P.P.* 1874, XLV [297], "Letter Addressed to Commodore Goodenough and Mr. Consul Layard," 15 August 1873.
91. *Fiji Gazette,* 13 December 1873.
92. Quoted in Routledge, *Matanitū,* 197.
93. ML FM4/1767, Goodenough Journals, 16 March 1874.
94. PRO, ADM 1/6303, Preliminary Report by Goodenough and Layard, 13 February [1874].
95. Routledge, *Matanitū,* 202; and Scarr, *Fiji: A Short History,* 74.
96. Roger C. Thompson, *Australian Imperialism in the Pacific: The Expansionist Era, 1820–1920* (Melbourne: Melbourne University Press, 1980), 21–34.
97. Ibid., 31.
98. ML, CY MSS, Parkes MSS, vol. 45, 312–313. This would not be the last naval-colonial collaboration, either; for example, in 1884 Commodore James Erskine, nephew of Admiral John Erskine, would declare a British protectorate in Papua New Guinea, an area "annexed" the previous year by the government of Queensland.

EPILOGUE

1. ML FM4/1767, Goodenough Journals, 25 June 1875.
2. Ibid., 12 August 1875.
3. ML FM4/1767, Goodenough Notebooks, transcript of Perry to Milne, 27 August 1875.
4. Ibid.
5. Ibid., "Extract from a letter of Nav'n Lieutenant H. Hosken, RN."
6. Ibid., Perry to Milne, 27 August 1875.
7. Ibid.
8. ML, Henderson, "Journal Written on HMS *Sappho,*" 824, 826.
9. The *Times,* 26 August 1875. This article was also carried by the *Army and Navy Gazette,* prompting an angry response from Admiral Phipps Hornby, a veteran of the Pacific Station; ibid., 29 August 1875.
10. ML FM4/1767, Goodenough Journals, *Newcastle Chronicle,* 26 August 1875.
11. *Allawarra Mercury,* 27 August 1875.
12. E.g., *The Sydney Morning Herald,* 27 August 1875.
13. *The Saturday Review,* 27 August 1875.
14. NMM, JOD/120, W. F. Carslake, Private Journal on Board *Pearl,* 1874–1875, entry for 30 August.
15. Henri Baudet, *Paradise on Earth: Some Thoughts on European Images of Non-European Man,* first English edition (New Haven and London: Yale University Press, 1965), 55.

Select Bibliography

ALL of the British-based records listed below are available on microfilm through the Australian Joint Copying Project at the National Library of Australia. Other records are available through the Pacific Manuscripts Bureau.

Since nineteenth-century British naval records may be unfamiliar to some readers of this book, I have annotated parts of the bibliography in hopes of promoting the richness of these records and inviting further research. Those interested in more detail should note several articles about Pacific naval archives published in the *Journal of Pacific History*, especially L. Cleland, "Royal Navy-Australian Station," 1 (1966), 183–184; Phyllis Mander-Jones, "Admiralty Station Manuscripts on the Pacific in the Public Record Office, London," 2 (1967), 170–171; Phyllis Mander-Jones and Judith Baskin, "Admiralty Records in the Public Record Office, London: Notes on Records Relating to Australia, New Zealand and the Pacific," 3 (1968), 162–165; and Barry M. Gough, "The Records of the Royal Navy's Pacific Station," 4 (1969), 146–153.

I have given only a select listing of primary and secondary references: all items referred to in the notes are included, along with selected background readings.

ARCHIVAL PRIMARY SOURCES

(AIM) *The Auckland Institute and Museum (Auckland, N.Z.)*
Robert Leeds Sinclair, "The True Account of the Loss of the Barque Harriet of Sydney," MS 279.

(AONSW) *The Archives Office of New South Wales (Sydney, Australia)*

Attorney General MSS (AGen 9/2697–9).

Colonial Secretary (Col Sec 1): Inwards Correspondence from 1871.

Colonial Secretary (Col Sec 4): In-Letters—Naval and Military, 1832–1859; Letters to Naval and Military Officers, 1832–1856; Letters to Naval and Military Officers, 1856–1875; Letters Sent to Clergy (1854–1856); Letters to New Zealand (1840–1856); Minutes of the Legislative Council; Governors' Papers, 1855–1861; Despatches from New Zealand, 1853–1862; Despatches to New Zealand, 1840–1841; Crown Solicitors' Judgment Books.

Governors (Gov 4): "Letters received from, and sent to, Officials and Private Persons," 1855–1880.

Supreme Court of New South Wales, Judges' Notebooks: Judge Stephen, Criminal (1851): 2/7020 (for R. *v.* John Charles Lewis); Judge Dickinson, Criminal (1854): 2/3114 (for R. *v.* John Ross).

(APL) *The Auckland City Public Library (Auckland, N.Z.)*

Governor Fitzroy Letterbook, 1845, and Governor Grey Letterbook, 1845–1853 (NZ MSS 227). Extensive correspondence with Home during the 1845–1846 uprising, letters from Home after his return to England, and a renewal of correspondence during Home's Senior Officership in 1851–1853.

Grey Letters (GL): Captain John Erskine (E23), Rev. John Inglis (I2), Captain John Maxwell (W1), and NZ MSS 227A, Captain Richard Oliver (O4).

Sir J. E. Home Correspondence (GL/NZ/H32): Includes detailed accounts of *North Star's* operations during the Maori uprising of 1845–1846, letters to Grey written after Home's return to England in 1847, and correspondence from Home's second south Pacific command in *Calliope*. Other letters from Home are in GL/NZ/F17 and GL/NZ/R11.

William Nihiol: "Journals, 1849–1851" (NZ MSS 132–134).

G. A. Selwyn: Letters, 1848–1861 (NZ MSS 740).

(ATL) *The Alexander Turnbull Library (Wellington, N.Z.)*

Richard Barrett: "Journal," MS Papers 1736.

Henry Gabriel Swainson: "Private Journal Commencing Jan 1st 1850 ending December 31st 1850, Henry Swainson, Her Majesty's Ship 'Havannah,' " QMS MS 1850–51/P.

Henry Gabriel Swainson letters: MS Papers 2373 and MS/SWA.

Philip D. Vigors: "Private Journal of a Four Months' Cruise in H.M.S. 'Havannah,' " QMS MS VIG 2081.

(BCRO) *Buckinghamshire County Record Office (Aylesbury, U.K.)*

Fremantle Family Papers (D/FR): This large archive, which consists of official and private correspondence, estate accounts, and other papers, includes a substantial collection from Captain Stephen Fremantle. Of the greatest importance are the large number of informal letters exchanged between Fremantle and Captain Henry Denham in 1854–1847, and the Governor of New South Wales, Sir William Denison. Both sides of each correspondence are included, providing a rare glimpse of the private opinions expressed by naval officers and their friends in the Australian Division.

(BLO) *Bodleian Library (Oxford, U.K.)*

Clarendon Deposit: "Papers, 1843–1870."

(BM) *The British Museum Manuscripts Department (London, U.K.)*

Halifax Papers: Add MS 49548, Correspondence with Captain Erskine, and Add MS 49551, letters from Captain Loring.

Stanmore Papers: Selected volumes, Add MSS 49204–49271, letters from various correspondents, including J. B. Thurston and Cdre. James Erskine.

(BUL) *Birmingham University Library (Birmingham, U.K.)*

Church Missionary Society Archives (CMS): Alfred Nesbit Brown Letters (1831–1839), C/N/026/1–100; Henry Williams Letters (1823–1842) C/N/093/1–61 and C/N/095/1–86; Henry Williams Journals (1830–1840) C/N/093/201–231 and C/N/095/117–226; Mission Letterbooks (Sydney) (1834–1836), C/N/M7–M8; Marsden Correspondence: Micro Acc 16, especially reel 3.

(CAF) *Central Archives of Fiji and the Western Pacific High Commission (Suva, Fiji, and Sydney, Australia)*

These records were consulted at the Mitchell Library in Sydney, and the reference numbers are all for ML manuscripts or microfilm. Many of the original papers are still in Fiji.

Cakobau Government Records: Ministry of Lands and Works (also naval and military affairs), outwards correspondence 1873, MSS A6970–A6971; Chief Secretary's Office and Ministry of Foreign Relations outwards correspondence, 1872–1874, MSS A6965–A6966, 6975–1/2, 6978; Chief Secretary's Office and Colonial Secretary's Office inwards correspondence 1871–1875 (FM4/2134–2143); Chief Secretary's Office, naval and consular inwards correspondence 1871–1874 (FM4/2143–2145, 2147–2151); Chief Secretary's Office and Ministry of Foreign Relations, general outwards correspondence, 1871–1874 (FM4/2146)

Fiji Gazette: 1872–1874, FM4/4018.

Richard Philp: Diary 1872, FM4/2559.

Robert S. Swanston: Journals 1857–1866 and 1874–1885, FM4/2558.

John Thurston MSS: List of contents at A2923–10; MSS at FM4/3579.

Edwin J. Turpin: Diary and narratives, 1870–c. 1894, FM4/3042.

(CUL) *Cambridge University Library (Cambridge, U.K.)*

Brewster Collection and G. K. Roth Papers (Add 8780): "Paciffic [*sic*] History," notes by a trader at Aneityum, New Hebrides, in 1883 and Brewster's notes on "Jimmy the Devil," both in Box 10.

(HOA) *U.K. Hydrographic Office Archives (Taunton, U.K.)*

This collection is one of the most neglected sources of information about British contacts with Pacific islanders. I have made use of selected volumes of the Remark Books, but the collection is vast and includes a large amount of original correspondence. Volumes consulted include

Remark Books 1844 to 1845: HMS *North Star* (Capt. Sir James Everard Home).

Remark Books 1848 to 1850: HMS *Calypso* (Capt. H. Worth and R. Knox, master); HMS *Dido* (Capt. J. Maxwell); HMS *Fly* (Cdr. R. Oliver and W. Luke, master); HMS *Havannah* (Capt. J. Erskine and W. Hilliard, master).

Remark Books 1855 to 1856: HMS *Juno* (Capt. S. Fremantle).

(JRL) *John Rylands University Library of Manchester (Manchester, U.K.)*

Methodist Archives and Research Centre (MAM): MAM Diaries, Walter Lawry Journal; MAM Individual Collections, John Hunt.

(ML) *The Mitchell Library (Sydney, Australia)*

Archival Estrays: These items were removed from the main government collections, often by colonial officials themselves, and are now found in various collections at the ML: Letterbooks from the Attorney General's office 1831–1884 (A165); NSW Law Office letterbook, 1865–1868 (A843, CY Reel 2573); Dixson MSS SP/193 "Documents re outrages at Rotumah Island"; SP/194 "Papers re ss Islands"; SP/195 "Pacific Islands." Also in this category is the file "Official Manuscripts, 1839–1854" (A1384, CY Reel 736), which contains, among other things, Captain Denham's report "Proceedings of H.M.S. *Herald*" on his search for Benjamin Boyd in 1854–1855.

Belmore MSS: Private and semi-private letterbooks, with letters from naval officers and others, 1868–1872 (A2542, vols. 1–3, CY Reel 496).

John Brazier: "Notes on the Cruize of H.M.S. Blanche, from Sydney, through the South Sea Islands, May 12–Nov 15, 1872," B512, CY Reel 681.

Rev. George Brown MSS: ML Doc 3261; A1686–1, CY Reel 2766; A1686–10/11/12, CY Reel 2759.

Rev. David Cargill: "Journal," 1832–1838, MS CY A1817.

Rev. James Cosh: Correspondence, MSS 1484, CY Reel 779.

Sir William Denison MSS: FM3/795.

R.A. Derrick: "Extracts from Letter Books of H.B.M. Consular Office, Levuka, Fiji, 1863–1869," A3167.

Rev. M. Dyson Journals: A2579–A2582.

Miles Franklin MSS: MSS 364/1.

J. W. Gambier: "Logs of HMS Retribution and Iris, 1855–1861," A2027.

R. P. Gilson MSS: PMB 1003, esp. reel 3, folders 33–41.

Commodore J. G. Goodenough MSS: Journals 1873–1875, and copies of letters with newspaper cuttings about Goodenough's death (compiled by his wife) at MSS 889/6–8, FM4/1767–1768.

Henry Gunton: "Diary of an Expedition to New Zealand in H.M.S. Alligator Aug–Nov 1834," MS A2892 (Micro FM 3/56).

Rev. David Hazlewood: "Journals," 1842–1850, MSS B568–B570.

Lt. Francis Hayter: Logbook and Journal 1871–1873, PMB 626.

Lt. Frank Henderson: "Journal written on HMS *Sappho*, 1875–76," CY MSS 369.

Francis Hixon: Logs of HMS *Havannah* 1848–1851 (A2748/2–3, CY Reel 2093) and Remark Books HMS *Torch* 1854–1855 and *Herald* 1855–1860 (A2748/3, B1131, CY Reel 2093).

Henry John Hoare: Journals of HMS *Dido, Clio* and *Pearl*, 1871–1874; A1761–1762, CY Reel 1307.

Admiral P.P. King Papers: Letters 1824–1855, FM4/66.

Rev. Walter Lawry: Diary 1851, B939.

Rev. Richard B. Lyth: "Journals," 1845–1853 (MS CY B535, 536–1, B541); "Daybooks," 1849–1854 (MS CY B538, B545); "Letters, 1836–1854" (MS 6658 and MS A836, CY Reel 108); "Notices" (B559); and historian George Henderson's MS notes on the Lyth journals (MS CY B536–2).

Macarthur Papers: Letters to James Macarthur (MS A2923–A2936); Letters to Emily Macarthur (MS A4346).

Rev. S. Macfarlane: Journals 1859–1869, A833, A893.

Melanesian Mission: "Island Voyages of the 'Southern Cross' 1874–77," PMB Doc 216; and general MSS, PMB 559.

Rev. Peter Milne: Letters 1869–1893, PMB 197.

Charles Moore: "Diary of a Cruise in HMS Havannah to the South Sea Islands," MS B786.

George Morrison MSS: ML MSS 312.

New Hebrides Presbyterian Mission: Synod Minutes 1857–1938, PMB 31 and PMB Doc 218; Annual Reports 1871–1901, PMB Doc 218.

Rev. Henry Nisbet: Correspondence and diaries 1835–1876, ML MSS 3093.

Rev. George Nobbs: Correspondence, A2881–1, 6.

Sir Henry Parkes: Correspondence, ML MSS 246.

George L. Ryder: "Pioneering in the South Seas," MSS 2868.

Captain Shepherd: "Journal of the Sparrowhawk," ML MSS 2831, CY Reel 2538.

Joseph Woods Smith: Remark Book, HMS *Herald*, 1852–1857; ML MSS 3214, CY Reel 1676.

Steel Family: Correspondence, ML MSS 28/1.

Steinberger MSS: FM4/200.

John Thomas: Correspondence 1825–1835, ML MS A1959, CY Reel 782.

Sir Edward Deas Thompson: Correspondence 1792–1883, A1531–3, CY Reels 721 and 813.

The Towns Papers: Outward Letters (General): Uncatalogued MSS Set 307, items 111–120; Outward Letters (Colonial): Set 307, items 40–42; Private Letterbooks: ML MS 88605, item 87; Incoming correspondence: ML MSS 1274/4, MSS 1279/16, MSS 1279/6–7; and Set 307, items 152–186, 189, 194.

R. H. Walpole MSS: Log HMS *Blanche* 1873, log HMS *Pearl* 1873–1875, ML MSS 2466/1.

Rev. Joseph Waterhouse: Papers, ML MSS 554.

Rev. James Watkin: Papers, ML MSS 713.

J. C. Williams: Papers, PMB 24.

Rev. Thomas Williams: "Journals," 1839–1852, B588–1 and B589.

(MM) *The Melanesian Mission (SOAS, U.K.)*

Correspondence Inward (miscellaneous), 1862–1875; Rev. Robert Codrington MSS, journals and letters, 1867–1882.

(NANZ) *The National Archives of New Zealand (Wellington, N.Z.)*

Archives of the British Consul, Samoa, 1847–1916 (BCS): Inward Correspondence, 1847–1876, Micro S/3512 (BCS 2/1); Letters to Samoan Government and Chiefs, 1857–1874, Micro S3556 (BCS 4/1); General Outwards Correspondence, 1859–1874, Micro S 2558 (BCS 5/1); Miscellaneous Papers, Micro S3623 (BCS 7/2).

Archives of the Colonial Secretaries (cs): Inwards correspondence, 1848–1852 (CS/1).
Archives of the Governors General (G): Naval and Military Letters, 1846–1853 (G16/1); Despatches to Gipps from Hobson (G36/1); Governor's Miscellaneous Outward Letters (G36/3); Outwards Letters to Naval and Military Officers (G33/1); Inwards Letters from Selwyn and Others (G19/1).
Archives of the Executive Council (EC): Council Minutes, 1841–1855 (EC/1).
Gore-Browne Papers (GB): Letters from Australia, 1858 (GB/1).
Royal Navy Australia Station Records (RNAS): These documents were left with the senior British naval officer in New Zealand after the last commander in chief of the Australia Station left in 1913. Much of the local correspondence and administrative material is not found in the Admiralty collection at the Public Record Office in Britain, making this a unique record of the Royal Navy's relationship with Australia. The collection is available on microfilm (but with different numbering schemes) at the NANZ and the Mitchell Library in Sydney. Both sets of references are given below; only files used for this book are cited:
    Vol. 13, "Pacific Islands, 1857–76" (NANZ Micro 3460, ML FM4/1654).
    Vol. 21, "Kidnapping, 1869–75" (Micro 3469, FM4/1663).
    Vol. 22, "Labour Traffic and Pearl Fisheries, 1873–80" (Micro 3470, FM4/1664).
    Vol. 28, "Fiji, 1868–79" (Micro 3476, FM4/1670).
    Vol. 32, "New Caledonia, 1870–83" (Micro 3479, FM4/1673).
    Vol. 33, "New Hebrides, 1873–79" (Micro 3480, FM4/1674).
    Vol. 43, "Index" (Micro 3488, FM 4/1682).
U.S. Government National Archives Holdings (RG): U.S. Consuls, Bay of Islands and Auckland, 1838–1906, Micro Z/2606–2619 (RG 59); U.S. Consul in Apia (Samoa), 1843–1906, Micro Z/2621–2647 (RG 59); Despatches from U.S. Consuls in Samoa, 1850–1856, Micro Z/2658–2660 (RG 59); Naval Secretary's letters from the Commander-in-Chief, Brazils Station, 1854–1857, Micro Z/2670–2671 (RG 84); Naval Secretary's letters from Commanders, 1857–1876, Micro Z/2672–2675 (RG 84).

(NLA) *The National Library of Australia (Canberra, Australia)*

Catherine Dengate: "British Naval Vessels in the Pacific Islands, 1800–1900: A Provisional Index to Source Material," filmed by the Pacific Manuscripts Bureau, PMB 516.
Rev. John Geddie: Diaries, MS 2180.
G. H. Inskip: "Private Journal 1849–1850," NLA MS 3784.
Alexander Kerr: Correspondence 1848–1851, NLA MS 7257.
Richard and Mary Ann Lyth: Correspondence 1829–1856, NLA MS 6658.

(NMM) *The National Maritime Museum (Greenwich, U.K.)*

Bellasis Papers and Admiral Richard Aldworth Oliver Papers (BEL); John Lort Stokes Papers (STK); Admiral Phipps Hornby Papers (PHI); William Hans Blake Papers (BLK).

(PRO) *The Public Record Office (Kew, London, U.K.)*

(ADM 1) Admiralty and Secretariat Papers: This class consists of all incoming correspondence from naval officers, British government departments (mainly the Colonial and Foreign Offices), the Admiralty solicitor, and other correspondents. This book makes use of most volumes from 1829 to 1875, with selected earlier volumes, but readers should note that material from 1830 to 1858 is incomplete. The Admiralty discarded most of the correspondence during "weeding" at the end of the nineteenth century, keeping only those items that seemed important at the time. For this reason, the index system found in ADM 12 (see below) does not always reflect the actual content of the volumes.

(ADM 2) Admiralty and Secretariat—Outgoing Correspondence: Parts of this collection are incomplete, but the following were particularly useful (and indexed): General Instructions (1823–1878): ADM 2/1329–1330; Military Branch—Foreign Stations (1829–1859): ADM 2/1590–1616; and Political and Secret Branch (1825–1857): ADM 2/1695–1705.

(ADM 7) Admiralty and Secretariat—Miscellanea: ADM 7/851 and 7/852: John MacGillivray, "Voyage of H.M.S. Herald under the command of Capt. H. Mangles Denham RN, being a Private Journal kept by John MacGillivray, Naturalist."

(ADM 12) Admiralty Index and Digest: All incoming correspondence was logged in the indexes, and notes were made in the digests about what the correspondence contained (for example, "report of proceedings") and whether it was forwarded to another government department. The incomplete state of ADM 1 makes these registers an invaluable guide to the original correspondence. They also indicate when captains' reports were copied to the Foreign or Colonial Office. I used selected volumes covering 1827–1875.

(ADM 13) Admiralty and Secretariat: Secret Correspondence: Port and Standing Instructions 1823–1850 (ADM 13/2–3); Station Orders 1860–1878 (ADM 13/5–6); Military Branch, Foreign Stations, 1867–1869 (ADM 13/39–40); and "Paper left by the Earl of Auckland expressing his views on our Naval Means," 1 December 1847 (ADM 13/185).

(ADM 50) Admirals' Journals: Until 1854 these are indexed by name; after that date, by station. Volumes consulted were ADM 50/213–225 for Rear Admiral Sir G. F. Seymour, and ADM 50/229 for Rear Admiral Richard Thomas.

(ADM 53) Ships' Logs, 1790–1885: Selected volumes from logs of the following vessels:

Basilisk, 1871–1874 (53/10289–10291).
Blanche, 1868–1869 (53/9888).
Bramble, 1850–1851 (53/3679).
Brisk, 1865–1868 (53/9276–9278).
Calypso, 1847–1849 (53/2327–2331).
Challenger, 1866–1869 (53/9742–9744).
Cordelia, 1858–1860 (53/7175–7178).
Curaçoa, 1864–1866 (53/8748).
Dido, 1847–1849 (53/2407–2411).
Falcon, 1867 (53/9193).
Favorite, 1837–1839 (53/539).
Fly, 1848–1851 (53/3665–3673).
Havannah, 1848–1851 (53/3629–3636).
Iris, 1856–1859 (53/6901–6902).
Juno, 1855–1857 (53/5896–5897).
Pearl, 1873–1875 (53/10742–10744).
Rosario, 1870–1871 (53/9892–9893 and 10491).

(ADM 122) Australia Station: General 1866–1879 (ADM 122/1); Queensland 1868–1884 (ADM 122/11); Samoa 1855–1879 (ADM 122/12). Most of the records have been transferred to

New Zealand (see National Archives of New Zealand, Royal Navy Australia Station Records above).

(ADM 125) China Station: Cocos or Keelings Islands and Seychelles, 1830–1839 (ADM 125/131); Australian Division Records, 1856–1858 (ADM 125/135).

(ADM 172) Pacific Station: "Pacific 1845–1857, Navigator's, Friendly, and Feejee Islands" (ADM 172/3); "Correspondence between Rear Adm. Sir G. F. Seymour. . . and the Admiralty from 14th May 1844 to 31st Dec 1845" (ADM 172/4). Most of the records have been transferred to the British Columbia Archives and Records Service in Canada.

(CO) Colonial Office Records: Fiji (CO 83); New South Wales (CO 201); New Zealand (CO 209); Queensland (CO 234/21); Crown Law Officers' Opinions (CO 305); Index to Crown Law Officers' Opinions (CO 323); Memoranda Relating to North American and Australian Colonies (CO 325); Indices to NSW Correspondence (CO 714); and Confidential Print, Miscellaneous (CO 885).

(FO) Foreign Office Records: Pacific Islands (FO 58); General (FO 83), especially FO 83/130 "Sailing Letters 1832–52"; America—United States (FO 97), especially FO 97/497 "Report on British Jurisdiction in Foreign States" and "Memorandum on Her Majesty's Jurisdiction in Western Polynesia"; Printed Correspondence Relative to the Society Islands, 1822–1843 (FO 534).

(RGS) *The Royal Geographical Society (London, U.K.)*

Journal MSS: Captain Henry Worth, "Account of a Visit in Septr 1848 to the Georgian, Navigators, Feejee and Friendly Islands."
Library MSS: Capt. F. R. M. Crozier papers and letters.

(RH) *Rhodes House Library (Oxford, U.K.)*

Papers of the British and Foreign Aborigines' Protection Society, 1837–88 (APS): MSS Brit. Emp. s. 18 and s. 22.
Sir Thomas F. Buxton MSS, 1834–1837: MSS Br. Emp. s. 444.
R. H. Codrington diaries, 1869–1882: MSS Pacific s. 2.
R. H. Codrington correspondence, 1867–1887: MSS Pacific s. 4.

(SCL) *Selwyn College Library (Cambridge, U.K.)*

Selwyn Papers: Box D contains letters from Bishop George Selwyn to his father, describing various island cruises.

(SOAS) *The School of Oriental and African Studies (London, U.K.)*

This is the repository for all official reports and correspondence of the London Missionary Society (later incorporated into the Council for World Mission) and the Wesleyan Methodist Missionary Society. Given the close relationship between naval officers and British missionaries in the islands, these papers were a rich source of information on Royal Navy activities and the humanitarianism its officers often shared with missions.

London Missionary Society (CWM): South Seas Correspondence, Incoming Letters, 1796–1927; South Seas Journals, 1796–1889; South Seas Reports, 1866–1939.
Wesleyan Methodist Missionary Society (WMMS): From FBN Australasian Correspondence: Australia, 1812–1842 (FBN 1); Australia, 1852–1864 (FBN 3); Australia, 1864–1889

(FBN 4); Fiji, 1835–1842 (FBN 5); Fiji, 1843–1884 (FBN 6); Samoa 1839–1870 (FBN 11); Tonga, 1822–1835 (FBN 12); Tonga, 1835–1843 (FBN 13); Tonga, 1843–1887 (FBN 14); James Calvert papers (Special Series FBN 35); John Hunt Papers (Special Series FBN 36).

PRINTED PRIMARY SOURCES

Great Britain Parliamentary Papers (P.P.)

"Report from the Select Committee on Aborigines (British Settlements)," 1836 VII [538].

"Report from the Select Committee on Aborigines (British Settlements), 1837 VII [425].

"Report from the Select Committee of the House of Lords, Appointed to Inquire into the Present State of the Islands of New Zealand," 1838 XXI [680].

"Correspondence Relating to the Fiji Islands," 1862 XXXVI [701].

"Correspondence Relating to Importation of South Sea Islanders into Queensland," 1868/69 XLIII [408].

"Further Correspondence Respecting the Deportation of South Sea Islanders," 1871 XIX [399].

"Correspondence and Documents Relating to the Fiji Islands," 1871 XLVII [777].

"Reports of Proceedings of H.M.S. 'Rosario' during Cruise among Islands, between 1st November 1871 and 12th February 1872," 1872 XXXIX [543].

"Fiji Islands (Instructions to Naval Officers)," 1873 XLII [76].

"Communications Respecting Outrages Committed upon Natives Received from Governors of Australian Colonies, Senior Naval Officers Commanding in Australia and China, and H.M. Consuls in Pacific," 1873 L [51].

"South Sea Islands," 1873 L [244].

"Letter Addressed to Commodore Goodenough and Mr. Consul Layard," 1874 XLV [297].

"Report of Commodore Goodenough and Mr. Consul Layard, on Offer of Cession from Fiji Islands to British Crown," 1874 XLV [323].

Hansard's Parliamentary Debates, third series. London: Baldwin and Cradock, 1829–1891.

Historical Records of Australia. Sydney: Commonwealth Parliamentary Library, 1914–1925.

Historical Records of New South Wales. Sydney: Government Printer, 1892–1901.

The Navy List. London: Her Majesty's Stationery Officer, 1829–1875.

The Queen's Regulations and the Admiralty Instructions for the Government of Her Majesty's Naval Service. London: Her Majesty's Stationery Office, 1862.

The Statutes of the United Kingdom of Great Britain and Ireland. London: George Eyre, 1817–1875.

SECONDARY SOURCES

[Aborigines Protection Society]. *Aboriginal Museum and Library*. London [1838].

————. *England and Her Colonies: Considered in Relation to the Aborigines, with a Proposal for Affording Them Medical Relief*. London [1841].

————. *Extracts from the Papers and Proceedings of the Aborigines Protection Society.* London: William Ball, Arnold and Co., 1839–1859.

————. *On the British Colonization of New Zealand.* London: Smith and Elder, 1846.

————. *Transactions.* London, 1838–1859.

Adams, Peter. *Fatal Necessity: British Intervention in New Zealand, 1830–1847.* Auckland and Oxford: Auckland University Press and Oxford University Press, 1977.

Adams, Ron. *In the Land of Strangers: A Century of European Contact with Tanna, 1774–1874.* Canberra: Australian National University Press, 1984.

————. "Nokwai—Sacrifice to Empire." In Donna Merwick, ed., *Dangerous Liaisons: Essays in Honour of Greg Dening,* 23–40. Melbourne: History Department, University of Melbourne, 1994.

Aldrich, Robert. *The French Presence in the South Pacific, 1842–1940.* Basingstoke: Macmillan, 1990.

Allen, William, and Thomson, T. R. H. *A Narrative of the Expedition Sent by Her Majesty's Government to the River Niger in 1841.* 2 vols. London: R. Bentley, 1848.

Anderson, Olive. "The Growth of Christian Militarism in Mid-Victorian Britain." *The English Historical Review* 338 (1971), 46–72.

[Anonymous]. Isles of the Pacific. Melbourne: n.p., 1861.

The Anti-Slavery Reporter. U.K., 1840–1875.

Arens, W. *The Man-Eating Myth: Anthropology and Anthropophagy.* Oxford and New York: Oxford University Press, 1979.

Arthur, William. *What Is Fiji, the Sovereignty of Which Is Offered to Her Majesty?* London: Hamilton, Adams, 1859.

[Ashwell, B. Y.] *Isles of the Pacific: Account of the Melanesian Mission.* Melbourne: Samuel Mullen, 1861.

The Australian Dictionary of Biography, vol. 4. Melbourne: Melbourne University Press, 1972.

Bach, John. *The Australia Station: A History of the Royal Navy in the South West Pacific, 1821–1913.* Kensington, N.S.W.: University of New South Wales Press, 1986.

————. "The Royal Navy in the Pacific Islands." *Journal of Pacific History* 3 (1968), 3–20.

Bach, John. "The Royal Navy in the South Pacific: 1826–1876." Ph.D. thesis, University of New South Wales, 1964.

Bannister, Saxe. *British Colonization and Coloured Tribes.* London: William Ball, 1838.

————. *Humane Policy, or, Justice to the Aborigines.* London: T. and G. Underwood, 1830.

Barker, Francis, Peter Hulme, and Margaret Iversen, eds. *Colonial Discourse/Postcolonial Theory.* Manchester and New York: Manchester University Press, 1994.

Bartlett, C. J. *Great Britain and Sea Power, 1815–1853.* Oxford: Clarendon, 1963.

————. "Mid Victorian Reappraisal of Naval Policy." In Kenneth Bourne and D. C. Watt, eds., *Studies in International History,* 189–208. London: Longmans, 1967.

Bastide, Roger. "Color, Racism and Christianity." *Daedalus* 96:2 (1967), 319–320.

Baudet, Henri. *Paradise on Earth: Some Thoughts on European Images of Non-European Man.* New Haven: Yale University Press, 1965.

Beaglehole, J. C. *The Exploration of the Pacific.* Third ed. London: A. and C. Black, 1966.

Beecham, John. *Remarks upon the Latest Official Documents Relating to New Zealand.* London: James Nichols, 1838.

Beechey, F. W. *Narrative of a Voyage to the Pacific and Beering's Strait . . . in the Ship "Blossom."* American ed. Philadelphia: Carey, 1832.

Behrman, Cynthia Fansler. *Victorian Myths of the Sea*. Athens, Ohio, 1977.

Belcher, Sir Edward. *Narrative of a Voyage Round the World*. 2 vols. London: H. Colburn, 1843.

Belich, James. *Making Peoples: A History of the New Zealanders from Polynesian Settlement to the End of the Nineteenth Century*. Auckland, London: Penguin, 1996.

————. *The New Zealand Wars and the Victorian Interpretation of Racial Conflict*. Auckland: Penguin, 1988.

Bennett, Judith. *Wealth of the Solomons: History of a Pacific Archipelago, 1800–1978*. Honolulu: University of Hawai'i Press, 1987.

Best, Elsdon. *The Maori Canoe*. Wellington: A. R. Shearer, 1976.

Biersack, Aletta. "Introduction: History and Theory in Anthropology." In her *Clio in Oceania: Toward a Historical Anthropology*, 1–36. Washington: Smithsonian, 1991.

Bolt, Christine. *Victorian Attitudes to Race*. London: Routledge and Kegan Paul, 1971.

Bourne, Kenneth. *The Foreign Policy of Victorian England, 1830–1902*. Oxford: Clarendon, 1970.

Bourne, Kenneth and D. C. Watt, eds. *Studies in International History*. London: Longmans, 1967.

Boutilier, James, Daniel T. Hughes, and Sharon W. Tiffany, eds. *Mission, Church and Sect in Oceania*. Ann Arbor: University of Michigan Press, 1978.

Bradley, Ian. *The Call to Seriousness: The Evangelical Impact on the Victorians*. London: Cape, 1976.

Brantlinger, Patrick. *Crusoe's Footsteps: Cultural Studies in Britain and America* New York and London: Routledge, 1990.

Brass, Tom. "The Return of 'Merrie Melanesia': A Comment on a Review of a Review" *Journal of Pacific History* 31:2 (1996), 215–223.

Brenchley, Julius. *Jottings during the Cruise of H.M.S. Curaçoa among the South Sea Islands in 1865*. London: Longmans, Green and Co., 1873.

Brewster, A. B. *King of the Cannibal Isles*. London: Robert Hale, 1937.

Bristow, Joseph. *Empire Boys: Adventures in a Man's World*. London: Harper Collins Academic, 1991.

Britton, Henry. *Fiji in 1870*. Melbourne: Samuel Mullen, 1870.

Broeze, Frank. "Australia, Asia and the Pacific: The Maritime World of Robert Towns, 1843–1873." *Australian Historical Studies* 24:95 (1990), 221–238.

Brookes, J. I. *International Rivalry in the Pacific Islands, 1800–1875*. New York: Russell and Russell, 1941.

Brown, George. *George Brown, D.D. Pioneer-Missionary and Explorer: An Autobiography*. London: Hodder and Stoughton, 1908.

————. *Melanesians and Polynesians*. New York: Benjamin Blom, 1972.

Burke, Peter. *History and Social Theory*. Ithaca, N.Y.: Cornell University Press, 1992.

Burns, Patricia. *Fatal Success: A History of the New Zealand Company*. Auckland: Heinemann Reed, 1989.

Buzacott, Aaron. *Mission Life in the Islands of the Pacific*. London: John Snow, 1866.

Calvert, James. *Mission History*. Vol. 2 of *Fiji and the Fijians*. With Thomas Williams. London: Alexander Heylin, 1858.

————. *Missionary Labours among the Cannibals; Extended, with Notices of Recent Events*. Ed. George Stringer Rowe. London: Hodder and Stoughton, 1870.

Cameron, Ian. *Lost Paradise: The Exploration of the Pacific*. London: Century, 1987.

Campbell, I. C. "The Alleged Imperialism of George Tupou I." *Journal of Pacific History* 25:2 (1990), 159–175.

———. "British Treaties with Polynesians in the Nineteenth Century." In William Renwick, ed. *Sovereignty and Indigenous Rights: The Treaty of Waitangi in International Contexts*, 67–82. Wellington: Victoria University Press, 1991.

———. "European Transculturists in Polynesia, 1789–ca. 1840." Ph.D. thesis, University of Adelaide, 1976.

———. "The Historiography of Charles Savage." *Journal of the Polynesian Society* 89:2 (1980), 143–166.

———. *A History of the Pacific Islands*. Christchurch: University of Canterbury Press, 1989.

———. "Savages Noble and Ignoble: The Preconceptions of Early European Voyagers in Polynesia." *Pacific Studies* 4:1 (1980), 45–59.

Campbell, John. *Maritime Discovery and Christian Missions Considered in Their Mutual Relations*. London: John Snow, 1840.

[Cargill, David]. *The Diaries and Correspondence of David Cargill, 1832–1843*. Ed. Albert J. Schutz. Canberra: Australian National University Press, 1977.

Cargill, David. *A Refutation of Chevalier Dillon's Slanderous Attacks on the Wesleyan Missionaries in the Friendly Islands*. London: James Nichols, 1842.

Cary, William S. *Wrecked on the Feejees*. Nantucket: Inquirer and Mirror Press, 1922.

Cell, John. *British Colonial Administration in the Mid-Nineteenth Century*. New Haven and London: Yale University Press, 1970.

———. "The Imperial Conscience." In Peter Marsh, ed. *The Conscience of the Victorian State*, 173–213. Hassocks: Harvester Press, 1979.

Chappell, David. "Shipboard Relations between Pacific Island Women and Euroamerican Men, 1767–1887." *Journal of Pacific History* 27:2 (1992), 131–149.

Chatterton, Lady Georgiana. *Memorials Personal and Historical*. London: Hurst and Blackett, 1861.

Cheyne, Andrew. *A Description of Islands in the Western Pacific Ocean*. London: J. D. Potter, 1852.

———. *The Trading Voyages of Andrew Cheyne, 1841–1844*. Ed. Dorothy Shineberg. Honolulu: University of Hawai'i Press, 1971.

Church, Ian. *Heartland of Aotea: Maori and European in South Taranaki before the Taranaki Wars*. Hawera, N.Z.: Hawera Historical Society, 1992.

Church Missionary Juvenile Instructor. U.K., 1840–1875.

Clifford, James, and George E. Marcus. *Writing Culture: The Poetics and Politics of Ethnography*. Berkeley, Los Angeles, and London: University of California Press, 1986.

Codrington, R. H. *The Melanesians*. Oxford: Clarendon, 1891.

The Colonial Intelligencer; or, Aborigines' Friend. UK, 1838–1875.

Connell, John. *New Caledonia or Kanaky? The Political History of a French Colony*. Canberra: Research School of Pacific Studies, 1987.

Colenso, William. *Ethnology: On the Maori Races of New Zealand*. New Zealand Exhibition, 1865.

Cook, James. *The Journals of Captain James Cook:* vol. 3, *The Voyage of the Resolution and Discovery, 1776–1780*. Ed. J. C. Beaglehole. Cambridge: Hakluyt, 1967.

Corris, Peter. *Passage, Port and Plantation: A History of Solomon Islands Labour Migration, 1870–1914*. Melbourne: Melbourne University Press, 1973.

Coulter, John. *Adventures in the Pacific*. Dublin: William Curry, Junior and Co., 1845.

———. *Adventures on the Western Coast of South America*. London: Longman, Brown, Green and Longmans, 1847.

Course, A. G. *The Merchant Navy: A Social History*. London: F. Muller, 1963.

[Craik, George]. *The New Zealanders*. London: C. Knight, 1830.

Crocombe, Ron, and Marjorie Crocombe, eds. *The Works of Ta'unga*. Canberra: Australian National University Press, 1968.

Cummins, H. G. "Holy War: Peter Dillon and the 1837 Massacres in Tonga." *Journal of Pacific History* 12 (1977), 25–39.

———. "Tongan Society at the Time of European Contact." In Noel Rutherford, ed., *Friendly Islands: A History of Tonga*, 63–89. Melbourne and New York: Oxford University Press, 1977.

Curtin, Philip. *The Image of Africa: British Ideas and Action, 1780–1850*. Madison: University of Wisconsin Press, 1965.

David, Andrew. *The Voyage of HMS Herald to Australia and the South-west Pacific*. Melbourne: Miegunyah Press, 1995.

Davidson, J. W. "European Penetration of the South Pacific, 1779–1842." Ph.D. thesis, Cambridge University, 1942.

———. *Peter Dillon of Vanikoro: Chevalier of the South Seas*. Melbourne and London: Oxford University Press, 1975.

———. "Problems of Pacific History." *Journal of Pacific History* 1 (1966), 5–21.

Davidson, J. W., and Deryck Scarr, eds. *Pacific Islands Portraits*. Wellington: A. H. and A. W. Reed, 1970.

Daws, Gavan. *Shoal of Time: A History of the Hawaiian Islands*. New York: Macmillan, 1968.

Dening, Greg. "A Poetic for Histories: Transformations That Present the Past." In Aletta Biersack, ed., *Clio in Oceania: Toward a Historical Anthropology*, 347–380. Washington: Smithsonian, 1991.

———. *History's Anthropology: The Death of William Gooch*. Lanham: University Press of America, 1988.

———. *Islands and Beaches: Discourse on a Silent Land*. Melbourne: Melbourne University Press, 1980.

———. *Mr. Bligh's Bad Language*. Cambridge: Canto, 1994.

———. *Performances*. Chicago: University of Chicago Press, 1996.

Denman, Joseph. *The African Squadron and Mr. Hutt's Committee*. Second ed. London: John Mortimer, [1850].

Derrick. R. A. *A History of Fiji*. Suva: Printing and Stationery Department, 1946.

Diamond, Marion. *Creative Meddler: The Life and Fantasies of Charles St. Julian*. Melbourne: Melbourne University Press, 1990.

———. *The Seahorse and the Wanderer: Ben Boyd in Australia*. Melbourne: Melbourne University Press, 1988.

Diapea, William. *Cannibal Jack: The True Autobiography of a White Man in the South Seas*. London: Faber and Gwyer, 1928.

Dieffenbach, Ernest. *New Zealand and Its Native Population*. London: Smith, Elder, 1841.

Dillon, Peter. *Letter to Richard More O'Farrell*. . . . [London, 1841].

Don, Alexander. *Peter Milne (1834–1924) Missionary to Nguna, New Hebrides*. Dunedin: Foreign Missions Committee PCNZ, 1927.

Douglas, Bronwen. " 'Almost Constantly at War?' An Ethnographic Perspective on Fighting in New Caledonia." *Journal of Pacific History* 25:1 (1990), 22–46.

———. "A Contact History of the Balad People of New Caledonia, 1774–1845." *Journal of the Polynesian Society* 70 (1970), 180–200.

———. "The Export Trade in Tropical Products in New Caledonia, 1841–1872." *Journal de la Société des Océanistes* 27:31 (1971), 157–170.

Dunmore, John. *French Explorers in the Pacific*. 2 vols. Oxford: Clarendon, 1965, 1969.

———. *Pacific Explorer: The Life of Jean-François de La Pérouse, 1741–1788*. Palmerston North, 1985.

———. *Who's Who in Pacific Navigation*. Honolulu: University of Hawai'i Press, 1991.

The Earl [of Pembroke] and the Doctor [G. H. Kingsley]. *South Sea Bubbles*. Second ed. London: Bentley and Son, 1872.

Earle, Augustus. *Nine Months Residence in New Zealand in 1827*. Christchurch: Whitcombe, 1909; first publ. 1829.

The Edinburgh Review. U.K., 1840–1875.

Ellis, William. *The History of the London Missionary Society*. 2 vols. London: John Snow, 1844.

———. *Narrative of a Tour through Hawaii*. London: Fisher, Son and Jackson, 1826.

———. *Polynesian Researches*. 2 vols. London: Fisher, Son and Jackson, 1829.

———. *A Vindication of the South Sea Missions*. London: F. Westley and A. H. Davis, 1831.

Erskine, John Elphinstone. *Journal of a Cruise among the Islands of the Western Pacific*. London: Dawsons, 1967; orig. publ. 1853.

An Examination of Charges against the American Missionaries at the Sandwich Islands As Alleged in the Voyage of the Ship Blonde and in the London Quarterly Review. Cambridge: Hilliard, Metcalf and Company, 1827.

Faivre, J. P. *L'Expansion française dans le Pacifique de 1800 à 1842*. Paris [1954].

Fanshawe, Alice E. J. *Admiral Sir Edward Gennys Fanshawe*. London: Spottiswoode and Co., 1904.

Farmer, Sarah S. *Tonga and the Friendly Islands with a Sketch of Their Mission History*. London: Hamilton, Adams and Co., 1860.

Fieldhouse, D. K. *The Colonial Empires: A Comparative Survey from the Eighteenth Century*. London: Weidenfeld and Nicolson, 1966.

———. *Economics and Empire, 1830–1914*. Second ed. London: Macmillan, 1984.

Fiji Times. Fiji, 1873–1875.

Findlay, G. G., and W. W. Holdsworth. *Wesleyan Methodist Missionary Society*. 5 vols. London: Epworth, 1921.

Fisher, Robin, and Hugh Johnston, eds. *Captain Cook and His Times*. Seattle: University of Washington Press, 1979.

———. *From Maps to Metaphors: The Pacific World of George Vancouver*. Vancouver: University of British Columbia Press, 1993.

Fitzroy, Robert. *A Narrative of the Voyage of H.M.S. Beagle*. Folio Society edition, London, 1977; first publ. 1839.

Foljambe, Lord G. C. *Three Years on the Australian Station*. London: Hatchard, 1868.

Forbes, Litton. *Two Years in Fiji*. London: Longmans, 1875.

Ford, Boris. *The Romantic Age in Britain*. Cambridge: Cambridge University Press, 1992.

Forster, Colin. "French Penal Policy and the Origins of the French Presence in New Caledonia." *Journal of Pacific History* 26:2 (1991), 135–150.

Fox, Charles Elliot. *Lords of the Southern Isles*. London: A. R. Mowbray and Co., 1958.

Fox, Grace. *British Admirals and Chinese Pirates, 1832–1869*. London: Kegan Paul, Trench, Trubner, 1940.

France, Peter. *The Charter of the Land: Custom and Colonization in Fiji*. Melbourne and London: Oxford University Press, 1969.

Frost, Alan. *Botany Bay Mirages: Illusions of Australia's Convict Beginnings*. Melbourne: Melbourne University Press, 1994.

———. *Convicts and Empire: A Naval Question, 1776–1811*. Melbourne: Oxford University Press, 1980.

———. "New South Wales as *Terra Nullius:* The British Denial of Aboriginal Land Rights." *Historical Studies* 19:77 (1981), 513–523.

Froude, James Anthony. *Oceana, or England and Her Colonies*. London: Longmans and Co., 1886.

Furnas, J. C. *Anatomy of Paradise*. New York: William Sloane, 1948.

Gailey, Christine Ward. *Kinship to Kingship: Gender Hierarchy and State Formation in the Tongan Islands*. Austin: University of Texas Press, 1987.

Galbraith, John S. *Reluctant Empire: British Policy on the South African Frontier, 1834–1854*. Englewood Cliffs, N.J.: Prentice Hall, 1963.

Galbraith, John S., with George Bennett. "The Humanitarian Impulse to Imperialism." In Robin Winks, ed., *The Age of Imperialism: Gold, God, Glory,* 71–76. Berkeley: University of California Press, 1963.

Gallagher, John. "Fowell Buxton and the New African Policy." *Cambridge Historical Journal* 10 (1950), 36–58.

Gallagher, John, and Ronald Robinson. "The Imperialism of Free Trade. *Economic History Review* 6:1 (1953), 1–15.

Gardenhire, W. C. *Fiji and the Fijians, and Travels among the Cannibals*. San Francisco: Sterett, 1871.

Gardiner, Leslie. *The British Admiralty*. Edinburgh and London: William Blackwood and Sons, 1968.

Garrett, John. *To Live among the Stars: Christian Origins in Oceania*. Geneva and Suva: World Council of Churches/Institute of Pacific Studies, 1982.

The Gentleman's Magazine. U.K., 1830–1875.

Gilding, Michael. "The Massacre of the *Mystery:* A Case Study in Contact Relations." *Journal of Pacific History* 17 (1982), 66–85.

Giles, W. E. *A Cruize in a Queensland Labour Vessel to the South Seas*. Canberra: Australian National University Press, 1968.

Gilson, R. P. *Samoa, 1830 to 1900: The Politics of a Multi-Racial Community*. Melbourne: Oxford University Press, 1970.

Girouard, Mark. *The Return to Camelot: Chivalry and the English Gentleman*. London and New York: Yale University Press, 1981.

Gonnard, René. *La légende du bon sauvage.* Paris: Librairie de Medicis, 1946.

Goodenough, Mrs. V., ed. *Journal of Commodore Goodenough.* London: King, 1876.

Gordon, Robert, and Mervyn Meggitt. *Law and Order in the New Guinea Highlands: Encounters with Enga.* Hanover, N.H.: University Press of New England, 1985.

Graham, Gerald S. *The China Station: War and Diplomacy, 1830–1860.* Oxford: Clarendon, 1978.

————. "Peculiar Interlude." In Deryck M. Schreuder, ed., *"Imperialisms": Explorations in European Expansion and Empire,* 56–66. Sydney: History Department, University of Sydney, 1992.

————. *The Politics of Naval Supremacy: Studies in British Naval Ascendancy.* Cambridge: Cambridge University Press, 1965.

————. *Tides of Empire.* Montreal: McGill-Queen's University Press, 1972.

Graham, Gerald S., and R. A. Humphreys, eds. *The Navy and South America, 1807–1823* London: Navy Records Society, 1962.

[Graham, Maria]. *The Voyage of H.M.S. Blonde to the Sandwich Islands.* London: John Murray, 1826.

Grattan, C. Hartley. *The South West Pacific to 1900.* Ann Arbor: University of Michigan Press, 1963.

Graves, Adrian. "The Nature and Origins of Pacific Islands Labour Migration to Queensland, 1863–1906." In Shula Marks and Peter Richardson, eds., *International Labour Migration: Historical Perspectives.* (Hounslow: Institute of Commonwealth Studies, 1984), 112–139.

Grey, Lord Henry George. *The Colonial Policy of Lord John Russell's Administration.* New York: Augustus Kelley, 1970; orig. publ. 1853.

Gunson, Niel. "The *hau* Concept of Leadership of Western Polynesia." *Journal of Pacific History* 14 (1979), 28–49.

————. *Messengers of Grace: Evangelical Missionaries in the South Seas, 1797–1860.* Melbourne and Oxford: Oxford University Press, 1978.

————. "Missionary Interest in British Expansion in the South Pacific in the Nineteenth Century." *Journal of Religious History* 3:4 (1965), 296–313.

Hall, William. *A Treatise on International Law.* Third ed. Oxford: Clarendon, 1890.

Halstead, J. P. *The Second British Empire: Trade, Philanthropy and Good Government.* Westport, Conn: Greenwood Press, 1983.

Hamilton, C. I. "Naval Hagiography and the Victorian Hero." *The Historical Journal* 23:2 (1980), 381–398.

Hardy, John, and Alan Frost, eds. *European Voyaging towards Australia.* Canberra: Australian Academy of the Humanities, 1990.

Harvey, Thomas. *The Polynesian Slave Trade: Its Character and Tendencies.* Leeds: McCorquodale, 1872.

Headrick, Daniel R. *The Invisible Weapon: Telecommunications and International Politics, 1851–1945.* New York and Oxford: Oxford University Press, 1991.

————. *The Tentacles of Progress; Technology Transfer in the Age of Imperialism, 1850–1940.* New York and Oxford: Oxford University Press, 1988.

————. *The Tools of Empire: Technology and European Imperialism in the Nineteenth Century.* New York and Oxford: Oxford University Press, 1981.

Hempenstall, Peter. " 'My Place': Finding a Voice within Pacific Colonial Studies." In Brij V. Lal, ed., *Pacific Islands History: Journeys and Transformations*, 70–73. Canberra: Journal of Pacific History, 1992.

Henderson, G. C. *Fiji and the Fijians, 1835–1856*. Sydney: Angus and Robertson, 1931.

Herschel, John F. W., ed. *The Admiralty Manual of Scientific Enquiry*. London: John Murray, 1851.

Hilliard, David. "Bishop G. A. Selwyn and the Melanesian Mission." *New Zealand Journal of History* 4 (1970), 120–137.

————. *God's Gentlemen: A History of the Melanesian Mission, 1849–1942*. St. Lucia, Qld: University of Queensland Press, 1978.

————. "John Coleridge Patteson: Missionary Bishop of Melanesia." In Davidson and Scarr, eds., *Pacific Islands Portraits*, 177–200.

Hilton, Boyd. *The Age of Atonement: The Influence of Evangelicalism on Social and Economic Thought, 1795–1865*. Oxford: Clarendon, 1988.

Hinds, Samuel. *The Latest Official Documents Relating to New Zealand*. London: J. W. Parker, 1838.

Hobsbawm, Eric, and Terence Ranger, eds. *The Invention of Tradition*. Second ed. Cambridge and New York: Cambridge University Press, 1983.

Hood, T. H. *Notes of a Cruise in H.M.S. Fawn*. Edinburgh: Edmonston and Douglas, 1863.

Hope, James L. A. *In Quest of Coolies*. 2nd ed. London: Henry King, 1872.

Hopkins, Manley. *Hawaii: The Past, Present, and Future of Its Island-Kingdom*. London: Longman, Green, Longman, and Roberts, 1862.

Howe, K. R. "The Fate of the 'Savage' in Pacific Historiography." *The New Zealand Journal of History* 11:2 (1977), 137–154.

————. "Firearms and Indigenous Warfare: A Case Study." *Journal of Pacific History* 9 (1974), 21–38.

————. "The Future of Pacific Islands History: A Personal View." in Lal, ed., *Pacific Islands History*, 225–242.

————. "The Intellectual Discovery and Exploration of Polynesia." In Fisher and Johnston, eds., *From Maps to Metaphors*, 245–262.

————. *The Loyalty Islands: A History of Culture Contacts, 1830–1900*. Honolulu: University Press of Hawai'i, 1977.

————. *Where the Waves Fall: A New South Sea Islands History from First Settlement to Colonial Rule*. Honolulu: University of Hawai'i Press, 1984.

Howe, K. R., Robert C. Kiste, and Brij V. Lal, eds. *Tides of History: The Pacific Islands in the Twentieth Century*. St. Leonards, N.S.W.: Allen and Unwin, 1994.

Howell, Raymond. *The Royal Navy and the Slave Trade*. London: Croom Helm, 1987.

Howitt, William. *Colonization and Christianity: A Popular History of the Treatment of the Natives by the Europeans in All Their Colonies*. London: Longman, Orme, Brown, Green and Longman's, 1838.

Hügel, Anatole von. *The Fiji Journals of Baron Anatole Von Hügel, 1875–1877*. Ed. Jane Roth and Steven Hooper. Suva: Oceania Printers, with Cambridge Museum of Archaeology and Anthropology, 1989.

Hügel, Baron Charles von. *New Holland Journal*. Ed. and trans. Dymphna Clark. Melbourne: Miegunyah Press, 1994.

Hunt, John. *Memoir of the Rev. William Cross.* London: John Mason, 1846.

Hviding, Edvard. *Guardians of Marovo Lagoon: Practice, Place, and Politics in Maritime Melanesia.* Honolulu: University of Hawai'i Press, 1996.

Inglis, John. *In the New Hebrides: Reminiscences of Missionary Life and Work.* London: T. Nelson and Sons, 1887.

James, Lawrence. *The Rise and Fall of the British Empire.* London: Little, Brown, 1994.

Jenkyns, Henry. *British Rule and Jurisdiction beyond the Seas.* Oxford: Clarendon, 1902.

Johnston, W. Ross. *Sovereignty and Protection: A Study of British Jurisdictional Imperialism in the Later Nineteenth Century.* Durham, N.C.: Duke University Press, 1973.

Jolly, Margaret, and Martha Macintyre, eds. *Family and Gender in the Pacific: Domestic Contradictions and the Colonial Impact.* Cambridge: Cambridge University Press, 1989.

Journal and Letters of the Reverend Isaac Rooney. Fairbanks: University of Alaska Press, [1985].

Journal of Civilization. U.K., 1840–1842.

Journal of the Royal Geographical Society. U.K., 1833–1875.

Kay, John. *The Slave Trade in the New Hebrides.* Edinburgh: Edmonston and Douglas, 1872.

Kelly, John. *A Politics of Virtue: Hinduism, Sexuality, and Countercolonial Discourse in Fiji.* Chicago: University of Chicago Press, 1991.

———. "Fear of Culture: British Regulation of Indian Marriage in Post-Indenture Fiji." *Ethnohistory* 36:4 (1989), 372–391.

Kennedy, Paul. *The Rise and Fall of British Naval Mastery.* London: Fontana, 1991; first publ. 1976.

Keppel, Henry. *A Visit to the Indian Archipelago, in H.M. Ship Maeander.* London: Bentley, 1853.

Kiernan, V. G. *European Empires from Conquest to Collapse, 1815–1960.* Leicester: Leicester University Press, 1982.

———. *The Lords of Human Kind: Black Man, Yellow Man, and White Man in an Age of Empire.* London: Weidenfield and Nicholson, 1969.

Knapman, Claudia. *White Women in Fiji, 1835–1930: The Ruin of Empire?* Sydney and London: Allen and Unwin, 1968.

[Koivi, Jamie]. *Quarterdeck Cambridge: The Quest of Captain Francis Price Blackwood, RN.* Royston: Ellisons' Editions, 1991.

Kotzebue, Otto von. *A New Voyage round the World.* London: H. Colbum and R. Bentley, 1830.

———. *A Voyage of Discovery into the South Seas and Beering's Straits.* 3 vols. London: Longman, Hurst, Rees, Orme, and Brown, 1821.

Kuklick, Henrika. *The Savage Within: The Social History of British Anthropology, 1885–1945.* Cambridge: Cambridge University Press, 1991.

Lal, Brij V., ed. *Pacific Islands History: Journeys and Transformations.* Canberra: Journal of Pacific History, 1992.

Lambie, K. R. *History of Samoa.* Apia: Commercial Printers, 1979.

Laracy, Hugh. "The Catholic Mission." In Noel Rutherford, ed., *Friendly Islands: A History of Tonga,* 136–153. Melbourne: Oxford University Press, 1977.

Latham, Robert Gordon. *Natural History of the Varieties of Man.* London: J. Van Voorst, 1850.

Lātūkefu, Sione. *Church and State in Tonga.* Canberra: Australian National University Press, 1974.

Lawry, Walter. *Friendly and Feejee Islands: A Missionary Visit to Various Stations in the South Seas in the Year 1847.* London: John Mason, 1850.

———. Missions in the Tonga and Feejee Islands. New York: Lane and Scott, 1852.

———. *A Second Missionary Visit to the Friendly and Fiji Islands in the Year MDCCL.* London: John Mason, 1851.

Leckie, Jacqueline. "Workers in Colonial Fiji: 1870–1970." In Clive Moore, Jacqueline Leckie, and Doug Munro, eds., *Labour in the South Pacific,* 47–66. Townsville: James Cook University of Northern Queensland Press, 1990.

Legge, J. D. *Britain in Fiji, 1858–1880.* London: Macmillan, 1958.

Legge, J. Gordon. *A Selection of Supreme Court Cases in New South Wales from 1825 to 1862.* 2 vols. Sydney: Charles Potter, 1896.

Lewis, Michael. *England's Sea-Officers: The Story of the Naval Profession.* London: Allen and Unwin, 1939.

———. *The History of the British Navy.* London: Allen and Unwin, 1959.

———. *The Navy in Transition, 1814–1864: A Social History.* London: Hodder and Stoughton, 1965.

Lindley, M. F. *The Acquisition and Government of Backward Territory in International Law.* London: Longmans and Co., 1926.

Linnekin, Jocelyn. "Ignoble Savages and Other European Visions: The La Pérouse Affair in Samoan History." *Journal of Pacific History* 26:1 (1991), 3–26.

Lloyd, Christopher. *The Navy and the Slave Trade: The Suppression of the African Slave Trade in the Nineteenth Century.* London: Cass, 1968.

Lorimer, Douglas. *Colour, Class and the Victorians: English Attitudes to the Negro in the Mid-nineteenth Century.* Leicester: Leicester University Press, 1978.

Lowenthal, David. *The Past Is a Foreign Country.* Cambridge: Cambridge University Press, 1985.

Lubbock, Alfred Basil. *Bully Hayes: South Sea Pirate.* London: Martin Hopkinson, 1931.

[Lucatt, E.] *Rovings in the Pacific from 1837 to 1849.* 2 vols. London: Longman, 1851.

MacAllan, Richard. "British Relations with the Hawaiian Kingdom, 1790–1850." M.Phil. thesis, University of London, 1992.

McIntyre, W. David. *The Imperial Frontier in the Tropics, 1865–1875.* London, Melbourne, Toronto: Macmillan, 1967.

———. "New Light on Commodore Goodenough's Mission to Fiji, 1873–74." *Historical Studies* 39 (1962), 270–288.

Mackay, David. *In the Wake of Cook: Exploration, Science and Empire, 1780–1801.* London: Croom Helm, 1985.

Madden, A. F. "The Attitude of the Evangelicals to the Empire and Imperial Problems, 1820–1850." D.Phil. thesis, Oxford, 1950.

Madden, Frederick, and Fieldhouse, D. K. *Imperial Reconstruction, 1763–1840.* Vol. 3 of *Select Documents on the Constitutional History of the British Empire and Commonwealth.* London and New York: Greenwood Press, 1987.

Malone, R. Edmond. *Three Years' Cruise in the Australasian Colonies.* London: Bentley, 1854.

[Manning, F. E.] *Old New Zealand*. London: Bentley, 1876.

Marcus, George E., and Michael M. J. Fischer. *Anthropology as Cultural Critique: An Experimental Moment in the Human Sciences*. Chicago and London: University of Chicago Press, 1986.

Mariner, William. *An Account of the Natives of the Tonga Islands in the South Pacific Ocean.* Ed. John Martin. 2 vols. London: John Murray, 1817.

Markham, Albert Hastings. *The Cruise of the Rosario amongst the New Hebrides and Santa Cruz Islands*. London: S. Low, Marston, Low and Searle, 1873.

Markham, Clements R. *Commodore J. G. Goodenough: A Brief Memoir*. Portsmouth: J. Griffin and Co., 1876.

Marks, Shula, and Peter Richardson, eds. *International Labour Migration: Historical Perspectives*. Hounslow: Institute of Commonwealth Studies, 1984.

Marsh, Peter, ed. *The Conscience of the Victorian State*. Hassocks: Harvester Press, 1979.

Marshall, John. *Royal Naval Biography*. 11 vols. London: Longman, Hurst, Rees, Orme, and Brown, 1823–1829.

Marshall, P. J., and Glyndwr Williams. *The Great Map of Mankind: British Perceptions of the World in the Age of Enlightenment*. London: Dent, 1982.

Marshall, William Barrett. *A Personal Narrative of Two Visits to New Zealand in His Majesty's Ship Alligator*. London: J. Nisbet, 1835.

Martin, John. *An Account of the Natives of the Tonga Islands . . . Arranged from Extensive Communications of Mr. William Mariner*. 2 vols. London: J. Martin, 1817.

Mason, Philip. *The English Gentleman: The Rise and Fall of an Ideal*. London: Andre Deutsch, 1982.

Masterman, Sylvia. *The Origin of International Rivalry in Samoa, 1845–1884*. London: Allen and Unwin, 1934.

Maude, H. E. *Of Islands and Men: Studies in Pacific History*. Melbourne and New York: Oxford University Press, 1968.

————. *Slavers in Paradise: The Peruvian Slave Trade in Polynesia, 1862–1864*. Stanford: Stanford University Press, 1981.

[Mbulu, Joeli]. *The Autobiography of a Native Minister in the South Seas*. London: T. Woolmer, 1884.

Meade, Herbert. *A Ride through the Disturbed Districts of New Zealand, Together with Some Account of the South Sea Islands*. London: John Murray, 1870.

Meek, Ronald L. *Social Science and the Ignoble Savage*. Cambridge and New York: Cambridge University Press, 1976.

Melanesian Mission, *Report of the Melanesian Mission for the Years 1861–1862*. London: Rivingtons, 1863.

Melbourne Argues. Australia, 1857–1875.

Meleiseā, Malama. *The Making of Modern Samoa: Traditional Authority and Colonial Administration in the Modern History of Western Samoa*. Suva: Institute of Pacific Studies, 1987.

————. "Pacific Historiography: An Indigenous View." *Journal of Pacific Studies* 4 (1978), 25–43.

Mellersh, H. E. L. *Fitzroy of the Beagle*. London: Rupert Hart-Davis, 1968.

Merivale, Herman. *Lectures on Colonization and Colonies*. 2 vols. London: Longman, 1841–1842; second ed. 1861.

Merwick, Donna, ed. *Dangerous Liaisons: Essays in Honour of Greg Dening*. Melbourne: History Department, University of Melbourne, 1994.

Methodist Missionary Notices. U.K., 1822–1875.

Miller, Char, ed. *Missions and Missionaries in the Pacific*. New York: Edwin Mellen Press, 1985.

Miller, Harold. *Race Conflict in New Zealand, 1814–1865*. Auckland: Blackwood and Janet Paul, 1966.

Miller, John. *Early Victorian New Zealand: A Study of Racial Tension and Social Attitudes, 1839–52*. Oxford: Oxford University Press, 1958.

Milner, John, and Oswald W. Brierly. *The Cruise of HMS Galatea*. London: Allen, 1869.

Moore, Clive. "Pacific Islanders in Nineteenth Century Queensland." In Moore et al., eds., *Labour in the South Pacific*, 144–147.

Moore, Clive, Jacqueline Leckie, and Doug Munro, eds. *Labour in the South Pacific*. Townsville: James Cook University of Northern Queensland Press, 1990.

Moorehead, Alan. *The Fatal Impact: An Account of the Invasion of the South Pacific, 1767–1840*. Second ed. New York: Harper and Row, 1987.

Moresby, John. *Discoveries and Surveys in New Guinea and the D'Entrecasteaux Islands*. London: John Murray, 1876.

———. *Two Admirals*. London: John Murray, 1909.

Morrell, Benjamin. *A Narrative of Four Voyages to the South Sea*. New York: J. and J. Harper, 1832.

Morrell, W. P. *Britain in the Pacific Islands*. Oxford: Oxford University Press, 1960.

———. *British Colonial Policy in the Age of Peel and Russell*. London: Cass, 1966.

Morris, R. O. "Surveying Ships of the Royal Navy from Cook to the Computer Age." *Mariner's Mirror* 72:4 (1986), 385–408.

Morton, Harry. *The Wind Commands: Sailors and Sailing Ships in the Pacific*. Vancouver: University of British Columbia Press, 1975.

[Moss, F. J.]. *A Month in Fiji by a Recent Visitor*. Melbourne: Mullen, 1868.

Motte, Standish. *Outline of a System of Legislation for Securing Protection to the Aboriginal Inhabitants of All Countries Colonized by Great Britain*. London: John Murray, 1840.

Murray, A. W. *Forty Years' Mission Work in Polynesia and New Guinea from 1835 to 1875*. London: James Nisbet, 1876.

———. *Missions in Western Polynesia*. London: John Snow, 1863.

The Nautical Magazine. U.K., 1833–1860.

Nettleton, Joseph. *John Hunt: Pioneer, Missionary and Saint*. London: C. H. Kelly, 1906.

Newbury, Colin. "Aspects of French Policy in the Pacific, 1853–1906." *Pacific Historical Review* 27:1 (1958), 45–56.

———. *Tahiti Nui: Change and Survival in French Polynesia, 1767–1945*. Honolulu: University Press of Hawai'i, 1980.

O'Byrne, William Richard. *A Naval Biographical Dictionary*. 3 vols. London, [1849].

Oliver, Douglas L. *The Pacific Islands*. Honolulu: University Press of Hawai'i, 1975; first publ. 1961.

[Oliver, James, and W. G. Dix] *Wreck of the Glide with Recollections of the Fijis and of Wallis Island*. New York and London: Wiley and Putnam, 1848.

Oliver, W. H., ed. *The Dictionary of New Zealand Biography*, vol. 1. Wellington: Department of Internal Affairs, 1990.

Orange, Claudia. *The Treaty of Waitangi*. Wellington: Allen and Unwin, 1987.

Orlebar, John. *A Midshipman's Journal on Board H.M.S. Seringapatam, during the Year 1830*. San Diego: Tofua, 1976; first publ. 1833.

Orme, William. *Defence of the Missions in the South Sea and Sandwich Islands*. London: B. J. Holdsworth, 1827.

Owen, Edward Roger John, and Robert Baldwin Sutcliffe, eds. *Studies in the Theory of Imperialism*. London: Longman, 1972.

Padfield, Peter. *Rule Britannia: The Victorian and Edwardian Navy*. London: Routledge and Kegan Paul, 1981.

Palmer, George. *Kidnapping in the South Seas*. Edinburgh: Edmonston and Douglas, 1871.

Parnaby, O. W. *Britain and the Labor Trade in the Southwest Pacific*. Durham: Duke University Press, 1964.

Paton, James, ed. *John G. Paton, D.D. Missionary to the New Hebrides: An Autobiography*. London: Banner of Truth Trust, 1965. Reprint ed.

Patterson, George. *Memoirs of the Rev. S. F. Johnston, the Rev. J. W. Matheson, and Mrs. Mary Johnston Matheson*. Philadelphia: Martien, n.d.

————. *Missionary Life among the Cannibals*. Toronto: James Campbell, 1882.

Platt, D. C. M. *The Cinderella Service: British Consuls since 1825*. Harlow: Longman, 1971.

————. *Finance, Trade and Politics in British Foreign Policy, 1815–1914*. Oxford: Oxford University Press, 1968.

Porter, Andrew. " 'Commerce and Christianity': The Rise and Fall of a Nineteenth-Century Missionary Slogan." *The Historical Journal* 28:3 (1985), 597–621.

————. *European Imperialism, 1860–1914*. London: Macmillan, 1994.

————. "Religion and Empire: British Expansion in the Long Nineteenth Century, 1780–1914." *Journal of Imperial and Commonwealth History* 20:3 (1992), 370–390.

Poyer, Lin. "The Ngatik Massacre." *Journal of Pacific History* 20 (1985), 4–22.

Prakash, Gyan. *After Colonialism: Imperial Histories and Postcolonial Displacements*. Princeton, N.J.: Princeton University Press, 1995.

Preston, Anthony, and John Major. *Send a Gunboat! A Study of the Gunboat and Its Role in British Policy, 1854–1904*. London: Longmans, 1967.

Price, A. Grenfell. *The Western Invasions of the Pacific and Its Continents*. Oxford: Clarendon, 1963.

Prichard, James Cowles. *The Natural History of Man*. Third ed. London: Hippolyte Baillier, 1848.

————. *Researches into the Physical History of Man*. Ed. George W. Stocking. Chicago and London: University of Chicago Press, 1973; orig. publ. 1813.

Pritchard, George. *The Aggressions of the French at Tahiti and Other Islands of the Pacific*. Ed. Paul de Deckker. Auckland and Oxford: Auckland University Press and Oxford University Press, 1983.

————. *The Missionary's Reward; or, the Success of the Gospel in the Pacific*. London: John Snow, 1844.

Pritchard, W. T. "A Consulate among the Fijis." *The Overland Monthly* 2:3 (1869), 235–238.

————. *Polynesian Reminiscences*. London: Chapman and Hall, 1866.

The Quarterly Review. U.K., 1840–1860.

Rabinow, Paul. "Representations Are Social Facts: Modernity and Post-Modernity in Anthropology." In James Clifford and George E. Marcus, *Writing Culture: The Poetics and Politics of Ethnography*, 240–247. Berkeley, Los Angeles, and London: University of California Press, 1986.

Ralston, Caroline. *Grass Huts and Warehouses: Pacific Beach Communities of the Nineteenth Century*. Canberra: Australian National University Press, 1977.

Rigby, B. "Private Interests and the Origins of American Involvement in Samoa." *Journal of Pacific History* 8 (1973), 75–87.

Roberts, David. *Paternalism in Early Victorian England*. London: Croom Helm, 1979.

Robinson, Ronald. "Non-European Foundations of European Imperialism: Sketch for a Theory of Collaboration." In E. R. J. Owen and R. B. Sutcliffe, *Studies in the Theory of Imperialism*, 117–140. London: Longman, 1972.

Rockwell, E. A. "Trade with the Cannibals." *The Overland Monthly* 2:3 (1869), 240–247.

Rodger, N. A. M. *The Admiralty*. Lavenham: T. Dalton, 1979.

Ross, Angus. *New Zealand Aspirations in the Pacific in the Nineteenth Century*. Oxford: Clarendon, 1964.

Routledge, David. "American Influence on the Politics of Fiji, 1849–1874." *Journal of Pacific Studies* 4 (1978), 66–88.

———. "The Failure of Cakobau, Chief of Bau, to Become King of Fiji." In W. A. Wood and P. S. O'Connor, eds., *W. P. Morrell: A Tribute*, 125–139. Dunedin: University of Otago Press, 1973.

———. *Matanitū: The Struggle for Power in Early Fiji*. Suva: Institute of Pacific Studies, 1985.

———. "Negotiations Leading to the Cession of Fiji." *Journal of Imperial and Commonwealth History* 2:3 (1974), 278–293.

Rowe, George Stringer. *James Calvert of Fiji*. London: C. H. Kelly, 1893.

Rutherford, J. *Sir George Grey, K.C.B., 1812–1898*. London: Cassell, 1961.

Rutherford, Noel, ed. *Friendly Islands: A History of Tonga*. Melbourne: Oxford University Press, 1977.

Sahlins, Marshall. "The Discovery of the True Savage." In Merwick, ed., *Dangerous Liaisons*, 41–94.

———. "The Return of the Event, Again; with Reflections on the Beginnings of the Great Fijian War of 1843 to 1855. . . ." In Aletta Biersack, ed., *Clio in Oceania: Toward a Historical Anthropology*, 37–100. Washington: Smithsonian, 1991.

Salmond, Anne. *Two Worlds: First Meetings between Maori and Europeans, 1642–1772*. London: Viking, 1991.

Samson, Jane. "British Voices and Indigenous Rights: Debating Aboriginal Legal Status in Nineteenth-Century Australia and Canada." *Cultures of the Commonwealth* 2 (1996–1997), 5–16.

———. "The 1834 Cruise of HMS *Alligator:* The Bible and the Flag." *The Northern Mariner* 3:4 (1993), 37–47.

———. "Imperial Benevolence: The Royal Navy and the South Pacific Labour Trade, 1867–1872." *The Great Circle* 18:1 (1997), 14–29.

———. " 'Protective Supremacy': The Royal Navy, Pacific Islanders, and the Limits of Benevolence, 1829–1859." Ph.D. thesis, University of London, 1994.

———. "Rescuing Fijian Women? The British Anti-slavery Proclamation of 1852." *Journal of Pacific History* 30:1 (1995), 22–38.

Saunders, Kay. "The Workers' Paradox: Indentured Labour in the Queensland Sugar Industry to 1920." In her *Indentured Labour in the British Empire, 1834–1920*. London: Croom Helm, 1984.

Scarr, Deryck. "Cakobau and Maʻafu: Contenders for Pre-eminence in Fiji," 95–126. In Davidson and Scarr, *Pacific Islands Portraits*.

———. *Fiji: A Short History*. Sydney and London: Allen and Unwin, 1984.

———. *Fragments of Empire: A History of the Western Pacific High Commission, 1877–1914*. Canberra: Australian National University Press, 1967.

———. *The History of the Pacific Islands: Kingdoms of the Reefs*. Melbourne: Macmillan, 1990.

———. *I, the Very Bayonet*. Vol. 1 of *The Majesty of Colour: A Life of John Bates Thurston*. Canberra: Australian National University Press, 1973.

———. "John Bates Thurston, Commodore J. G. Goodenough, and Rampant Anglo-Saxons in Fiji." *Historical Studies: Australia and New Zealand* 11:43 (1964), 361–382.

———. "Recruits and Recruiters: A Portrait of the Labour Trade." In Davidson and Scarr, eds. *Pacific Islands Portraits*, 95–126.

Scholefield, Guy H. *The Pacific, Its Past and Future and the Policy of the Great Powers from the Eighteenth Century*. London: Murray, 1919.

Seemann, Berthold. *Viti: An Account of a Government Mission to the Vitian or Fijian Islands, 1860–1861*. Folkestone and London: Dawson's, 1973; orig. publ. 1862.

Semmel, Bernard. *Liberalism and Naval Strategy: Ideology, Interest and Sea Power during the Pax Britannica*. Boston and London: Allen and Unwin, 1986.

Sherrin, Richard A. A. *Early History of New Zealand from Earliest Times to 1840*. Ed. Thomson W. Leys. Auckland: H. Brett, 1890.

Shineberg, Dorothy. "Guns and Men in Melanesia." *Journal of Pacific History* 6 (1971), 61–82.

———. *They Came for Sandalwood: A Study of the Sandalwood Trade in the South-west Pacific, 1830–1865*. Melbourne: Melbourne University Press, 1967.

———, ed. *The Trading Voyages of Andrew Cheyne, 1841–1844*. Wellington and Auckland: A. H. and A. W. Reed, 1971.

Shipley, Conway. *Sketches in the Pacific*. London: T. McStan, 1851.

Short, Robert. *The Slave Trade in the Pacific*. London: George Levey, 1870.

Simpson, Alexander. *Narrative of a Journey round the World during the Years 1841 and 1842*. 2 vols. London: Henry Colburn, 1847.

———. *The Sandwich Islands*. London: Smith, Elder and Co., 1843.

Smith, Bernard. *European Vision and the South Pacific, 1768–1850*. Second ed. New Haven and London: Yale University Press, 1985.

———. *Imagining the Pacific in the Wake of the Cook Voyages*. New Haven and London: Yale University Press, 1992.

Smith, S. Percy. *Maori Wars of the Nineteenth Century*. Second ed. Christchurch: Whitcombe and Tombs, 1910.

Society for the Propagation of Christian Knowledge. *Life of Bishop Patteson*. London: SPCK, n.d.

Society of Friends. *Further Information Respecting the Aborigines.* London: Harvey and Darton, 1839.

Spate, O. H. K. *Paradise Found and Lost.* Vol. 3 of *The Pacific since Magellan.* London: Routledge, 1988.

Stanley, Brian. *The Bible and the Flag: Protestant Missions and British Imperialism in the Nineteenth and Twentieth Centuries.* Leicester: Apollos, 1990.

———. " 'Commerce and Christianity': Providence Theory, the Missionary Movement, and the Imperialism of Free Trade, 1842–1860." *The Historical Journal* 26:1 (1983), 71–94.

Steel, Robert. *The New Hebrides and Christian Missions.* London: J. Nisbet, 1880.

Steven, Margaret. *Trade, Tactics and Territory: Britain in the Pacific, 1780–1823.* Melbourne: Melbourne University Press, 1983.

Stewart, Charles S. *Journal of a Residence in the Sandwich Islands.* London: H. Fisher, Son and Jackson, 1828.

Stock, Eugene. *The History of the Church Missionary Society.* 4 vols. London: CMS, 1899–1916.

Stocking, George. *Victorian Anthropology.* New York and London: Macmillan, 1987.

Stoughton, J. *British Influence and Responsibility.* London: John Snow, 1850.

Sydney Gazette. Australia, 1800–1840.

Sydney Morning Herald. Australia, 1840–1875.

Tate, Merze. *The United States and the Hawaiian Kingdom: A Political History.* New Haven: Yale University Press, 1965.

Temperley, Howard. *British Anti-Slavery, 1833–1870.* Harlow: Longman, 1972.

———. *White Dreams, Black Africa: The Anti-Slavery Expedition to the River Niger, 1841–1842.* New Haven and London: Yale University Press, 1991.

Thomas, Nicholas. *Colonialism's Culture: Anthropology, Travel and Government.* Cambridge: Polity Press, 1994.

———. "Fear and Loathing in the Postcolonial Pacific." *Meanjin* 51:2 (1992), 265–276.

Thompson, Roger C. *Australian Imperialism in the Pacific: The Expansionist Era, 1820–1920.* Melbourne: Melbourne University Press, 1980.

The Times. U.K., 1850–1875.

Towns, Robert. *South Sea Island Immigration for Cotton Culture.* Sydney: Reading and Wellbank, n.d.

Trood, Thomas. *Island Reminiscences.* Sydney: McCarron, Stewart, 1912.

Tucker, H. W. *Memoir of the Life and Episcopate of George Augustus Selwyn, D.D.* New York: Pott, Young, 1879; first publ. 1875.

Turley, David. *The Culture of English Antislavery, 1780–1860.* New York and London: Routledge, 1991.

Turner, George. *Nineteen Years in Polynesia: Missionary Life, Travels and Researches in the Islands of the Pacific.* London: John Snow, 1861.

———. *Samoa a Hundred Years Ago and Long Before.* London: Macmillan, 1884.

Tyerman, Daniel, and George Bennett, *Voyages and Travels round the World.* London: London Missionary Society, 1841.

Vason, George. *An Authentic Narrative of Four Years' Residence at Tongataboo.* Ed. S. Piggott. London: Longman, Hurst, Rees, Orme and Longman's, 1810.

Vattel, Emerich de. *The Law of Nations*. London: G. G. J. and J. Robinson, 1793.

Vernon, R. *James Calvert; or, from Dark to Dawn in Fiji*. London: S. W. Partridge, n.d.

"Vindex." *Fiji: Its Political Aspect from 1870–1873*. Levuka: Griffiths, 1873.

Wagner, Roy. *The Invention of Culture*. Chicago: University of Chicago Press, 1980.

Waldegrave, William. "A Contrast and Its Lessons." In *The Church Missionary Juvenile Instructor*, 35–36. London, 1862.

———. "Extracts from a Private Journal Kept on Board H.M.S. Seringapatam in the Pacific, 1830." *Journal of the Royal Geographical Society*, 3 (1833), 168–196.

Wallace, J. H. *Early History of New Zealand from 1840 to 1845*. Ed. Thomson W. Leys. Auckland: H. Brett, 1890.

Wallis, Mary. *Life in Feejee: Or Five Years among the Cannibals*. Boston: W. Heath, 1851.

Walpole, Frederick. *Four Years in the Pacific in Her Majesty's Ship Collingwood from 1844 to 1848*. London: Richard Bentley, 1849.

Ward, John M. *British Policy in the South Pacific, 1786–1893*. Sydney: Australasian, 1948.

Waterhouse, Joseph. *The King and People of Fiji*. London: Wesleyan Conference, 1866.

Wawn, William T. *The South Sea Islanders and the Queensland Labour Trade*. London: Swan Sonnenschein, 1893.

West, Thomas. *Ten Years in South-Central Polynesia*. London: J. Nisbet, 1865.

Whitmee, S. J. *A Missionary Cruise in the South Pacific*. Sydney: Cook, 1871.

Wilkes, Charles. *Narrative of the United States Exploring Expedition*. 5 vols. Philadelphia: Lea and Blanchard, 1844.

———. *Defence . . . of . . . C. W. to the Charges on which he has been tried, etc.* [Washington], 1842.

Williams, David Owen. "Racial Ideas in Early Victorian England." *Ethnic and Racial Studies*, 5:2 (1982), 196–212.

Williams, Glyndwr. "English Attitudes to Indigenous Peoples of the Pacific." In John Hardy and Alan Frost, eds., *European Voyaging towards Australia*, 133–141. Canberra: Australian Academy of the Humanities, 1990.

———. " 'Savages Noble and Ignoble'; European Attitudes towards the Wider World before 1800." *Journal of Imperial and Commonwealth History* 6:3 (1978), 300–313.

Williams, John. *A Narrative of Missionary Enterprises in the South Sea Islands*. London: J. Snow and J. R. Leifchild, 1837.

Williams, Thomas. *The Islands and Their Inhabitants*. Vol. 1 of *Fiji and the Fijians*. With James Calvert. Second ed. London: Alexander Heylin, 1860.

Wilson, William F., ed. *With Lord Byron at the Sandwich Islands in 1825*. Honolulu: Petroglyph, 1922.

Wolffe, John. *God and Greater Britain: Religion and National Life in Britain and Ireland, 1843–1945*. London: Routledge, 1994.

Wood, C. F. *A Yachting Cruise in the South Seas*. London: King, 1875.

Wood, G. W. "Pax Britannica: The Royal Navy around 1860." In Wood and O'Connor, eds., *W. P. Morrell: A Tribute*, 51–68.

Wood, G. W., and P. S. O'Connor, eds. *W. P. Morrell: A Tribute*. Dunedin: University of Otago Press, 1973.

Woodward, Sir L. *The Age of Reform, 1815–1870*. Second ed. Oxford: Clarendon, 1962.

Wright, Harrison M. *New Zealand, 1796–1840: Early Years of Western Contact.* Cambridge, Mass: Harvard University Press, 1959.

Young, D. M. *The Colonial Office in the Early Nineteenth Century.* London: Longmans, 1961.

Young, John M. R. "Evanescent Ascendancy: The Planter Community in Fiji." In Davidson and Scarr, *Pacific Islands Portraits,* 147–175.

———. "Frontier Society in Fiji." Ph.D. thesis, University of Adelaide, 1968.

Index